NIALL QUINN
The Autobiography

NIALL QUINN

The Autobiography

headline

First published in 2002
by HEADLINE BOOK PUBLISHING

10 9 8 7 6 5 4 3 2 1

A CIP catalogue record for this title is available from the British Library

ISBN 0 7553 1044 6

Text design by Ben Cracknell
Typeset by Palimpsest Book Production Limited,
Polmont, Stirlingshire
Printed and bound in Great Britain by
Clays Ltd, St Ives plc

HEADLINE BOOK PUBLISHING
A division of Hodder Headline
338 Euston Road
London NW1 3BH

www.headline.co.uk
www.hodderheadline.com

For Gillo, Mikey and
Ash the Bash

CONTENTS

Acknowledgements   ix

Prologue: A Red Carnation   I

 1. Roots   9

 2. Ready for Take-off   23

 3. Opening Time   41

 4. Storm Country   59

 5. You Gotta Dance with Them what Brung You   75

 6. Every Time We Say Goodbye . . .   91

 7. Success Has Made a Failure of Our Home   109

 8. Just Because Your Wife Dies Doesn't Mean
    Your House Can't Burn Down Too   127

 9. Life but Not as We Know It   143

10. Twenty-four   159

11. The Perfect Storm   177

12. Movita, Me   191

13. Every Story Ends   207

14. Starter's Orders   225

15. Two Legs Bad   241

16. On the Edge of Something   265

17. Closing Time   279

Epilogue: After Hours   295

Index   303

ACKNOWLEDGEMENTS

My thanks to Tom Humphries – a literary giant disguised as a sports reporter.

A special word for Michael Kennedy, whose advice, friendship and generosity have been invaluable throughout my career.

Thanks also to Ian Marshall, Jonathan Harris, Bob Harris and Bob Murray, chairman of Sunderland AFC.

And to all the unsung heroes who coach the kids in the street, for the love of the game.

A RED CARNATION

I know some things all right if I could only think of them.
These guys say I'm crazy — crazy in the head like a sheep:
But I'm as happy as if I had good sense.
DAMON RUNYON, *TWO MEN NAMED COLLINS*

Summertime and I'm lingering on a field in the town of Suwon, somewhere in South Korea, gazing up at a cliff of green and white and orange, speckled with faces. Some people are crying, some are laughing; all the faces are red from excitement. I'm lingering because probably I'll never stand in a place like this again. This is goodbye — a guilty farewell.

The other players are slowly wandering off, heading towards the dressing rooms. They have their hands raised above their heads, clapping and saying goodbye as they vanish into the tunnel. I just stand here, taking it all in. Most of the lads have swapped jerseys, and Spanish red is draped over their shoulders. I've kept mine. It's my last Irish jersey. Years from now I'll take it out and these moments will come swimming back; the end of the good times.

*   *   *

When I was a kid — well, when I was somewhere between being just a kid and being a professional footballer — my father used to have chats with me every now and then. I was innocent and naive and at the time it seemed that every door I walked towards just opened for me. Da was concerned. He knew my nature.

'Don't do a Jack Doyle on it now, will ya,' he'd say. 'Don't do a Jack Doyle.'

Perversely, of course, Jack Doyle became a hero for me. Something about the way he strolled through life, always sticking to the sunny side of the street. That appealed to me. Jack won a fortune and threw it away again, he believed that a generous man never went to hell, he married the most beautiful woman in the world, and he entered each act of his life with the same bubbling optimism he had when he started out.

We had no nerves when we came here tonight. We were skittish and optimistic. During the week we sat down to watch the last game Spain played in this World Cup. They were up against South Africa and after a while they began to look awesome. So we wandered off and played pool.

We didn't care. We came here to give a passionate performance; we came here to do what we do. So Spain move the ball around one touch, two touch and olé. We do what we do.

Spain started well. They fancy that they might win this strange World Cup and for a little while we could believe that. Soon they score. It's a lovely glancing header from Morientes that just embarrasses us: they have a throw-in, they toss it to Puyol who controls it, digs it out with his feet and crosses it into the danger area. We've allowed them to throw a ball from level with the six-yard line to a player who's then allowed to turn and cross it; and we've thrown in a free header. Thank you for shopping with us. It's gut wrenching.

The bright side? This is the third time in four matches at this

World Cup that we have gone a goal down. We'd like to think that we have them where we want them. On the bench, we wrap our arms around each other. There's a great unity in this team, especially when we can feel our backs pressed to the wall. Nobody is moaning about things, but it's plain horrible to be watching from here. I'm beside Clinton Morrison and Eddie Corcoran. We kick every ball.

'He shoulda done this,' says Clinton.

'Get rid of it, get rid of it,' mutters Eddie.

Jack Doyle was a boxer, a singer, a movie star, a womaniser, a drinker and a charmer. He fought in front of 90,000 in White City in 1933, and thirty years later, when The Beatles played in Dublin for the first and only time, Jack had a crowd twice the size listening to him sing ballads two hundred yards away.

He came from Cobh in County Cork and his first job was hauling coal out of the bellies of boats on the quayside. He never forgot that. He never forgot the little row of houses that he came from or the dank poverty he grew up in. He never forgot it but the memory never made him mean.

It's going away from us, this game. Spain are controlling it. Damien Duff and Robbie Keane, our two forwards, can't buy an inch of space. We aren't creating anything but till they score again we're still in the game, hanging on by our fingernails.

Time for our tea and oranges. It's another first half when we've been outplayed. In the dressing room we are calm. The feeling is that we'll have to be adventurous now. The ball is still precious, we can't give away possession, we can't get beaten on the break, but we have to gamble – throw it away or win big.

It's a different feeling being 1–0 down to Spain at half-time from being 1–0 down on the other days. On those days we felt we hadn't performed. Today we're just not right tactically. Something has to change. We need to adjust.

In the dressing room Mick McCarthy has a quiet word with me – get yourself right, I'll be putting you on. Soon.

I weigh things up. Ian Harte on our left side has been placing fine passes in to Damien and Robbie but we haven't been able to get to the next point. Ian is playing well and he can put the ball wherever he wants it tonight. That's what I need from him.

We begin to play differently. I get my head up to win bits and pieces. Instead of our attacks breaking down thirty-five yards from goal, we're within twenty yards. I get a turn and snap a shot that doesn't have the power I want but . . .

I head a ball out to my right, and Damien latches on to it. He's as quick as a fish. The defender seems to hit him from behind. He tumbles. I'm not sure how hard the Spaniard really caught him, but he didn't catch the ball. It's from behind and they've been cutting Damien's feet from under him all night. We take the penalty without guilt. We need the break. It evaporates, though.

Casillas saves the penalty from Ian Harte.

Kevin Kilbane, my room-mate and friend, comes on to the rebound. I think that this is going to be the moment he deserves. He just needs to sidefoot the ball home. He hits it full on. Wide. It's like we've just had some good news. Nobody wants to see the senior players saying, 'For fuck's sake, Hartey,' or, 'What were you thinking, Kev?'

'Don't you worry,' we say. 'We have them.' I believe it, for a minute. Almost as soon as I went on, we won the penalty. Ian missed it but he's still passing well. We're on our way. Then Ian is taken off. So it's plan B – what was plan B?

Jack was six feet five inches tall. He'd earned three-quarters of a million pounds by the time of his thirtieth birthday. Later he'd walk the streets without any shoes but he always believed that something good was around the corner.

✻   ✻   ✻

I know we'll get another break. Time stops. I feel like I've been on the pitch about ten minutes, no more, when we win a free kick. The ball floats across. The referee whistles. I'm surprised. What the hell is he penalising us for now? I'm about to run to him to complain when I see that he's pointing to the penalty spot. Wow! Thank you, Mr Anders Frisk.

He's right, I suppose, but it happens twenty times a game that somebody yanks my jersey — twenty times, and harder than that. Hierro hasn't pulled me to the ground or hit me hard; he's just pulled my jersey up over my head. Mr Frisk must have tougher standards.

This is it, then; it's ours. Robbie Keane — Jesus, he's still a kid — just takes the ball, puts it down and wham. Not a second thought. Then it's over. Final whistle.

Mick McCarthy comes on. We huddle. Mick says we're going for this, we're going to pummel them. He tells Dave Connolly, you stay up front. Let's go out and give it everything, he says.

At kick-off for extra time, a Spanish player comes to the referee and asks for five minutes' grace. They have a player getting treatment.

'No,' says Mr Frisk.

They have only ten men. We're hammering them but we can't score — fifteen minutes and no punches landed. We start the second half and it's still eleven against ten. They are ragged, arguing with each other. The smiles, the high fives and easy confidence have all gone. I wink at Robbie Keane. This is ours. We have so much possession but it won't fall right. It's always rushed, there's always a deflection, somebody always turns away with their head in their hands.

So it goes to the tiebreaker — penalty kicks, five per team. I'm not knocking anyone out of the way here. I'm hanging back. Mick says who wants one, who'll take a penalty, and all the lads jump in. Dave Connolly says I'm having one. Kevin Kilbane says give me one. Gary Breen says no way. I keep my mouth shut.

Mick says to the boys that they've done everything that could be asked. There's no pressure whatsoever. Go up, pick a corner and stick to it. Nothing to lose. Good luck.

Perhaps he might have said, 'You've done nothing. Now we've to win this penalty competition.' Perhaps he might have said, 'Niall Quinn, you're taking one of these.'

Instead, I stand and watch with my arms around Mark Kinsella and Kenny Cunningham. If we're level after five apiece, I'll go sixth I tell myself.

It's history now. Dave Connolly hits his straight down the middle at Casillas. Mattie Holland misses. Kevin Kilbane misses. Mendieta scuffs one home for the Spanish. Our World Cup is over. Finito.

Our theme has been two words on a blackboard: no regrets. I have some, though, and I've just added another. My international career is finished. They are heroes, these kids who stepped up and had the guts to miss. I'm looking at them and saying to myself over and over again, 'Oh no, I've really fucked up here.' I've scored in these circumstances before – against Charlton at Wembley, against Everton once. Now I've chickened out. Right at the end of my career, I've funked it.

When Kevin put up his hand to take one, I thought Kevin's never taken a penalty before. I can't remember Kevin taking one. But you can't say, 'Kev, are you sure?' So I patted him on the back and said, 'This is yours. You've had a great tournament, you deserve this.' And I said yeah, that's it, I'll go sixth.

When we played Charlton in a play-off at Wembley, I remember saying all the way up to the penalty spot, right corner, right corner. Sasa Ilic, the Charlton keeper, dived so early I changed my mind and trickled it into the other corner. It's easy really, I told myself. The lads will be OK taking their penalties with the world watching them.

Why do I feel so guilty, then? I could have had one more kick, one more throw of the dice. Even if we got beaten it might have been a goal. When I twist and turn at night now, that's what I'll think about. Right at the end, when the money was piled high on the table, I lost it. I lost my nerve.

He would have taken a penalty. Jack Doyle would have taken one.

He went to jail. He went on the run. He fought while racked with VD. He took on America and lost. He decked Clark Gable and bedded Carole Lombard, but not in that order. He caroused with Cagney. He gambled. He ran horses. He backed losers. He loved Kipling:

> If you can make one heap of all your winnings
> And risk it on one turn of pitch-and-toss
> And lose, and start again at your beginnings
> And never breathe a word about your loss . . .

He went broke again and again and he died a pauper. He shrugged his massive shoulders and said that he'd come from nothing and that he would return to nothing. He took it all without bitterness and even in his destitute days he'd walk the streets of Dublin with a red carnation in his breast pocket, still a little swagger about him.

I loved that story.

CHAPTER ONE

ROOTS

Though we have the hay saved and Cork bate,
if twas aisy to save the hay, it was not aisy bate Cork.
JOHN MAHER, TIPPERARY HURLING CAPTAIN (1945)

It's a Wednesday night late in a bad season, and it's dark when I get home. I've parked the car at the front of the house and the glow of the dashboard clock tells me that it's just after 1 a.m. Tomorrow is a schoolday. Gillian and the kids are in bed, asleep hours ago.

Did Daddy win his match or lose his match? Tomorrow morning is early enough to find out about Daddy's work. Has he scored? Been sent off? Stunk the place out? Did Daddy's back hold up? Are his knees OK? Are his various nagging aches still there? Hey, Daddy is thirty-five and still playing professional football. What does Daddy expect?

I pad around the house quietly, make a cup of tea, glance at the papers and then put on my work boots. I know the way of course, out the back and up the gentle hill. There's just me and the pitch blackness of the countryside, just my footsteps in the tranquil silence.

They hear me coming. They sense my anticipation. I go up to the horses and they nuzzle their long faces against me. I give them hay and water them, talk to them, and just absorb the darkness. The close smell of the horses, the sounds of them breathing and moving about, takes me to a different world, eases every trouble. Tomorrow is a new morning. Saturday will be a new match. August will be a new season. Nothing is for ever.

The Football Association of Ireland have sent me an itinerary for the World Cup. An itinerary! This is one small step for mankind but one big step for the FAI. It augurs well – the itinerary has arrived on time and it has come to the right address. It may transpire that I won't be going and the itinerary is superfluous, but right now, it's exciting just to have one. It's the thought that counts. I'm included in somebody's football plans.

For sixteen years the routine has been different. The FAI likes to keep you guessing. Sometimes you can go on a playing trip for Ireland and there will be no itinerary, just a series of little surprises. Sometimes, when you get home, an itinerary will be lying in the hallway in a neat brown envelope. Occasionally, when you are heading away from the team on a Thursday morning with sore legs and a flight to catch, your itinerary might be pressed into your hand by a man in a blazer. On your way home, you can compare the plan for the trip with how it actually panned out – if you want to punish yourself, that is.

According to this grand itinerary, we are heading to Saipan to start our World Cup preparations. This could be good or it could be bad. I don't know where Saipan is. I don't know how far away it is. I don't know how big it is. Nobody knows these things, and anyway, I have a testimonial game to organise before then.

An itinerary is a licence to daydream, all the same. I look over the strange and unfamiliar names – Saipan, Izumo, Niigata, Chiba and so on – and wonder how these places will figure when the history of this Irish team is written. For most of the lads who will travel, this will be a beginning. For me, it will be the end. My knees tell me, my back tells me, my heart tells me – the end. In one of these places I will say goodbye to football.

Perhaps I'm skipping ahead of myself here. My last hurrah could have slipped by without me noticing. The Irish squad for this World Cup hasn't even been announced. Strictly speaking, only twenty-three players should be getting this itinerary and I fancy that if I have received one, there must be dozens of them in circulation, some of them in the hands of the type of player I hate – younger, fitter, faster, better. You know the sort.

This itinerary may be the last World Cup souvenir I will ever get. I have missed a few friendly games for Ireland recently and at club level for Sunderland I have been performing without bothering the headline writers. I am Mighty Quinn no more. Worse, I've been scraping by in a team inexplicably crippled by self-doubt. We have been bumping along just above the floor of the league table, listening to the ominous disenchantment of our fans, who can see through us suddenly. We're not the passionate, gutsy team we were a year or two ago. They can feel it. We can feel it.

I have this nagging twinge of a feeling that Saipan and Izumo and all the others might never mean anything much to me.

I notice the younger players now. I've kept an eye on the Irish kids Cliffie Byrne and Tommy Butler since they came to Sunderland with their spots and their homesickness. Once upon a time they were in awe of me and, if I had a mood to, I could make them dance on the palm of my hand. I'd steer them this way and that, bring them out occasionally for drinks and a meal, tip them off about what they needed to be doing to impress. Then we became equals, me playing the role of older brother in a big family, the pair of them feeling comfortable with taking the mickey out of the older members of the family.

Now Tommy and Cliffie are on the threshold of being first-team regulars and although we are friends and we don't play in the same position, I'm in their way a little. It used to be that if I had a good game, they'd seek me out and it would be 'top man, Niall' and 'you never lost it', and if I went badly, they'd pull the piss out of me, knowing that I'd have my revenge on them soon. Now I'm on a bad run and they don't say anything at all. They don't want to catch my eye. If the audience were to stand up and put their coats and hats on, it couldn't be a clearer hint that the show is over.

Mick McCarthy rings one evening to ask about my back and my other rusting parts. It's encouraging enough that he's calling and I ask him where Saipan is. Mick gives me a quick geography lesson. Saipan is a long way away but Mick seems happy to be heading there. It's spring and I've a lot to be doing. If the manager is happy, then I'm happy. I haven't given it another thought. I have a family to worry about first. I have a club that's getting sucked towards relegation to fret over. I have a back injury that has to be coddled and tickled. I have a testimonial game to organise. I have the players' pool negotiations for the World Cup to help with. Whatever will be, will be, I tell myself.

I feel old, though. Do you know that when I first went to Arsenal on trial there was still an iron curtain, Margaret Thatcher was still young, nobody could imagine a computer that was smaller than a large wardrobe, teams were allowed just one substitute and I used to travel home to Ireland by boat and train. I had been on a plane when I went to Fulham for a trial in 1983, but coming home with the advice ringing in my ears that I'd best get an ordinary job, I imagined it could be some time before I saw the inside of another one.

Football would have survived without me and I'd have survived without it. However, some people from Arsenal Football Club called to our door in Hillsbrook Drive in Perrystown, Crumlin and painted a pretty picture of the wonderland of professional football – mine to keep after a brief trial period. For me, there was the promise, at best, of glory and money and, at worst, of bragging rights to my friends. Arsenal still had a reputation then as the Irish club, having simultaneously hothoused three of the country's greatest talents in Frank Stapleton, David O'Leary and the incomparable Liam Brady. O'Leary was the only one left at the club by then, but I fancied tagging my name on to the list.

For my parents, there was Terry Neill's promise that I would be academically catered for in a new system which was being set up by a London Irish friend of his. The dean of this place of learning turned out to be Kate Hoey, the future Minister for Sport. Arsenal, the club of marble halls and old-style values, would act *in loco parentis* as they steered me through a series of academic courses with a little football on the side. The worst that could happen was that I would return home in a year or two's time qualified as a professor of something or other.

We all took what we wanted to hear from Arsenal's sales talk, and a little while later I departed for my fortnight's trial, leaving Dublin with a pocketful of high hopes. The fact that I was what newspaper reporters have always called 'gangly' and what my friends described as 'just bleedin' lanky' didn't stop me from wondering if the Arsenal of Stapleton, Brady and O'Leary wasn't about to become the esteemed firm of Stapleton, Brady, O'Leary and Quinn.

For a Dublin kid, it seemed that if you could make it anywhere, you could make it at Highbury. We'd all seen the photos of Stapleton, Brady and O'Leary in their young days at Arsenal, with their big hair and flapping flared trousers. They were Dubliners who'd made it as we watched. When Arsenal sold the dream, those pictures of the lads floated into my head. Look, son, here's some of our previous lucky winners.

I grew up in Crumlin, an historic spot. It was once a village outside Dublin but, as the city grew, Crumlin became part of its fabric. It was burned to the ground by Walter Fitzgerald, leader of a marauding clan from Wicklow, in the year 1565. For his troubles, Walter was hanged soon afterwards. Crumlin grew again and prospered and we remained wary about Wicklow people.

The first slice of good luck that life handed me was to be reared in Crumlin. The place was an old-style mix of terraced and semi-detached houses built at a time when people still valued space and green fields. Even if we did most of our playing on the streets, there were plenty of green napkins for us to go to when the occasion demanded.

It was 1983 when Arsenal came to the door and the prospect of leaving home for England just never seemed that daunting. In the eighties, it seemed as if we were being reared for emigration, fattened for the boat to England or the plane to America. If I was going to London to work as a footballer, well, I was going to a job at least. I was doing what we Irish had always done.

Let me tell you something about my dad, a Tipperary hurler. He played for a little club in Tipperary called Rahealty and when he was still a kid he appeared in the 1952 and 1953 All Ireland Minor (under eighteen) finals, winning both. He captained Tipperary in the second game and those sides he played for were described as among the best ever to come out of Tipperary at that level. They were the foundation of the glory years that were just around the corner.

Tipperary is the home of hurling. By the age of eighteen, my father, Billy Quinn, was a superstar. By then he was playing for the Tipperary senior team, and in 1954 he scored three goals in a National League final against Kilkenny. For anyone who doesn't know the game, imagine growing up near Anfield and at eighteen scoring three goals for Liverpool in an FA Cup final against Manchester United. It's like that but it means more. It's more important, more tribal, more beautiful. Dad pinched his scores from under the nose of a legendary Kilkenny full-back named Paddy 'Diamond' Hayden. Eighteen years old and Billy Quinn had it made. Nearly fifty years later, people still come up to Dad and talk to him about that day. That's how much it meant.

Outside it was 1954, though. It was the old Ireland – poor, grey, and run by the Catholic Church. My mother was a teacher and when she wanted to marry my father, the rules dreamed up by the priests and enforced by the politicians demanded that she resign from her teaching post. No married woman would keep a man from a job.

So Billy Quinn and Mary Condon threw it all in and emigrated. My ma gave up a good teaching job, my da gave up hurling and they left for England, cashed in their chips for a life, like so many others. They lived in Strood, near Rochester in Kent, and Da worked as a steel erector for McAlpine's. It was cold, hard work that squeezed the romance of hurling right out of him.

When Jack Lynch lifted the marriage ban on female teachers in 1959, they moved to Dublin but it was too late and too far for my father to pick up the golden thread of his hurling career. Still young, he missed out on being part of one of the greatest and most fabled of Tipperary teams. Tipp would win five All Ireland titles between 1958 and 1965, all of them without Billy Quinn who was by now working in Bolands bakery in Dublin and dabbling in club hurling at the weekends while he supported a family that would eventually comprise three daughters and a son.

I think of the young Billy Quinn a lot these days, now that I'm coming to the end of my sporting career. He must have his regrets and his what-might-have-been moments, yet he passed on the love of hurling. What he missed out on never soured him. I remember childhood Sundays, propped in the car beside him, driving to hurling matches in Tipperary, Kilkenny, Cork, Limerick, anywhere there was a good game to be enjoyed. I played Gaelic football and hurling, the games of the GAA, under his approving eye.

When this World Cup is over and done with, I'll start the second half of my life. By then I'll be a former soccer pro. I know that I'll always be a GAA man, though. The things that stirred Da and his people before him will always stir me. In a moment I'd trade these last nineteen years of soccer for the chance to score the winning point in a Munster final one sunny day in Thurles, me wearing the blue and yellow of Tipperary and watching the poppy red jerseys of Cork wilt all around me as the ball sails over.

Now it's Friday morning, 17 May 2002 – time for different dreams to unfold. We have a few crazy days behind us and some crazier ones ahead. On Tuesday night we played my charity game at the Stadium of Light in Sunderland. A couple of hours before that, I threw some clothes, some toiletries, some footwear and some books into the bag I'll live out of for the next five or six weeks.

Last night we played Nigeria in a harmless send-off friendly at Lansdowne Road and afterwards had a few quiet drinks with our families before this early start. It was raining then. It's raining now.

The consensus from our loved ones is that this trip, this World Cup, is the adventure of a lifetime. There's a monsoon outside this morning, though, and we haven't had enough sleep. Also it's election day in Ireland, and the news for the next forty-eight hours will be about recounts, cliffhanger seats and lost deposits. Nobody will care about jaded footballers and the long season they are trying to shake from their bones.

This is Ireland's third World Cup, the first since the economic boom time arrived. Somehow we sense that it means less; the old excited innocence of our first great adventure twelve years ago is gone. Ireland is a more confident place nowadays and we don't feel that having our soccer team in the World Cup finals makes us one of the great nations on the earth. As a nation, we're pretty cocky, anyway, right now.

So the mood is downbeat, and besides, little things that happened this week have sown a seed. We all know it's there, taking root beneath our feet, but we don't talk about it. We ignore the signs and cross our fingers.

It started with this business of my charity game in Sunderland on Tuesday night. A long time ago, I played in a testimonial match for Frank Stapleton. The former Scottish centre-half Gordon McQueen once said about Frank (unfairly) that he gets up in the morning and smiles at himself in the mirror just to get it out of the way for the day. Well, however miserable Frank was, the crowd that turned up for his testimonial was even more miserable. It was no way to say goodbye. I decided then that if I ever put together a career long enough to merit one of these testimonial games, I wouldn't pin my future on the proceeds, such as they might be. Instead, I'd give them away in exchange, or in penance, for all the good times.

It was a modest enough idea and it just sat at the back of my mind for years. As luck would have it, my testimonial came around. I'm an old-timer at a bad time for football. We millionaires have been muttering about a strike. Two Leeds players have been tried for assaulting an Asian student. Some Chelsea players end up in court following 'a nightclub incident'. There is a common perception that players are rich, spoiled and out of touch with the real world.

Against this backdrop, I, who have had the most privileged of lives, the most carefree of existences for nearly twenty years, have managed to get myself painted as a living saint for keeping my promise to myself.

It's embarrassing and awkward. When I close my eyes, I can see lads in dressing rooms up and down the country pointing to their newspapers and hear them saying what I'd say about myself – 'Who does that twat think he is?'

Yet the evening of my charity game was perfect. We're on the way to collecting one million pounds for children's hospitals in Sunderland and in Dublin. The players have all waived their match fees. Instead of a little present afterwards, they'll all be receiving a letter from a sick child. It's not much to set against a gloriously misspent youth, just a small good thing. As I keep saying, it's not my money to give away anyway. It's other people's. Donations, tax relief, tickets sold – we just channelled it and took the credit.

As usual, there are flies in the ointment. Amid a general and generous chorus of approval for the whole thing, the media have decided that on the night, there was something missing. It was a night with everything but the boy, everything but Roy Keane.

Roy is our best player, our most interesting player, our only true superstar and the subject of maybe 70 per cent of the stories and rumours written about this Irish team. That he wasn't at my testimonial game doesn't surprise me or hurt me. He explained in a subsequent interview that he was injured, and wanted to spend the time with his family rather than sitting in the stands. But his absence is a story and people aren't going to let go.

On Wednesday, when we arrived in Dublin to prepare to play Nigeria, the media were looking backwards instead of forwards. Virtually all the Irish papers were stalking the tasty but spiky prey. They pounded Roy for not appearing in Sunderland. His absence is being billed as some sort of artful insult to me. The game, which was advertised as 'A Night With Niall', should apparently have been sold as 'A Night Without Roy'.

It's uncomfortable. At the best of times, Roy isn't one to go around beaming about good press clippings. It's safe to say he won't be pleased with this crop of negatives.

The testimonial game took place on Tuesday. Roy had already been asked to play against Nigeria two nights later and was, I think, not entirely happy about it. He's had a long season at Manchester United, which ended in bitter disappointment. How bitter some of us can only guess at. Roy is more driven and more obsessed by success than the rest of us. None of us here is walking around with the jingle of medals in our pockets. Two nights ago, the European Champions League final was just something for us to watch on the television. Roy is different. He rails against failure and rages for success. Sometimes I wonder if he might even despise the rest of us for not having the same brooding, obsessive passion that he has, but we need him and he needs us. So we rub along.

Anyway, he'll be disappointed, and his knee will be troubling him. It makes him look bad to have played against Nigeria and not to have played in my testimonial game; but he can't win. It will make him look bad, too, if he misses another friendly for Ireland.

In truth, I'm a little surprised he's here at all. Some extra rest in Manchester with his wife, Theresa, and the kids, a little extra treatment on his knee, a chance to avoid all this hullabaloo and join us a week into the trip would have been a viable alternative. That was more what I'd have expected Roy to do.

Instead, he's here and he's in the wars. Supposedly, there is tension between us. I am, if the papers are to be believed, 'fuming' over Roy's failure to appear in Sunderland. I'm not. In the press conference after the game, nobody even asked me about Roy, let alone whether I was giving off fumes about him. I've thought about Roy and the whole testimonial issue, but I don't believe I've ever 'fumed'.

A few weeks ago, Roy refused to cooperate in writing an article for the programme of the game. Cathal Dervan, the Irish journalist, was organising the articles for me. Cathal and Roy have a history that almost amounts to a feud. Once Cathal urged a Lansdowne Road crowd to boo Roy's every touch in a game against Iceland. So probably Cathal should have known that Roy wouldn't deal with him in writing a piece for the programme, but he asked anyway, given the nature of the event. Word came back through Michael Kennedy, the Irish-born solicitor who acts as an agent for both Roy and me. The message was sorry, Roy wouldn't be doing any articles with Cathal Dervan.

I hadn't fully appreciated the antipathy between them. I hoped that Roy would offer to do the piece with somebody else (maybe I should have suggested this, and he probably didn't realise it either as time was tight), and I got a little bit wound up about it, stomped around the kitchen for five minutes announcing that there was no way I was travelling to the World Cup with that mean hoor as my captain. Gillian reminded me that, first, I might not be asked to travel to the World Cup anyway, and second, if I was, wild horses wouldn't keep me away. So I've moved on. Roy has had a busy time of it and, in retrospect, I understand him not playing ball with Cathal Dervan. Footballers have longer memories than journalists do.

Anyway, Roy and I have had an Oprah moment. Roy arrived in Dublin on the evening before the Nigeria game. As usual Mick Byrne, our physio and Roy's close friend, picked him up at the airport and whisked him down to the Holiday Inn. I was just getting into bed when Mick knocked at my door. He told me that I needed to speak to Roy.

I have one foot in the bed and I say to Mick, 'Sorry? Did you say I need to speak to Roy?' Mick is agitated.

'Don't be awkward,' Mick says. 'He needs to speak to you.'

'Well, why doesn't he come here, then?'

'Just go, will ya,' says Mick.

And I do. The mountain must go to Mohammed. I follow Mick down the corridor to Roy's room. He's sitting there, tense and uncomfortable, and he says to me, 'No hard feelings. I thought Mick [McCarthy] knew.'

I'm a little bit surprised. I thought this was something about which nothing would ever be said, but Roy is obviously making an effort and I appreciate that.

'Yeah, Mick did know,' I say. 'It's not a problem, Roy.'

I can see he's embarrassed about this whole conversation so we keep it short, very short.

'Cheers,' I say, and leave him sitting there.

Not sleepy now, I wander down and have a bowl of soup with a few of the lads who are still up and about. Roy wanders in a couple of minutes later and does the same. It's easier and less awkward when there are other players about. There are no bad feelings. I appreciate that the excruciating encounter in his room was tough for him. I make a little mental note to let the press guys know tomorrow that there is no problem between us. Just in case.

CHAPTER TWO

READY FOR TAKE-OFF

What if this is as good as it gets?
JACK NICHOLSON, *AS GOOD AS IT GETS*

For some time now I have been clicking on the teletext on the day of Irish squad announcements. Always it's the same. 'Oh no,' I'll say, 'there's been a terrible mistake. They've picked me again.'

When I meet up with the lads I'll joke that it's harder to get off this team than it was to get on; best that I say it before they do. Some of the younger lads think that the triangular tournament in which I made my debut back in 1986 was held to celebrate the invention of the wheel.

This morning we are just about ready to set off from Dublin airport when I notice Roy. We are at a chaotic reception that somebody has thrown for us, and Roy is kicking off about the players having to carry all their bags through the public area, and about the media being at this supposedly private party. It strikes me that he has a point, but only Roy would have the energy or the intensity to make it. It's messy here today, even this early in the morning, but let's just get through it.

The Nigeria game last night was one of those tentative, dutiful games that's not quite real. Everyone's mind was somewhere else. None of us wanted to get injured or bruised. It was raining, the pitch was greasy and it was no time to be a hero. We surrendered a long unbeaten record at home and forgot about it immediately. This morning the Taoiseach, Bertie Ahern, is buzzing about, looking for face time with the footballers. There are people dressed in leprechaun suits, there are fans with drink taken, and there are bewildered American tourists. The flight is delayed. We're all pissed off but Roy is probably the only one among us who will bother fighting the battle.

He's had his victories. It was Roy who ended the slightly surreal situation, which had gone on for so long that the rest of us hardly noticed, whereby the players sat in economy seats and the FAI suits parked their ample behinds in the first-class section. It was Roy who got our training ground in Dublin improved and got us into better hotels for the longer stays. All this is done to make sure the players are properly looked after, so they can perform well. He has an appetite for these situations. The rest of us are happy just to grumble — except me, of course. My approach is different. I'm the optimist. That's my role in the group. At half-time I always think that we'll go on to win the game. When we lose, I'm the one who says that we'll get them the next time. When we fail to qualify for a tournament, it's me who goes around telling everyone to take a look at what we've learned.

I'm on this trip as much as a good-vibes man as a centre-forward. When things go bad I am to burst into a chorus of 'Always Look On the Bright Side of Life'. My job will be to jolly people along and to play the odd bit of football if an emergency arises. I'm happy with that. I'm thirty-five and going to the World Cup. Even if it's part of an Elderly in the Community scheme, I'm happy to be going.

It's a strange way to approach my last World Cup but then it's strange to be having a last World Cup. Going back to the mid nineties, if I'd cared to, I could have collected a thick sheaf of newspaper articles mentioning my imminent retirement. So although I have a poorly defined task, it's something I'll enjoy doing. I'll just feel my way along, like a blind man at an orgy. I'm not the captain of the team. I'm not the star player. I'm not the one with the most appearances. I'm the oldest, though, and I enjoy working with young players. I like the idea of this team taking up some of the spirit and atmosphere of the team I came into back in 1986.

It's a tradition thing. I like the thought that some of these kids will be part of the continuity and the future of Irish soccer. Soon after I came into the Irish team, I played and roomed with Liam Brady. He was coming to the end of a career that began when he was a kid in a team in which Johnny Giles was the king. In turn, Johnny's international career can be traced back to 1959 when it overlapped with that of Charlie Hurley after whom our training ground in Sunderland is named. Charlie played with the great Liam Whelan of Manchester United. Liam died in the Munich air disaster but his short career caught the end of Con Martin's time in the green jersey. And so on and so on back through time, each little bit of experience being added to the rest, until here we are with a young team ranked among the top twenty in the world, on our way to the greatest show soccer has to offer.

The prospect of doing this job, of adding my small sum to the pool and of perhaps playing a few minutes, has kept me going at this level for the past few months while my back has ached and my form has dipped. In spring, not for the first time, I spoke to Mick McCarthy and told him that retirement didn't scare me, that he owed me nothing. I said I'd prefer to call it a day rather than deprive a younger and fitter player of a place at the World Cup. In the rearview mirror, I could make out the faces of the players who will do my job on the pitch in the years to come — Gary Doherty of

Spurs, Richie Sadlier of Millwall, and, coming up behind, Jon Daly of Stockport.

If it all sounds noble, it was no hardship. I was sore and dispirited, and I'd already taken enough from the game. Earlier in the winter, on my birthday in fact, I had played at Lansdowne Road against Cyprus and scored the goal that made me the country's top scorer ever. That night, out of habit, I went for a few quiet drinks in Keogh's in Dublin and the entire team (except Roy, who now likes to avoid such occasions) turned up to have a drink with me and my family and friends. The next month we travelled to Iran for the second part of a two-legged play-off to secure our qualification for the World Cup. I was there for those things. If my career had ended at that point, with me being witness to the birth of a new team and becoming the short-term holder (surely) of the Irish scoring record, I would happily have shuffled off.

I'd been there in Iceland in 1986 when we won a small triangular tournament, the first senior international competition Ireland had ever won. I was there two years later when we went to the European Championship for the first time; I was on the pitch when we beat England in Stuttgart. I was part of our first World Cup voyage two years later and poked home a goal to tell the grandchildren about. Who could complain about that?

It's like this. All my dreams have crystallised for me. One by one, they've come true. I remember as a young kid one of my first romances with soccer began when Manortown United rounded up a bunch of us to take to Dalymount Park, the old home of Irish soccer. It was October 1974 and I wasn't long past the excitement of my eighth birthday. Ireland were to play the USSR in a European Championship qualifier.

We begged to be allowed to go to Dalymount because the club coach got us cheap tickets and going there was in every way better than being in school. The skies were the smoggy Dublin grey that they always were back then, and the stern old stands in rickety

Dalymount were sharp, angular, dark and rusty. It was the single most glamorous place on earth, and that day it shook to what we used to call the Dalymount Roar. Liam Brady made his debut and Don Givens scored three goals. For many of us, that match was a landmark in our footballing memories. I was awestruck by this world.

Dublin had won the All Ireland title in Gaelic football the previous month. A handful of the players had been driven out to the Eight Acres near us in Crumlin and they'd stood in a trailer waving the Cup at us as they were driven around the field at speed. We chased after them all the way and our young heads were still crammed full of that close encounter with such unlikely glory. Irish soccer was distinctly unfashionable, but Don Givens slipped into our imaginations.

He was a hero, a natural old-fashioned goalscorer who got nineteen international goals while playing fewer matches than I did. He played with lesser players than I did, too, but Don looked the part. He looked half like a centre-forward and half like an Italian matinee idol. He carried the louche glamour of that eccentric Queens Park Rangers team he played with at the time. I can see him now with his sideburns and his sweated hair hanging down to his eyebrows, and those three stripes running down to the cuff of his long-sleeved Irish jersey. Was it any wonder we didn't draw distinctions between Müller, Cruyff and Don Givens?

Don was a wonder but by the time he retired Frank Stapleton had almost shouldered him out of my memory. In his prime, Frank was by turns to be found in the colours of Arsenal, Manchester United and Ajax. He seemed to be on a grand tour of the clubs that young boys dreamed of playing for.

More exciting – for me, if not for him – was the fact that Frank was the first professional whose path ever crossed mine. I was playing for the Dublin Under-14 team and won the Player of the Month award, the prize for which, that month and every month, was a coaching weekend sponsored by McVitie's, the biscuit people.

It all fell perfectly. The course took place in August during the school holidays and was given by Malcolm 'Supermac' Macdonald, then the manager of Fulham, and my hero, Frank Stapleton. Supermac, well, I could take or leave Supermac (and not long later, it transpired that he felt the same way about me). Frank was a superstar. He was all coiled power and strong shoulders and professional intensity. We spent a couple of days at University College Dublin being coached and I spent the whole time trying to impress Frank. I'm not sure if it was the pay-off but, when it was time to go home, I received the prestigious honour of being chosen as 'Player of the Weekend'.

Ten years later, Frank eclipsed Don Givens when he scored his twentieth goal in a pre World Cup friendly in Malta. It was Frank's final appearance for Ireland. He came on to score Ireland's third and final goal. I scored the first.

I'd just left Arsenal where my early days as a professional had been spent in constant competition with the memory of Frank. Frank could do these things when he was your age, I was told. Frank used to practise on his own over there. Frank scored this many when he was your age. He was always the yardstick.

It was Frank's record I beat on my thirty-fifth birthday, and if there was ever a time when it would have been natural to slip away, that was it. But Mick urged me to hang on. You'll be in retirement for a long time, he said, don't hurry yourself getting there.

In the last couple of months, both Gary Doherty and Richie Sadlier have been blighted by injury. So here I am, about to board a plane for a twenty-three-hour journey to an island none of us has ever heard of.

Just one more taste of World Cup action would be good but I have got used to the idea that I may travel all that way and not play. I have got used to the notion that I may never wear an Irish jersey again, that I may never kick a ball in anger again. I plan to do what I can and then go back to Sunderland and negotiate a decent deal for my retirement. I'm at peace with all that, easy with the notion that I'll never change at Crewe again.

Getting changed at Crewe used to entertain me. The last time I played at Gresty Road was on the coldest night in living memory. Nobody wanted to get changed. There was an arctic wind howling through the dressing room; polar bears were romping on the glacier outside. The lads prayed for a postponement. None came.

The dressing room could have been designed by Dickens. Dark, cold and dank, the watery light coming from the inadequate bulb above our heads barely illuminated a table, some old wooden benches and a bath that could take three people if they were intimately acquainted or wanted to get that way.

After the game, as we sat on the benches, I felt the sweat on my head turning icy. I rubbed my hands hoping to feel some life in them before dawn. My fingers were too numb to undo my mud-caked laces. That was a problem because by the time I coaxed some life back into them, my laces would most likely be frozen together. I might end up breaking them off. Meanwhile, I leaned forward, afraid that the sweat on my back would fuse me to the ice-cold wall. It was that sort of night. Our breath fogged the room and the only words we used were curses.

I loved every minute. I sat there taking it all in. I felt like one of the Yorkshiremen in the old Monty Python sketch: 'Ee, this is luxury, this is. When I were a lad, we used t'change in yon coal mines, three miles down and three miles back up, in bare feet . . .'

This was the game I loved and those are the times I miss most, the times when the game shares its essential character with you, when it's not all moneyed, airbrushed and antiseptic. At Gresty Road, I could see the game I fell in love with. It had colour, personality and romance.

Trivia question: the first player ever sent off in an FA Cup final and the first player ever sent off in the Premiership went to the same school. Name the players and their school.

If you said Kevin Moran, Niall Quinn and Drimnagh Castle in Dublin, you've just won a sunshine holiday.

You wouldn't think a school could prepare you for this life, but Drimnagh Castle did. We didn't lack heroes or role models among the alumni. We lacked a posh changing area but not examples of sporting success. Kevin Moran was a Gaelic football superstar before he ever left for Manchester United. Before that, he was a Drimnagh Castle kid. Gerry Ryan was a local hero who played for Bohemians and went on to play for Brighton in the 1983 Cup final. Kevin played for Manchester United in that same match. Two from our school playing in the FA Cup final – who wouldn't have dreams? Eamon Coughlan was the world 5000 metres champion and unlucky fourth-place finisher in just about every other great race he ran.

They all passed through Drimnagh Castle before my best friend Dave Whelan and I ever got there. They knew the same changing rooms that we knew. They put down the days in the same class-rooms and then changed for games in the old moat-bound castle, the ancient tumbledown pile that is the area's best landmark. If you stayed quiet for a moment, a rat would barrel across the floor, in no hurry either. He would come out with a fine sense of entitle-ment. There was no concrete on the floor, just rat droppings and mud. We were the intruders.

We played every sport with the same enthusiasm. Television was a last resort when it came to entertainment. Computer games hadn't progressed beyond the monotony of Space Invaders, we weren't bookish and girls were for later.

If you were to rewind and look for us in the Crumlin of the late seventies and early eighties, you'd find us pedalling for miles with golf clubs on our backs. At Ballinascorney we'd manage forty-five holes between dawn and dusk before scorching home again.

You could look for us tapping a sliotar (the ball used in hurling) around on the street, or ball juggling under the street lights outside the home of some girl one of us was trying to impress. We could serenade with footballs. We'd be the ones hopping like cat burglars over the wall of Molly 'rob the ball' Murphy's house to retrieve our football before she confiscated it for ever.

If you could go back there, we'd be easy to find. We were too innocent, too damn sappy to drink cider in the fields; we were too scared to take drugs and too straight looking to be offered them anyway. We'd be on the streets taking penalties at each other, using the pillars to a driveway as goalposts; or we'd be picking teams for endless games, the original jumpers-for-goalposts kids. Five half-time, ten the winner? Next goal wins? Fly keeper or stick? A goal or over the post? Your ma's calling you.

When we weren't playing, we'd be getting frogmarched down to Crumlin Hospital by an exasperated parent. Another broken finger needed splinting or fresh gash needed sewing up. I broke every one of my fingers at sometime or other once I started hurling – took a perverse pride in every snap.

Sport links all my childhood memories together. My family were immersed in sport. School was one long celebration of it. All week we played school games. I think at one stage, early in my secondary education when I was still eligible to do so, I played on just about every team that Drimnagh Castle had. This followed the pattern of primary school, which had finished with our glorious annexation of the Geraldine Cup, the top Gaelic football trophy at that age level. It was a job that involved my first playing outing to Croke Park. I suppose Wembley would be London's equivalent of Croke Park, minus the nationalist history. The thrill of playing there never quite went away.

On Saturdays, I'd tumble out of bed early to walk Paddy Croke's greyhounds. Paddy was an old hurler from Tipperary who had pitched up in Dublin and wound up back in 1961 playing on the last Dublin senior team to play in an All Ireland final. Luck being the way it is, he was playing against Tipperary. Dublin lost by a point and the game in the city never quite recovered.

I'd walk Paddy's dogs and I'd be back in time to get to my hurling game at 11 a.m. After that, I'd cycle to a Gaelic football game for one o'clock, and then on to soccer later in the afternoon. Sundays it would begin again, and if it didn't, Dad would ferret out a game to go to somewhere in the country and we'd set off, talking hurling and football as we went.

As kids, we played everything, and in the excited commentary that ran through our heads as we played, we could be anybody we wanted to be. We listened to Michael O'Hehir and then Michael O'Muircheartaigh commentate on football and hurling; we got our soccer through *Match of the Day* and *The Big Match*. When we played we always had a soundtrack to accompany our heroics.

Mainly they were good times but sometimes they were end-of-the-world tragic. For instance, I was sent off in the semi-final of the All Ireland soccer championships against Falcarragh Community School from Donegal. The game was played on a Saturday and the final was set for the next day. For me, it all finished on the Saturday. We won the semi-final on penalties but by then I had been dismissed for fighting off the ball. I was marking a guy named Eddie McGinley who was already something of a star. He'd played League of Ireland for Finn Harps when he was seventeen and that was experience enough for him to be able to fold me up and put me in his pocket for the afternoon. This wasn't how I'd imagined things going and I didn't handle it well. I fell to fouling him, and from there we progressed quickly to exchanging blows. We were hauled apart and when play resumed, I told Eddie to get back to digging potatoes.

Looking back, I'm surprised that I had that piece of economic history to hand, but not as surprised as Eddie was. Eddie lost it. He reacted as if he was the orphaned son of two potato diggers. He administered a good hiding to me. We both got sent off and I missed the final the next day when we beat Summerhill of Sligo 6–0. I watched each goal sail in and my lower lip got closer to the floor each time.

By then, I felt like a footballer with a good future behind me – sixteen years old and all washed up. The previous Easter I'd had what I assumed would be my one shot at the big time. Fulham Football Club wrote to me. Their manager, Malcolm Macdonald, had mentioned my name after the McVitie's weekend. I was to go over and show Mr Supermac and company whether or not I could do it all with the big boys.

I wasn't the most mature of sixteen year olds. The letter was a passport for showing off at school for about a week – genuine letterhead, genuine signature, yes, I was in correspondence with a genuine professional football club. I wasn't actually sure what travelling to Fulham would involve, and it took months for the trial to come about. My audience in school grew bored with seeing my letter and finally lost interest altogether. Christmas came and went. Finally, word came – Easter in London. Fulham were going at something of a gallop in the old Second Division and looked likely to force their way back into the top flight. I imagined that this somehow concerned me, that next season I would be playing for the league title instead of just for promotion.

Malcolm Macdonald himself met me at the airport. I had a goofy grin on my face and a feeling of irrepressible excitement in my head. First time on an aeroplane! Supermac on the Tarmac! Top o' the world, Ma! Top o' the world!

I was whisked off to the club, introduced to some faces I'd only ever seen on football cards and then deposited in some digs that the club used. A young fella from Liverpool who was hoping to make the grade as a goalkeeper was there, too, and we were lumped in together.

Next morning, the first thing that became clear was that Fulham were broke. No wonder the manager was meeting a sixteen-year-old triallist personally at the airport; the taxi fare would have tipped the club over into bankruptcy. We trained in the local park and twenty minutes into the session everyone grabbed the cones and footballs and fled across the fields like three-card-trick men who've spotted a policeman's hat. They ran and, taken by surprise, I followed. These professionals and their training techniques!

Helter skelter we got back to the ground, where I was told that a park ranger had appeared on the horizon. Aha! So we went off to another park and continued the session. The adrenaline rush of being among the outlaws of the public-parks system just added to the excitement for me.

Fulham gave me the full experience. Just because I was on trial didn't mean that I wouldn't get to clean boots after training. It never struck me to object. I spat and polished as if my career depended on it.

I played a game for the youth team and it went sweetly enough. Then they moved me up a rung and put me into a reserve game against Charlton in the Football Combination. I didn't get eaten alive, but I certainly got nibbled daintily.

The next game was against Queens Park Rangers reserves. I was auditioning as a centre-half and I found myself marking Clive Allen. He was wonderful. He scored five and I remember him driving away afterwards in his Ford Capri with the groovy go faster stripes. The man has everything, I thought. Years later, when we were playing together at Manchester City, I asked Clive if he remembered that day. He remembered the goals. He didn't remember me.

Next day, Malcolm Macdonald invited me in to his office. The conversation was short and frank.

'Son,' said Supermac, 'you've no future in football. Go home, get yourself a good education. Forget about this life. I wanted to call you in here to tell it to you straight. Man to man. See, there's two ways of doing this. There's the polite way and there's the truthful way. I'll give it to you the truthful way, son. As long as you have a hole in your arse, you will never make a footballer.' He handed me a signed football. 'Here's a souvenir of your time in football.'

I should have been insulted but I assumed that Malcolm

Macdonald knew best. Fulham blew promotion that year; they lost five of their final nine games. Leicester City went up instead. Supermac didn't know everything.

Luckily, the hole in my backside was no impediment to my enjoyment of the equal-opportunities sports of football and hurling. All my friends in the GAA suffered from the same handicap. We all played happily.

I was happier than most. Although reared in Dublin, I was brought up mainly as a Tipperary person. This is important. When it comes to sport, Tipperary people believe hurling to be the greatest game in the world. When it comes to hurling, Tipperary people believe themselves to be the chosen tribe. Generally speaking, in the lottery of life, Tipp people believe themselves to be the big winners and I had a share of the ticket. Other people, poor souls born in other counties, think we're arrogant. Not being from Tipp, they can't understand that Tipp's hurling history is a burden and a responsibility which all Tipp people must bear.

How great and beautiful a game is hurling? One image will do. It's said that Tipperary's greatest-ever goalkeeper was Skinny Meara from Toomevara. It is said, too, that Skinny trained in the summertime by opening the doors of his barn, standing in the great gap and stopping swallows from flying in and out. That was one hundred years ago almost. The game is faster now.

In 1984, in the summer after I went to Arsenal, I travelled with Dad to a famous Munster final in Thurles. At the time, Tipperary were coming to the end of a long period in the wilderness, a bad time that included a stretch of nine years when the county team went without winning a single championship match. That Sunday we travelled to Thurles more in hope than in confidence. Tipp were to play Cork. You are never confident against Cork.

The game is remembered with a wince by all Tipp people, even now. Five minutes left and a veteran called Noel O'Dwyer put Tipperary four points ahead. This was it. This surely was the end of the bad times. Dad was beside himself. I have seldom seen him so excited. All around us, Tipperary people were beginning to celebrate. Men were shedding tears, hands were being pumped, fists were being shaken. No more feigning humility! We were back! At the best of times, a Munster championship is worth celebrating, but to end a famine with a Munster championship win against Cork? That's the Tipperary idea of heaven. The hay saved and Cork beat. Perfect!

But the sky fell in. Cork scored a point. Then they equalised with a goal. Then Tipp had possession through Mick Doyle, the son of the legendary John Doyle, but somehow it was lost and Cork raced to the other end of the field where the Tipp goalie John Sheedy made a wonderful save only to see a famous Cork forward by the name of Seanie O'Leary sweep the ball home. Cork added another point from a free and then it was over.

Four points up; four points down. My father, always first out the gate after a big game as he went in search of a decent pub and some good hurling conversation, just wilted. The air left him. I remember him sitting at the top of the terrace as Semple Stadium emptied, and he looked desolate, like a man whose entire tribe had been cursed. There and then you could see the meaning of it all.

When I began playing soccer with Manortown United, I kept it a secret from my da for a couple of years because, like many GAA people at the time, he was no great fan of soccer. My mother would smuggle me to games with Manortown, relieved I think that I was playing a more gentle sport than football or hurling.

Despite my wanton experimentation, we remained a fundamentalist GAA family and hurling was the high religion. Dad had been a real prospect with the greatest of hurling counties and, for me, the idea of hurling for Dublin at minor level and later at senior level was always more exciting than the notion of playing for Fulham.

Perhaps you have to be from these parts to understand how Gaelic sports touch Irish lives. People live, eat and breathe hurling and football, completely amateur games that whip up the passion in people's hearts because they are about where you are from and what sort of person you are. I am convinced that, if you have an experienced eye, you can identify those of us in the Premiership and beyond who played a lot of Gaelic games when growing up. There's Kevin Moran, Denis Irwin, Steve Staunton, Colin Healy at Celtic, Martin O'Neill, Packie Bonner, Pat Jennings; we all played. In fact, and there are a few Irish people who won't like hearing this, I think the ethos of Gaelic games has influenced Irish international teams over the last twenty years.

I'm saying the games are better. I'm not saying those of us who play them are better, just different. In soccer, with the trial system and the way that money trickles down even to the lowest levels of the game, the individual comes first. When you hurl or when you play football for your home place, when you do it purely for the love of it and the tradition of it, you develop a different feel for sport. Some of that sensibility comes through in Irish teams.

My own moment in the sun came in the summer of 1983. I was still sixteen and I made the Dublin minor hurling side. We reached the Leinster final, beating Kilkenny along the way, quite an achievement for a team from Dublin where the game is weak. We beat Westmeath in the semi-final and faced the provincial decider against Wexford. I scored three goals and five points as we won our first Leinster title in eighteen years. As it became clear that we actually had a good side, I enjoyed a mild form of celebrity for a few weeks. That summer I could see nothing in my future but hurling, hurling, hurling.

By the time the All Ireland final came about in September, I hadn't played soccer for months. I crashed to earth quickly. Galway beat us handily. I was marked by Sean Treacy, who went on to be one of Galway's greatest players at senior level. I could tell he enjoyed devouring the Dublin kid who'd been in all the papers. I scarcely caught sight of the ball throughout the game and we lost badly. I promised myself I would be back for more.

But nineteen years of soccer got in the way and when I think of a hurling career now, I think of retiring to Kildare and playing in goals for a local junior team. Junior hurling in Kildare is the bottom of the ladder – in Tipperary, they'd be reluctant to call it hurling – but it would be nice to feel the thrill of the game just a few more times, to feel the uncluttered purity of an amateur sport again.

This morning I could live with that quiet life. When we got to the airport, we were ushered up into what we were promised would be a private lounge but it's crammed now with press and punters and various hangers-on and liggers who are here to see us off. A few times I catch sight of Roy out of the corner of my eye. He's still very agitated. There are people milling about here who have slaughtered him in the papers all week, and whatever amount of front we all bring to this job, I know it's hurting him. I see him complaining to a couple of journalists. Rather them than me.

Finally, we get on board. We're no sooner settled than we are in Amsterdam for a two-hour stopover. Again we're wondering why are we here, why we are wandering these corridors for two hours. I'm not sure if it's true but it's said that when we knocked Holland out of the World Cup qualifying stages, the FAI did a deal with the Dutch FA and bought their flight tickets off them. If it's true, I hope they got good value. We could do without this delay.

At last, it's on to the big plane to Tokyo where we will have another stop for an hour or so. Early in the journey, Roy makes his way downstairs and tears into another journalist or two. Dispatches say that the word 'scum' gets used a lot.

I'm here as the vibes man. Perhaps I should go and smooth things over. Maybe not. The flight is too long or life is too short. Either way, I stretch my legs out, shut my eyes and let the time go by. I think of a story – it seems so long ago now that it should begin with the words once upon a time.

Once upon a time when we were both young and broke and out of the team at Arsenal, Paul Merson and I went to Ascot and lost what little cash we had. The last race of the day was a maiden hurdle with thirty-one runners. I fell back on science to save me. I took my last tenner in the world and did a reverse forecast bet using the number of my flat (6) and the number of our hall door in Dublin (23).

I queued and handed over the money, with Merse, already skint, beside me like a bodyguard. We'd come away from the hatch when Merse noticed that the ticket had the wrong numbers. Instead of horses six and twenty-three, I'd been given six and twenty-seven.

'Leave it or change it?' I said.

'Nah, change it, Niall.'

So we queue again, explain the mistake, get it changed. You can guess the rest — six beats twenty-seven for first. They come home at 100 to 1 and 66 to 1 respectively. My tenner would have become £25,000. I could only laugh. Merse looked suicidal. He could scarcely speak. When we got back to the car, we found I'd left the lights on all day and it wouldn't start. I laughed some more. I laughed till I cried. Merse almost went over the edge. Two friends have never been more mystified by each other.

That's what I like about football. That's why most of the time I enjoy Roy. The media allow us a narrow range of character types; anyone outside that range gets hammered, screwed, caricatured or laughed at. But it's the guys at the extremes who make life interesting. They make the journey shorter.

CHAPTER THREE

OPENING TIME

You, me and the bottle makes three tonight.
BIG BAD VOODOO DADDY

The front entrance of the Saipan Hyatt is at the end of a dusty road that teems with girls who offer massages to passers-by. The hotel's rear entrance leads on to the beach. Tonight we are going to a barbecue out back and then toddling out through the front to get drunk, very drunk. For some reason, it reminds me of the first big night out I ever had with a team. I was sixteen and we were in Hawaii, on our way to Australia. We were staying in a hotel that fronted on to a street busy with prostitutes, and backed on to the beach. We were going out the front door with the intention of getting drunk, very drunk.

I was rooming with my friend Tom O'Donovan. Tom is a prison officer in Mountjoy Jail now but he still has the same streak of lunacy running through him that he had then. I remember him in Hawaii chatting to the prostitutes, asking them about what sort of a job it was, could you get promoted, how much job satisfaction was there, how would you get a start, would it be worth his while. All the time I'm beside him, trying to push him along. I'd seen *Hawaii Five O.* I knew that the evil pimp would be along to murder us at any moment just for making jokes on his patch. Worse, one of the coaches might see us.

It was 1983, the summer in which we reached the All Ireland minor hurling final, and I was captain of the Dublin Colleges Under-18 Gaelic football side, the first Irish representative side to tour Australia. Today, an Irish senior team travels to Australia every second autumn to play the Aussies at International Rules, an exciting hybrid of Aussie Rules and Gaelic Football. In the off years, the Aussies come to Ireland. It's a popular annual event for which we were the guinea pigs. We didn't play hybrid rules, we played pure Aussie Rules. Looking back, it was as much an opportunity for the Australians to beat us up and pick off our best players as it was anything else.

On the night in question, we were on our way to a nightclub. We got the hotel to hire an eight-seater taxi to take us to a popular nightspot. We were just kids and only eight of us had nerve enough to go. The taxi came with an assurance that the driver knew the owner of the club and it would be no problem slipping eight spotty underaged lads with sunburn past the bouncers, no problem at all.

This is the life, I thought as we drove through Hawaii. Five weeks in Australia and an All Ireland minor hurling final three weeks after I get home. The nightclub will be filled with beautiful and exotic women in grass skirts and they will place garlands of flowers around my neck and ask me if it's really true that I scored three goals and five points in the Leinster minor hurling final. I'll say yes, and I know Supermac, too.

It took about half an hour to get to the club, which was on the far side of Honolulu. We pulled up and took care of our driver big style. We had agreed a fee with him beforehand but, because it was all so clandestine and glamorous and he was getting us in with the in-crowd, we almost doubled it with a massive tip. We handed over the money with many matey nods and winks.

To be fair, we glided into the nightclub as promised – 'Evening, sir, and how are you tonight?' Two things registered – the joint ain't jumping and it's empty except for us. They were playing 'Beat It' by Michael Jackson – again and again and again.

We downed some drinks and raised a laugh among ourselves for being such losers. Collectively, we suffered the sort of spasms that, for Irishmen, pass as dancing. After a short while, we decided we might as well cut our losses and slink home for an early night. So we scooted back down to the ground-floor exit in a novel way. The club had one of those glass lifts that travel up and down the exterior of the building. We all piled in, paddies on tour. On the way down, Tom spotted something familiar just down the street a little bit – our hotel. We looked at each other, eight suckers descending in a glass lift, and agreed that this night out, from beginning to end, would be our little secret.

There's a point to this story; I'm sure there is. The point is that an Irish World Cup team is different from other World Cup teams. We do things differently. We're more easygoing. I don't know why but I think it suits us. I think that the day we are the same as everyone else is the day we will have lost our edge.

Imagine the English World Cup squad flying for twenty-three hours to an island in the western Pacific. OK, most likely it wouldn't happen at all but just imagine Becks, Rio and the boys. There would be advance parties and heavy security, and their five spin doctors would be spinning like spiders. The island would be closed off while the media and the paparazzi peeped at players from zeppelins cruising overhead.

Us? We travelled to the point of exhaustion, leaving Dublin on Friday morning, getting to Saipan on Saturday afternoon. Tonight we have a barbecue for the media. Then most of the team and probably most of the media will go to a pub and drink together till dawn. If anybody writes about it, they'll be given a quiet dignified burial on the beach. We're different. That's all I'm saying. My experience is that no harm comes from the difference. We thrive on it.

Back in 1983 (different time, different sport, but the same race of people and the same bad habits) we flew from Hawaii to Melbourne where we were farmed out to families in private houses. Tom and I stayed in the home of Melbourne Football Club chairman Dick Seddon. What sticks in the memory is the fact that he had a lift in his house. The house was that big. He could have taken in our whole twenty-six-man squad if he'd wanted to.

We trained every day and played our first match about a week into the tour. The Australians battered us. We went to the Territories and I was deposited in the home of a man who lived in the bush about five miles away from the nearest sign of life. I was petrified until . . . well, it sounds too much like the beginning of a dirty joke but out in the bush he had a sixteen-year-old daughter who was the most beautiful creature I'd ever seen. We became friends but I know that to this day there are people who were on that trip who regard her as Quinny's imaginary friend.

Australia was sensational. Apart, that is, from a kangaroo hunting tour, which made me physically sick. I was captain so I got to make a lot of speeches. We moved on to Sydney where the host family kindly took Tom and me on guided tours of the seediest areas. They got us drunk in King's Cross. I went to bed wondering what I'd write when it came to the annual 'what I did on my summer holidays' essay back in school. The next morning I trained with a hangover for the first time – not ideal but something I would soon master.

I got used to getting away with things, to leading a charmed life. We lost our first four matches in Australia but learned from each one. Our fifth game was against Melbourne at the MCG. We played as the curtain-raiser to a big AFL game and I kicked a score right at the buzzer, which allowed us to come away with a draw and train for the second time with a hangover. We won the final four games and travelled home as a successful side.

The way we did things then relates to this Irish World Cup team and its predecessors. We're not buttoned down and rigid. We have a little wildness in us. We have a feel for the far side. We are professional footballers but we are a group of people, too, and bonding together is as important as training together.

We're not perfect and things here in Saipan aren't perfect. There's been some mix-up with our training gear. The training pitch, which has been built specially for us, is a little on the bumpy side and there are no spare goalposts. Bits and pieces of stuff we need haven't arrived, and some of us are finding the plane journey hard to shake from our limbs.

Last night we had a team meeting at which Dr Martin Walsh, who's been putting us back together for years now, spoke to us about hydration and what we should drink while we are living and training in this heat and humidity. The FAI have special drinks for us. They just haven't arrived yet. This sets Roy off. We're leaving the room and he's moaning, 'It's fucking wrong. It's a mess. It's a disaster.'

I catch up with him. 'Jaysus, Roy, it's no big deal. C'mon, we're all in this together. Let's make the most of it. We'll get through it. Have a laugh at it.'

It's not the easiest thing to do. I get away with it this time.

'I'm just saying it's wrong,' he says. 'That's all.'

He sees Mick to discuss all the problems and I hope that resolves it. Roy is the captain and channelling them through the manager is the best way of dealing with them, instead of moaning all day.

The barbecue with the media tonight is a disaster in some ways. Roy has been against it for obvious reasons and he has made his displeasure known. In fairness, he comes along anyway and sits with the rest of us through an awkward hour or two of speeches and entertainment.

Roy hasn't been drinking for some time now so we keep it low key about what we have planned for the rest of the evening. Meanwhile, the local cabaret artists put on an exhibition of bad jokes and hula dancing. The entertainment ends with Robbie Keane, a couple of journalists and some girls in grass skirts all dancing together on the stage. Robbie looks like the only one who can actually dance.

There is a quick break for the bar. The players circulate dutifully for a little bit, Roy slips off into the night and then some of the lads make a fairly theatrical show of yawning and stretching and pretending to be heading off to bed. We reconvene half an hour later in an English-style bar downtown. It's called the Beefeater Bar and it's run by a hapless American called Carl.

Carl, you're about to have the longest night of your life.

Inside there's a dartboard, a pool table and a jukebox. Most of the squad arrive and we set about some serious bonding. By the morning, we'll be leglessly bonded. Roy has a point about things being wrong but this is a week mainly of rest and recreation between the end of a long season and the start of a World Cup. It doesn't have to be perfect.

Today and yesterday we trained with no footballs. We did some running and some exercises, no problem. We don't have footballs and we don't have the right training gear but the skies are blue, the beach is perfect, the hotel is fine and we're on our way to the World Cup. Relax.

I know about the complaints Roy is submitting but I don't care that much. The training gear is an issue with Roy. He is furious over it, but for some of us it amounts to the difference between round necks and v necks for a couple of days. I'll wear what we have brought with us till the right gear arrives. I can live with it. Nobody will die.

Traditionally, this is the way we've been. We've never pampered ourselves. Under Jack Charlton, when we enjoyed ten years of good times, we were mostly ramshackle, and part of what made us tick was the disorganisation and the joy we got from pretending to the world that we weren't to be taken seriously. Then we'd go out on to a pitch and die for one another. I think that, because Roy has done so much with Manchester United and everything there seems to be perfect, he expects more to be laid on during these Irish trips, just as a starting point. When the rest of us don't get as wound up as he does, he wonders if we're as motivated as he is.

I don't think it means, as newspapers often claim, that Roy represents a new Ireland where everything is done in a pristine and perfect fashion, and the rest of us represent an old slapdash culture. We just have different ways of making the thing work.

Few people here, apart from Steve Staunton and me, will remember our training camp for the Italian World Cup twelve years ago. We went to Malta and used the same training base as Scotland. They had their orange cones, their dieticians and shrinks, their bags of balls and their synchronised exercises. We were doing our work just a pitch length away from them and we looked like Ragarse Rovers. The weather hadn't been obliging. It was mainly overcast so Jack hit on the idea of making us train while wearing three layers of tracksuits with heavy rain jackets over the lot. We bumbled about like Michelin men during the day, drank at night and looked askance at the Scots, all lean, mean and perfect.

In Italy, the Scots made their traditional first-round exit while we got to the quarter-finals and went out to the hosts in the Olympic Stadium in Rome. Human beings aren't an exact science. It doesn't have to be dead solid perfect. There's an intangible called spirit.

Suddenly, the Beefeater Bar goes quiet. The media have walked in. This is slightly awkward. We can't say that of all the bars in all the towns in all the world you had to choose ours. The Beefeater is about forty yards from the hotel. Still, it's uncomfortable. Silence breaks out for a while before we all decide this is silly. We stop being footballers. They stop being scribblers. We get the drinks in.

Carl, it's still going to be the longest night of your life.

When we lost the All Ireland minor final of 1983, the light went out of the world for a few days. Playing badly and losing put a dent into what had been one great adventure of a summer. I went back to school and settled down for the grey life of study, followed by the leaving certificate and then a dose of the real world. But a few days later, it all went crazy again. Bill Darby knocked on our door up in Crumlin.

'Yes?'

'I'm sorry. I've been waiting till you got the hurling out of the way before I came to ask.'

'What?'

'Would you like to go to Arsenal for a trial?'

I hadn't played soccer for six months. The Fulham experience had left its mark. I fancied playing minor football and hurling for Dublin the following summer. I had my exams to worry about. Immediately, I said yes.

Next thing I knew I was playing up front alongside this fairhaired kid for an Arsenal Under-18 team against Southall FC. I scored three. The kid scored six. We won 9–0. The kid came over to me afterwards. He was maybe a year younger than I was.

'I'm Paul Merson,' he said. 'We must be a million on to get a contract after this.'

Personally, I thought that this was a fine thing to say if you'd scored six and looked as good as Paul Merson did. But I was an old hand at this trial thing. I believed that I'd be found out quickly. Merse and I were fast friends from there on, though.

The trial was a two-week affair and my seventeenth birthday came up on the day after we played University College, London. We won 4–0 and I scored two, laid on two and got taken off at half-time. We didn't score in the second half. We didn't even create anything. So far, so good.

Next day, in an unlikely display of sentimentality, Arsenal let me train with their first team. Here's the birthday boy and here's his special treat. Immediately, I was suspicious. Malcolm Macdonald had given me a football to take home. At Arsenal they must allow you to train with the first team before they throw you back into the pond. Oh well! Not the end of the world. I decided to enjoy it anyway. We did a ball-control exercise and I remember Charlie Nicholas whacking the ball at me, again and again, and because I thought it was all over and the pressure was off, I was laughing, pulling it down and whacking it back to him. Maybe the professionals will wonder how come the club aren't keeping the lanky fella, I thought to myself.

At the end of the session Arsenal's youth-development coach, Steve Burtenshaw, crooked his finger at me. He put an arm round my shoulder.

'I think we can forget about next week, son,' he said. 'Just go home and get yourself sorted because we will be offering you a contract to come over to play for Arsenal.'

In the Beefeater Bar, Gary Kelly is conducting an art competition. We are all to draw a horse, or a 'haws' as Gary calls it in his broad Drogheda accent. Gary will judge the best drawing. It costs ten or twenty dollars to enter, depending on what Gary is thinking at the time.

We can scarcely draw we are laughing so much. Gary is one of the funniest people I have ever met and he's making up the competition rules as he goes along. Everyone has to keep their drawing private, extra marks are going for good-looking horses, Robbie Keane is disqualified because he's from Tallaght, home of the roaming piebalds, Ian Harte is bumped out because he's let somebody see his horse. We can hardly breathe we're laughing so hard.

✻   ✻   ✻

With Steve Burtenshaw's permission, I went home to Dublin and imagined the life of the professional footballer – a monastic existence of self-denial and self-discipline, which might eventually lead to oneness with the ball and a Ford Capri with go faster stripes.

The following week, Dick Seddon, the chairman of Melbourne with whom I'd stayed in Australia, arrived in Dublin. He was offering me an Aussie Rules scholarship – good money, good education, free trips home. I could have my own home with my own lift in it, eventually. Poor man. I could hardly pay attention.

Terry Neill, manager of Arsenal, and Steve Burtenshaw came to Dublin soon afterwards. They brought us to see Ireland play Holland at Dalymount the following week. I remember Gullit played as a libero and scored two of their three goals. Afterwards, we went to the Skylon Hotel and my mother pitched wits with Terry Neill. He was good. He'd pitched wits with other people's mothers. I'd get so many dusty books to read that the only thing that would stop me becoming asthmatic was the occasional ninety minutes in the fresh air that Arsenal could offer. I would also get £150 a week (that's sterling, missus) for the first two years, rising to an incredible £175 (again, I tell you, that's sterling) in the third year; plus a £5,000 sterling signing-on fee, doled out over the three years. Why, I would be as highly paid as a busy pizza delivery boy. I signed up. It was 12 October 1983.

Then, for some reason, I went back to school till I got FA clearance to go to Highbury. While I was strutting around school, a man called Greg Miller from the Sydney Swans Aussie Rules club called to the door. I'd done well in Sydney and they were keen to tap into the Irish emigrant market. He offered me an incredible deal – a signing-on fee of A$15,000 a year plus A$600 a week, a car, a rent-free apartment and free flights back. I would practically be governor of New South Wales.

I never gave it a thought. Then Dick Seddon came back again and upped his offer. It was too late. I'd lost my heart to Arsenal.

Dick switched his attention to Jimmy Stynes from Ballyboden. He went on to become one of the great figures in the Aussie game. I went on to place third in the Gary Kelly World Cup Horse Drawing Contest. Thus two great cultures benefited.

By the way, third isn't bad. Gary is a tough judge of a haws. He and Robbie Keane are serenading me at the moment. The pair of them can harmonise instinctively and they are singing some hokey country song about how they both thought that I could walk on water. It's a good piss-take on all the Saint Niall headlines my testimonial has attracted.

The testimonial is a fine source of fun for Gary, who actually did the same thing with his testimonial the week before. The difference is that Gary has only ever played for one club, so he has never picked up the handy money that goes with a move – and he actually deserved the testimonial Leeds United gave him. My testimonial proceeds were found money. What Gary gave away to cancer charities (his sister Mandy died of the disease) was earned money; his own earned money. Not just that, he sent me a huge cheque for my fund and just now he bumped me up to third in the haws drawing contest. Nevertheless, any time I go to buy a round he starts up.

'Forget it, Quinny. Leave it alone. It's over. No more good deeds. Get on with your life. We know how good you are. You've nothing to prove to us.'

His tribute song with Robbie on harmonies is just ending when The Commodores come schmaltzing out of the jukebox – 'You're once, twice, three times a lady'. We are waltzing with poolsticks, with the bored Russian barmaids, with each other. Of all the things The Commodores have done with their lives, I imagine that sparking an Irish sing-song in an English bar in Saipan at four in the morning is a first. We segue from The Commodores into 'The Green Fields of France' and on into 'The Summer Wind'.

We've switched to tequilas.

*　　*　　*

My Aunt Ailish and Uncle Mattie met me at Heathrow. Promisingly, we stopped for a pint on the way home from the airport. Mattie was a bar steward at the London Irish rugby club and had enlightened ideas about young athletes and drink.

Mattie and Ailish lived near Twickenham and getting to Highbury was something of an epic journey. I caught the bus at 6.15 a.m. from Twickenham to Hounslow West. Then I took the tube, the blue Piccadilly Line, from Hounslow West to Highbury, arriving at the club at 7.45. First thing, I'd do the kit. Then it was on the road at 8.30 to pick up the professionals who hadn't got cars. They gathered at Southgate at 9 a.m. It was twenty minutes to half an hour to London Colney. Once there, I'd lay out all the kit for training at 10.30.

I talk to young players about it now and make out it was a hardship, but truth to tell, I was too excited to know what it was. Streaking through London in the morning, I was shoehorned into a tube carriage filled with people going to work in offices and shops and on building sites. Me? Want to know my secret? I'm off to play for the Arsenal. I was giddy as a kite. I had signed as a professional and wasn't even supposed to be doing all the jobs that engaged me up until 10.30 in the morning. I threw myself into them anyway.

On the first day, I remember walking up from the tube station at Highbury. The train I'd just stepped from was leaving and another one, going the other way, passed it at speed. The uprush of wind they created caught me by surprise and nearly blew me away. I felt somebody tugging at my sleeve. It was David Rocastle. He remembered me from the trial and he'd run along the platform to catch up with me.

'You coming to play with us then?'

'Yeah.'

'Excellent.'

'Thanks.'

'One word, mate.'

'Yeah?'

'The duffel.'

'Yeah?'

'Honestly, mate. Lose it.'

'Serious?'

'Deadly.'

So I removed the brand new duffel coat that my mother had bought to shield her only son against the London winter. I walked back and handed it in to the ticket office. I picked it up that evening and never wore it again. Instead, I froze through the winter in a green combat jacket.

After a couple of weeks, I ceased to care whether Arsenal would start tending to my academic needs. I had jobs to do. Terry Neill would come in every afternoon and check the dressing rooms that we'd cleaned. I never imagined that the manager of a large football club would have such concerns but he'd come in and run his finger along the top of the pelmet, and if he found a speck of dust there you'd start again.

After a few weeks, he called me in to his office.

'How are you getting on, son?'

'Fine,' I said. 'Only trouble is nobody can understand a word I'm saying.'

'Sorry, son. What was that?'

'Just saying nobody can understand a word I'm saying.'

'Sorry, son. Slower. I didn't catch that.'

'NO-BODY CAN UNDER-STAND A WORD I SAY.'

'I'm sorry, son. Calm down, it's just a comprehension problem. Steve! Can you get in here a minute. Quinn here is trying to tell me something and I can't make it out.'

'I was just saying to the gaffer that nobody can understand a word I say.'

'What's that?' said Steve Burtenshaw. 'What did you just tell me?'

On it went. Several more experts on dialect and accent and speech impediment were called in. I spoke my sentence louder and slower each time. My cheeks went redder with every effort. Hours later, on the tube back towards Twickenham, the awful truth dawned on me.

It's bright outside the Beefeater Bar now. Carl has been trying to throw us out for maybe two hours. We have invented birthdays and toasts to secure another round from him. We have promised to show him new drinking games in order to get more. We have promised him we have somebody keeping an eye out for the cops. We have paid him ten dollars a drink. We have told him that a pint and a short is the traditional Irish going-home drink – a pint and a short and another pint. Then we'll be gone.

Carl can't move us. I believe he's had more drink than any of us. He's almost given up. We start fighting among ourselves. Some players and some journalists begin arguments. Ian Harte leans across the bar.

'Carl,' he says sadly. 'Why don't you just throw us all out?'

Carl looks at Hartey and knows he'd never last a night as a barman in Drogheda, County Louth.

Honestly, I thought they'd hail me as the next genius from the production line that gave Arsenal Brady, Stapleton and O'Leary. Instead, I had to contend with the legacy of Duffy. I never knew his first name but Duffy was from Dublin and he was a legend by the time I got to Highbury. On one two-week youth trip to France, Duffy had turned up carrying nothing more than a plastic bag with a brand new white cotton shirt and a toothbrush in it.

Every morning when training finished at London Colney, Duffy, who looked more frazzled every day, would skip the showers and sprint for the team coach. He'd persuade the driver to take him to Southgate while the other lads showered. The bus would be back in time for the regulars.

After a while, the club began to get a little concerned for Duffy's welfare and hygiene. Eventually, the landlady at the digs complained, too. An investigation was opened. At Southgate there was a bookies called Bashams. The bus driver reported that Duffy disappeared in there every day.

So one day, somebody from the club was delegated to follow Duffy. As usual, Duffy sprinted for the bus, covered in mud and sweat. The driver took him back to Southgate where Duffy leaped out, having changed on the way, and headed straight into Bashams. The club spy followed him inside, being careful to keep his distance, so he could ascertain the level of the kid's gambling problem. There was no sign of Duffy. The spy waited a while but Duffy had disappeared. Then suddenly their eyes met. The boy in the white coat, chalking the odds on the board for the bookie, was Duffy, my immediate predecessor.

It was a rough and tumble world and it took me a while to get used to it. I was bottom of the pecking order. There was Tony Donnelly, a kitman originally from Crumlin and a great guy, Terry Burton, the reserve-team manager, and Tommy Coleman, the youth-team coach. Tommy has a bar in Spain now. Terry and Tommy were the resident Cockney double act – geezers and wiseguys. They were never my cup of tea.

I was astonished by the casual hardness of life on the training ground. I became known as Wolfie because, in my combat jacket and with my lank hair, I reminded them of the TV character Citizen Smith. Other names weren't pleasant. The lads used to take it. There was no choice.

Cockney rhyming slang was Tommy Coleman's supposed genius.

'Quinn. I'd say you're a real Allied Irish Banker.'

'Yeah, I am.'

'Hear that, lads. He says he's an Allied Irish Banker.'

'Really?'

'Eh, yeah.'

'Had you down for a Midland Banker, son.'

'No. I'm an Allied Irish Banker.'

Even thirty seconds later when I'd got the hang of it all, it was easier just to play along with them, deadpan.

I made friends. We were all hopeful, all in the same boat. There was John Purdie from Corby, a good player who went to Wolves afterwards, and Jonathan Woods from Wales; and Dave Rocastle and Merse, of course. There was Rhys Wilmot, Kenny Veysey, Gus Caesar and Tony Rees, a funny lad from Wales. He'd come up every now and then and say mournfully, 'Really sorry, Niall. Just heard now.'

'What?'

'About you being let go.'

'Wha—?'

Gary Campbell was a great kid and a wonderful player from the north. He was to be the next big thing, but it never happened. He got the reputation of being too good-natured and too easygoing. Ahead of me was Paul Gorman from Crumlin, and David Cork and Tony Isaacs whom the lads fancied looked a little like Michael Jackson except with more style. Tony used to wear spats. There was Martin Keown, Martin Hayes, Nicky Hammond and Donato Russo.

I liked Donato. Back then, in the afternoons we used to go to a snooker hall above a bank in Southgate. Don never played snooker. I'd play a game or two and Don would mooch around. One day Don is bored. He puts fifty pence into a fruit machine and wins a hundred quid. Unbelievable! It's one of those machines that when you win the jackpot only a few quid comes out but all the bells and buzzers go off so that somebody from the desk comes along and pays you the balance. Don is confused by this and when the guy comes along Don is beside himself.

'You're ripping me off,' he says. 'There's only about ten quid here.'

The guy sizes Don up and explains the deal.

'What it is, son, is that ten per cent gets paid out here and the rest automatically goes into a chute, through the floor and into an account which is opened up for you downstairs in the bank. You now have ninety pounds' credit in the bank whenever you need it. Just go there and have a word.'

So Don goes down and queues up.

'I'm from the snooker club. The fruit machine? I just want to get my money.'

And, of course, there was Tony Adams. You knew Tony would make it. He was way ahead of all of us. He made his first-team debut at seventeen, not long after I arrived. He was as big as the senior players physically, he could run quicker than any of us, and he had the nerve to organise people.

In the mornings and the evenings, I'd listen out for Irish people on the tube. I'd hear somebody chatting and try to work out what county they were from. I never had the bottle to say hello but I longed to.

Things shocked me. Once I went to Euston Station to get the train home at Christmas. I went into the bar there and it was full of Irish down and outs. Over a pint, I half befriended a couple of them and bought a few drinks to kill the time. All they wanted from me was my birth certificate so they could claim benefit. I'd be asking why they didn't just go home, these Irish people with brown faces all crossed with cuts and scabs, and they were gently hustling me. I was seventeen with plenty to learn about football and more to learn about the real world outside. I was one step ahead of Donato Russo, though.

In the end, we throw ourselves out of the Beefeater Bar. It's bright in Saipan now but not yet warm. We're laughing and hooting. Some of us are still arguing. Others are singing. It's coming on for six in the morning and in a few hours, Mick will take us training in the heat.

I know the tricks of the trade by now. Get some fluids inside me. Get as much sleep as possible. Get more fluids in, and then go for it bald-headed in training, especially when Mick is watching.

It's a wonderful life.

CHAPTER FOUR

STORM COUNTRY

Mankind faces a crossroads. One path leads to despair and
utter hopelessness. The other path leads to extinction. Let us
pray that we choose correctly.
WOODY ALLEN

Not too long ago at Sunderland we had an apprentice with us from Dublin. He was a young fellow from the southside called Smith. He was known everywhere in the club as Smithy and he was good, but he couldn't handle the daily training.

In the summer, our pre-season training finishes each day with four laps of the entire training ground. Most days it nearly kills me. Unless you are Yifter the Shifter, you have to play it smart as you get older. You don't dally at the start, you hang on the shoulder of somebody good and you build up some credit because you know that for the last two laps you'll be wheezing back through the field. When that happens, you don't want Peter Reid kicking your tail all the way home.

Smithy didn't have the knowledge. Fatally, he was slow but honest. Every day Smithy came home last by a country mile. The poor kid was slower than a wet week. In a young player, a manager finds this discouraging. Peter was discouraged, so he experimented with advanced motivational techniques.

'Smithy,' he said, 'I'm going to join in today and if I beat you, there'll be effin' trouble.'

'Right, Gaffer,' says Smithy.

And off we all went.

I'm doing my usual trick, getting away to a good start while the lads are all still lolloping along chatting through the first lap. Soon I can hear Peter.

'Smithy, don't let me beat you, son. C'mon, Smithy.'

I glance back and Peter is jogging backwards about thirty yards ahead of Smithy. This is fine entertainment and as it's slowing everyone down, I make the most of it.

By the time we come around for our second lap we are ahead of Smithy by half a circuit of the training ground. We realise that in two more laps we'll have lapped him. That's unprecedented. Peter is further and further ahead of the kid, still jogging backwards some of the time, still roaring at him to move. 'Please don't let me beat you, Smithy,' he roars, and I can tell even from a distance that he's knocking a laugh out of this one.

Smithy is trundling along, giving forlorn looks, like a tortoise envying an elderly hare as a steamroller bears down from behind. He comes around by the main entrance for the second time and then a remarkable thing happens. The kid vanishes. He just runs straight out the gate, straight back to the digs, gets his stuff and is gone back to Ireland quicker than he's ever moved before.

We've never seen him again but we talk of him sometimes. Smithy. Who'd have thought you could just walk away?

We got a history lesson yesterday. For a small island in the middle of nowhere, Saipan has a story to tell that is ugly and shocking, like nothing we've heard before. We went off on a coach to see the parts of this little island where the ghosts still linger.

Back in the years after Pearl Harbor, the island of Saipan had some strategic value for America. Its neighbouring island, Tinian, is where the Enola Gay took off from to bomb Hiroshima. By the time the fighting for Saipan ended in the summer of 1944, 30,000 Japanese had died and some 14,000 Americans were either dead or wounded.

Then it got worse. Japanese civilians, who had been force-fed bewildering propaganda about the American invaders, began hurling themselves off the cliffs and promontories around the island. Two-thirds of the 12,000 Japanese civilians on the island chose to go out this way. Meanwhile, American interpreters begged them through loudhailers to surrender and Japanese snipers shot those having second thoughts from behind.

Since then the island's main claim to fame has been as one of the world's great sweatshops. Non-unionised workers from China were kept in compounds and paid a pittance to produce top-label goods for the American market.

We drove around the island looking at the Suicide Cliff and the Bonsai Cliffs and listening to the grim history of it all. It fairly knocked the giddiness out of us. We were thirty sombre souls by the time we got back to the hotel.

Otherwise, life here has settled into its own gentle routine. We train, we eat, we sleep. Tomorrow we might play golf. Every now and then three of us walk over to the media hotel and have a press conference where we drip-feed the press boys little tidbits about our lives and careers, answering all the obvious questions with all the obvious answers. It passes the time.

Training has picked up after the first couple of days. We have footballs. We have our drinks. We have our round-collared, or was it V-necked, shirts. The pitch is a couple of miles along the coast, and if you look carefully on the way, you can see the gun turret of an old American tank sticking out of the clear blue water just off one of the beaches. The pitch is still bumpy and parched but we'll get by for the week. Apart from when people roar in the dressing room that they are going to give it 100 per cent, football isn't actually a game of 100 per cent. It's about adapting to 90 per cent and compensating for 80 per cent and being 1 per cent better than the other guy and so on.

I know this because back home in Sunderland we train at the Charlie Hurley Training Ground at Whitburn. Let me just say that Whitburn is the north-east's response to global warming. From July through to May, we are there almost every day and it's always winter. If you can say that you have felt the heat of the sun on your neck half a dozen times in that time, you have a problem with exaggeration. Whitburn is cold and windy and sometimes the pitches take so much water that we have to decamp entirely and go to Manchester or somewhere to train. At other times, there's so much snow that Peter Reid comes to work mushing a team of huskies.

It's a happy place nonetheless. We love it. Peter Reid keeps the mood light and what makes a training place is the atmosphere within the team that uses it. Before we disintegrated last year and turned into a backbiting rabble, our squad was fun and we got more out of ourselves than the sum of our talents should have allowed.

Usually it feels that way with this Irish team, too, but right now the good stuff is seeping away. We're struggling to hold on to it.

It's Tuesday today and we're training in the afternoon. We come down to the lobby at about 3 p.m. and even in the lobby we can feel the heat outside. Mick wants us to train in the worst the weather has to offer.

The goalkeepers went to work early. There's only one set of goalposts at the training ground and when the whole squad is there it's hard to accommodate the needs of all the outfield players and three keepers. By the time we reach the training ground they've been working solidly for an hour. I notice Shay Given, drenched in sweat. He looks as though he's just lost a stone in weight.

It's one of those tense sessions. There's an atmosphere from the start. We know we are going to be pushed hard and we are all a little edgy. Ian 'Taff' Evans takes most of the session. Ian has the bark of a square-bashing sergeant and he enjoys the no-nonsense image – let's do this and let's do it quickly. C'mon, let's stop moaning like little old ladies. Let's just do it. Roy and Taff have never got along.

We run, we turn, we run some more. Taff works us hard before we get near the footballs. Then, after our one-touch exercises, Taff has us setting up attacking situations on the keeper. He'll roll a ball to Steven Reid, say, while Robbie Keane and I move towards a line-up of four defenders and a keeper. We all get to do this in turns, the forwards laying balls off for each other and so on. Finally, Taff announces the end of the exercise and the goalies are excused the ritual seven-a-side. The goalies are exhausted. Roy pops a gasket. He has smoke coming from his ears.

'Taff,' he screeches, 'for fuck's sake. Can't have a game without goalies.'

Taff is unmoved. Roy begins the practice match in a foul mood, and those of the rest of us, usually willing to jolly things along, just aren't in the mood today. We're playing an extra player at the back and getting on with it.

A couple of times it almost gets out of hand. Players dive in with tackles. At one stage, Robbie Keane takes a swing at me as I'm trying to hold him up in front of goal. He picks me up and we smile at each other but we know this is one of those games with a little spike in it. I'd do it again. So would Robbie. Some sessions are like that.

When it's over there are duties to perform. John White, a Dubliner who has lived on Saipan for a long time, has done much of the liaison work for us here. As a sort of thank you, Mick has asked him to bring along as many of the local children as possible today, to meet the players and kick some footballs around with us.

Mick, Damien Duff, a couple of the other lads and I move to one end of the training ground. The kids wander down shyly. It's not that we're big names, we mean nothing to them; they just don't know what to do. Damien starts doing some juggling tricks with the footballs and Mick is good with kids, and soon we have a little session going with them. It's a bit of fun at the end of the afternoon.

The other players are sitting on a tiny terrace of wooden benches under the shade of a little canvas shelter. Those of us playing with the kids are too far away to hear what's going on but it transpires not to be good.

Roy has come off the field after the practice session and had a cut off Packie Bonner, our goalkeeping coach. He has flung his bottle of water to the ground and proceeded to the canvas shelter where he's spotted Alan Kelly, our reserve keeper, sitting on a bench in the shade. Roy has started in again. He's furious. Roy wanted a harder session. He wanted goalies for the seven-a-side.

'We were tired,' says Alan.

'What do you want, a fucking medal? We're all tired. It's the fucking World Cup. Ye won't be too tired to play golf tomorrow.'

Alan has tried to look straight ahead, to disengage himself. Roy is too wound up, though. Finally, Alan says, 'Why don't you calm down?'

'Do you want to try and make me?' says Roy, and then he storms off, gets on to the team bus and sits on his own till everyone is ready.

Word of the spat passes around the team quickly. It's not an unusual occurrence. It's not like Mount Vesuvius has just erupted for the first time in a decade. We have spats all the time at training and Roy's mood has been dark all week. It's a talking point but not a sensation.

We take the bus back to the hotel, sweating and tired. As we finish our showers, we can see from the balconies of our rooms

Roy and Mick sitting at a table in the gardens, talking things over. Good. We wander down for tea and mill about the place for a while. There's no sign of Roy. Later, Mick Byrne comes to my room. He's almost in tears.

'Roy is going home.'

Fuck. Things can't be that bad. It can't be true, anyway. Roy has yearned for this World Cup. I've assumed he's tense partly because this is the big one for him. This is a world-class player in his prime, walking on to the great stage. He's not going to do a Smithy – run out the gate and disappear.

I say to Mick to ring Michael Kennedy; somebody, anybody, should ring Michael Kennedy. One of the few things Roy and I share is our affection and respect for Michael. Mick looks at me doubtfully, as though he'd expected more. He closes the door behind him, and up and down the corridor the talk begins. Word is that Colin Healy of Celtic will join the squad, and that Eddie Corcoran is already booking a ticket for Roy. That news should give a certain finality to the talk, but it doesn't. None of us really believes that Roy will go. You don't run out the gate a couple of weeks before a World Cup. Do you? Somewhere in the hotel, Roy is in his room on his own, making that decision.

I don't know if we should go and knock on his door and dissuade him. Probably not. He would want to be left alone right now. He was lighter and more fun when he came into the squad, but he's always occupied an awkward place in the group. He broke through as a slightly chubby, hard-tackling kid in 1991. At that point, the Irish team was well established – we'd been to a World Cup together the previous year – and Roy was years younger than anyone else in the team.

By the time the 1994 World Cup came around, Roy was a star at Manchester United, and the next intake of young players was never going to attract his affection. Jason McAteer, Phil Babb and Gary Kelly came in as a sort of comedy threesome just as Jack began to get a little indulgent with us. All three earned their keep on the field, but off the park they became known as the Three Amigos. Roy never reviewed their act kindly, though.

At that stage he roomed with Denis Irwin, also from Cork and also from Manchester United. When Denis packed it in, Roy asked could he room by himself, and has done so ever since.

Some months ago, I was asked to look into organising a package to the World Cup for the wives and families of the squad. Nobody had Roy's number and when he was asked about it he declined to give it. He made the arrangements for his brothers on his own, as he guards their, and his own, privacy closely. Not long after the players' pool got up and running for this World Cup, Roy's face began appearing in a campaign for 7 Up. I felt it was awkward because it might have ruled out the possibility of the squad concluding an exclusive soft-drinks deal with anybody else, and because not a penny of Roy's money hit the squad pool. He may have donated the money to charity; his deal may have been concluded long before the World Cup. But it seemed to me to run against the concept of the team pool. I asked Michael Kennedy about it. 'You know what Roy is like,' said Michael.

I lie on the bed and wonder what the young lads in the squad are making of all this. To me, Roy is just another spiky genius whom I've watched come up through the ranks. To Dave Connolly, Damien Duff, Steven Reid and the other young lads, he's some-thing of a god. Whatever happens, Roy is tough enough to look after himself. The rest of the squad I'm not so sure about.

Kids are less innocent than they used to be. They're born wise to the world now. They know how things work and they know their own worth. Damn, I remember Robbie Keane getting into this Irish team when he should have been just learning how to shave. He came out in the first five-a-side and treated us senior professionals like traffic cones laid out for him to dribble around. Every time he scored a goal he'd run around asking us, 'So where's John Aldridge? Who was John Aldridge? Who was Stapo? Bring 'em on!'

We loved him straight off, the crazy fox. When he was fourteen he had every club in England panting for his signature. He sized them up and chose Wolves because he figured that was where he'd get into the first team soonest. Not long after he turned seventeen, he scored two beauties against Norwich, and he's played for Coventry, Inter Milan, Leeds and Spurs since then. He's twenty-two now and he could buy and sell most of us. He'll be a star of this World Cup, as will Damien Duff. The two of them came into the senior squad together a few years ago on a trip to Olomouc in the Czech Republic. Duffer is quieter than Robbie. He sleeps for almost every second that he's not playing football. They are both so self-possessed and confident I wonder are they the same species as myself.

By instinct, at Sunderland I find that I follow the progress of the Irish kids a little more than I do with the other lads. We have a good crop of them and I'm free and easy with them when it comes to advice. Whether they want it or not, they get it.

The closest to making it right now is Thomas Butler. Tommy is from Coolock on the north side of Dublin, and it seems as if he's been knocking around here for years. Next year I think will be his season. He's a tidy, smart midfielder who brings the best out of the players around him. He has that football intelligence that you can't teach. In our relegation struggle of the past couple of months, he has come into an ailing team and made us better. It's taken the club a while to see his virtues but I think he's making it. Next season, Tommy, I tell him, next season.

Not so long ago he came to me one day at Whitburn, unhappy with his lot — he wasn't getting playing time, he wasn't getting a whole pile of money, he wasn't getting anywhere, and the manager had refused to speak to his agent, he said.

My eyebrows shot up. Tommy Butler has an agent? The boss refused to speak to this agent? Peter Reid is one of the good guys. He's not one for slamming down phones or making life hard for young players. Agents, though, are his Achilles' heel.

Tommy and I talked. He had heard a whisper that there might be an offer of a move out of the Premiership to First Division club Stockport, who have since become a quite convincing Second Division club. Tommy thought it would mean more football, more of everything. He couldn't understand why the manager was jerking him around.

Turns out that Tommy has had four agents since the start of the season. Turns out that the FA are looking into why he has had all these agents. Tommy has had so many agents that he doesn't know which way he is turning any more. With all that he's been hearing from the agents and the manager, he has lost his patience, fallen out of love with the idea of playing for a great club. Jesus, he's just a kid. This is a big hard industry.

Kevin Kyle is a big strong striker who came to Sunderland without a touch and worked and worked at his game to the point where he's been our top scorer in the reserves for two years, and has just won a cap for Scotland. Almost every day his agent would come to training, to watch him, to talk to him, to advise him gently. Then Kevin stepped over the threshold, got an international cap and traded in his old agent for somebody new and flashier. I asked why. Kevin said he felt he had to.

Who can argue? When a kid signs a deal now he is prey. At Sunderland, we get Ferrari salesmen and Porsche salesmen dropping by the ground. If you're due a decent fee of some sort, signing-on or transfer, they'll take you to lunch, talk to you about getting only one chance, the ultimate thrill, the status of being a footballer, the personal registration they'll throw in. And hey presto! A kid who had nothing a month ago is spinning into the Charlie Hurley training ground in a sports car that's too small to take all his gear. So he gets a sports utility vehicle for driving to the airport, and maybe buys a BMW as a runaround for the new girlfriend, having traded in the old one.

Old guys like me seem folksy by comparison. They are kids. It's a big bad world but even the ones who deal badly with it probably deal with it better than we did. I notice that about the game now.

Not so long after I went to Arsenal, Terry Neill got the sack; just like that. We played Walsall, or 'lowly Walsall' as the papers would have it, in the League Cup one night. Back then, the kids used to sit in a pen behind the glass dug-out and keep notes on the players who played in our position. I'd watch Tony Woodcock and Charlie Nicholas and write down what I was learning. There was a chance I'd be asked to produce the notes the following week. I mention this because Terry had just signed Tommy Caton and Tommy came along and sat with us behind the dug-out that night.

Walsall beat Arsenal. Next day Terry Neill was out of a job. Tommy Coleman called me and told me to stay home for a day or two till things sorted themselves out. I was awestruck. I'd just met Tommy Caton. Tommy had just signed. I wondered what would happen to him (in the end, he was to die a very sad death after so much went wrong in his life). It never struck me to fret about what would happen to me. Now when a manager leaves, every kid at a club is on the phone to his agent to discuss the implications. Back then, only three players at Arsenal had agents – Charlie Nicholas, Graham Rix and somebody else whose name I can't even recall. Only one player, Gus Caesar, had a mobile phone. Gus carried it around like a plumber's box. I think he had to go to the Cotswolds to find a hill high enough to get a decent reception on the thing.

Don Howe got Terry Neill's job and he signed Steve Williams and an established striker, Paul Mariner, almost straightaway. I suppose I moved down the pecking order by one place but nothing about the atmosphere of Arsenal changed much. The humour remained the same. Not long after he arrived, Mariner was central to setting up one of the younger apprentices at London Colney. The public phone was at the end of a corridor. If it rang while the team were in the canteen after a session, an apprentice would have to run and answer it. Paul Mariner had been there a week when the phone rang. An apprentice duly went down to answer it and came panting back a few seconds later.

'Paul Mariner. It's your wife.'

'Yeah? Just tell her to fuck off.'

'What?'

'You heard me.'

'Seriously.'

'I told you once. Tell her to fuck off.'

So the young lad walks slowly back up the corridor and now you can hear a pin drop in the canteen. We can hear his quavering voice.

'I'm sorry, Mrs Mariner, but he wants me to tell you to, erm, fuck off.'

At which point Don Howe's role kicks in. He sprints up and grabs the phone.

'I'm so sorry. I'm so very sorry. Son, what did you just say to this lady?'

'But Gaffer, but, but . . .'

'This is a decent club and we have decent manners here. You've tried to come between a man and his wife.'

All the while, I'm laughing. There, but for the grace of God, go I.

That's changed. Tommy Butler wouldn't fall for that. None of the lads here in Saipan would either.

My progress turned on small things. Don Howe moved Terry Burton up to be assistant coach and my youth-team coach, Tommy Coleman, moved up to become reserve-team coach. Inwardly I cheered. Tommy hadn't much time for me. As a kid at a club, you suss pretty quickly who rates you and who doesn't. Tommy didn't rate me.

To fill Tommy Coleman's job, Arsenal brought in a former Arsenal player who had moved on to Watford – Pat Rice. Pat joined a long list of people whom I have to thank for, at various stages, saving my career. Pat persuaded me to believe that I could be a footballer.

There was a gym behind the clock end at Highbury, an astro-turf gym. On Fridays, if they were playing at home, the first team would train there and late in the afternoon the teamsheets for the weekend would be pinned on the notice board there. For the rest of the week, we could use the gym for optional training in the afternoons.

If Tommy Coleman wanted me to train in the afternoon, I'd wriggle and squirm to get out of it, and frankly, Tommy didn't mind much. I don't think he saw Arsenal's future as hinging on my progress. Tommy was great for the more skilful players — Rocastle, Hayes, Thomas, Merson, Adams. I think they all benefited from his work. But for me, I don't think Tommy could see any potential there.

I don't know if Pat Rice saw potential or if he just wanted to get the best out of all of us but I responded. I'd be waiting for Pat to tell us there was training available in the afternoon. I wanted to show him.

Pat brought me to a wall outside the gym. This was the start of the Frank Stapleton Memorial Course in football skills. Frank would come to this wall every day and kick the ball against it one hundred times, keeping it off the floor all the way. I managed four before it dropped. Pat left me to it. I practised for a week or so till I got to a hundred. But I waited till I got to two hundred before I called Pat to have a look.

Pat changed our fitness, built us up, and nothing got past him. We used to have to do terrace runs, sprinting up the high grey cliffs of the North Bank. One long run went almost to the clouds, or so it seemed, up to a galvanised fence at the back. There were two paths up, forty yards apart. The winner had to slap the fence. One day, one of the lads got a big bamboo cane and left it at the top of the North Bank to bang the fence with, so he didn't have to go all the way. He got caught and everyone did double terrace runs. Another day, it was so smoggy you couldn't see twenty yards in front. We were supposed to be doing laps of Highbury but Pat couldn't see us. He knew us, though, and moved about in the fog quicker than we did, catching some of us taking a short cut by walking across the penalty area — double laps.

At London Colney, there is a cross-country run, which was the staple of our pre-season training. It took the average person thirty-five minutes to cover it. Brian Talbot could do it in under twenty. He'd have a quick shower and be waving to us from his car as we stood exhausted with our hands on our knees at the finish. I used to have to do it carrying a sandbag. I'd disappear out into the corn-fields on a summer's day wearing a waistcoat full of heavy sand. I never got any faster. I'd lose as much in sweat as I was supposed to gain in muscle.

In exasperation, Pat sent me off one day with stern words ringing in my ear — 'You have thirty minutes, Niall.' I ran to the first field of corn and lay down for a while, counting the clouds going by above. When I thought enough time had passed, I made my way over to the far side of the field and — surprise, surprise — suddenly came bursting from the corn, sprinting for home.

'What time, Pat?'

'Eh, just under twenty-four minutes, Niall.' Shit, got my timing wrong. 'Really looking forward to you beating your new record tomorrow, Niall.'

I think of my seventeen-year-old self, still learning the rudiments of the trade, and I think of Robbie Keane, down the corridor, who was a superstar when he was seventeen and who's looking forward to this World Cup like a kid looks forward to his birthday. The bigger they are, the harder he wants to make them fall. He's a tougher cookie than I ever could have been.

'What are you looking at, you big Crumlin knacker?' he'll say to me with a grin if he catches me watching him doing amazing tricks with a football. 'Hopin' you might learn something?' See?

If you took the stories of the twenty-three of us who are in this

World Cup squad, on the surface they would look the same, but underneath they would each have a Pat Rice figure somewhere, a lucky break here and a lucky break there – even Roy, even Robbie. When I talk to Tommy Butler or Cliffie Byrne or any of the other lads whose impatience with the game is drawing them away from it, this is what I try to explain. Everything in football is fluid. It changes. People get injured, people lose form, people get ahead of you, people move on. Keep working and the break will come.

Tommy points to another player just his age at the club, a first-teamer bought in from elsewhere. Tommy reckons he's better than him and he gets paid less. Right on both counts, but it'll change.

Cliffie has had two serious injuries already and he's twenty, but he's one of those implacable kids who'll end up captaining a club some day because he can organise and cajole people while he looks after his own game. I don't know if everyone at Sunderland sees what he has, but I see it. Give me a club and a chequebook and I'd buy him and play him next Saturday. But at Sunderland it might not happen for him.

Meanwhile, it's a tough world and the kids own it. They humiliate us in five-a-sides and watch us drive away in our big cars, or listen to us making arrangements for Saturday's away game. My only revenge these past few years has been my prowess at head tennis. I've been playing so long I am almost unbeatable, and after a session I like to rub it in.

'I'll be leaving the game soon, kids, and I'm wondering which one of you tossers I'll bequeath my first touch to? Which of you needs it the most, eh?'

They laugh but I wonder when they get back to Jim and Karen Mordey's lodging house at Roker if they don't roll their eyes at the memory of it and say to each other, 'Just how sad a bastard is Quinny?'

The season after Pat Rice arrived, the first game of the year for the youth team was against Cambridge. We played them at eleven in the morning at the Abbey Stadium in Cambridge and we won 6–0. I scored five of the goals. It was my second season with the youth set-up and I was mad to perform well for Pat Rice – and to show Tommy Coleman a thing or two. Alan Caven laid on all the goals. He's working in insurance now – not a story I tell to Cliffie, Tommy and the boys.

We were beaten in the semi-final of the Youth Cup that year by Stoke City but we won the Floodlit Cup and I scored thirty-odd for the season. I was on my way.

Something always changes; something always gives. That's why I'm lying here chatting to Kevin Kilbane and I'm calm. Roy won't go. He knows football. He knows it's not 100 per cent for 100 per cent of the time. It doesn't work that way. He knows things change, people, moods. We'll wake up tomorrow and laugh about this. Roy knows things that Smithy didn't, things that Tommy and Cliffie still have to learn. When Roy was a kid, he wrote to every one of the ninety-two clubs in the English League looking for a break, and he got one. He knows you don't go off the cliff, you don't run out the gate. You don't settle for Stockport.

CHAPTER FIVE

YOU GOTTA DANCE WITH THEM WHAT BRUNG YOU

You say you lost your faith
But that's not where it's at
You had no faith to lose
And you know it

BOB DYLAN, 'POSITIVELY 4TH STREET'

I've been blessed with interesting uncles. Mattie's brother Noel was a bachelor who lived in Ealing. Because of the amount of time I was spending travelling from Twickenham to Highbury every day, I moved into digs with a Mrs Thorburn, and when I had some time off I'd stay with Noel. Finally, I bought a flat in Enfield and stayed with Noel for a couple of months, until it was ready.

Noel always seemed to be at a loose end, which made him an ideal companion for a shiftless young footballer. We'd play golf together, drink together or just ride around in his Hillman Imp. He's taller than I am; we'd fold ourselves up like two concertinas and insert ourselves into his old car for our expeditions.

At other times, Noel would insist on walking everywhere. There must have been a hundred pubs on Ealing Broadway but there were just about three that suited Noel. He'd walk the length of the

Broadway, criss-crossing the road again and again, me striding along behind him. On nights out, we'd spend more time walking than drinking.

He played golf with the same energy. One day at Perivale Golf Club, Noel teed off and strode away towards the first green. Next thing, a ball hit Noel's bag from behind. We turned to see a large group of people waiting to play. So he picked the ball up, placed it on a tee and, facing them, swung at it with his driver. In the distance, nine lads dived one way, another eight or nine dived another.

'They won't be bothering us again, Niall,' Noel said solemnly, and played his approach shot.

At other times, I hung out with Robbie Gavin from Portobello, who once dated my sister. Robbie was an architect who'd emigrated in the same week as I did. He lived in Hendon and I'd go up there on a Saturday night for a session that would last till Sunday lunchtime, pay a quick visit to Mattie and Ailish and off out on Sunday night for the drink and ramble with Noel.

Six months after my eighteenth birthday, I paid £26,000 for the flat in Enfield. Arsenal helped with the mortgage. There's a word you don't hear around football training grounds any more – mortgage.

Independent at last! I missed Noel's, though. His house had a sitting room with nothing in it except floorboards and a fireplace. Every night when Noel came home from the pub, he'd take out all his loose change and put it on the floor. Then he'd get his old driver from the golf bag and he'd whack the coins one by one at the wall. He wasn't done till they'd all wedged into the plaster. He had an entire end wall decorated in this way – brown coins, silver coins, every sort of coin, violently driven in so that they looked like a cascade from a massive fruit machine. As I say, Uncle Noel is a bachelor.

Roy Keane is blessed with an interesting father. During the 1994 World Cup, I got to know Mossie Keane well. I wish sometimes that I was as hard and as stone-faced as Roy is. Sometimes, though, when I think of Mossie, I think of what Roy might have been if fame hadn't imprisoned him.

My ideal player is somebody with the enthusiasm and brashness of Robbie Keane, somebody who doesn't care what anyone thinks, who doesn't care for reputations, who wants to be marked by the best, who wants the world to bring it on. I never had that. And the ideal player would have the toughness of Roy, the mental strength he has. I never had that either. I'm fond of Roy. I'm fond of Robbie. I'm fond of Mossie. Maybe I take Robbie first for the fun side. He's natural company. Roy isn't, not usually, but when he lightens up, I can see his father in him.

I meet his dad in the lounge after most games at Lansdowne Road, and back in 1994 when I was injured, I spent a lot of time with him. We were thrown together a lot and we socialised. I remember one great night in the Cusack Stand Bar in New York City. We went there with Eamon Coughlan and Mossie let fly. He was singing and playing spoons and telling stories.

When this week with Roy started going wrong, I thought of Mossie. There's a wildness in him that Roy would still have if he hadn't become the centre of an industry and been forced to close down so much of his personality.

Two short stories show two sides of Roy. During qualifying for this World Cup we played Portugal at home and Estonia away in the space of a couple of days. In the course of the Portugal match, a draw in which Roy played incredibly well, Roy got booked. Eddie Corcoran, our liaison man, had gone on to Estonia that day as an advance ambassador to check that everything was OK for our arrival the following day. Eddie was the only Irishman watching the game in a bar in Tallinn and when Roy got yellow carded it meant that he wouldn't be travelling to Estonia. The story goes that a local said to Eddie that he must be devastated. Apparently, Eddie smiled, knowing this had its advantages. He knew his job was likely to be easier.

Back in Dublin, that same night was the first occasion for a long time that Roy came out with us. We wound up in the piano bar in Lillie's Bordello. Roy was wonderful company. He gave his shirt to a fan. He got up and sang Bob Dylan. He chatted and cracked jokes. Peter Reid was there and I remember him saying to me, 'Isn't Roy Keane a great guy.'

He is, and in a different time he might have been allowed to enjoy what he does a little more. I look at Roy and it seems to me that it's a long time since anyone let him live his life on his terms. I see him play and I think that I'd love to have that talent but I couldn't live with everything that goes with it. I couldn't pay the price.

It's never been the same life for me as it has been for Roy. When I went into my third year at Arsenal, I was suddenly, frighteningly, too old for the youth team. Like most kids, I was beginning to wonder if I'd ever make it. I was leaving Pat Rice's domain for a life in the reserves and I suspected that the reserves didn't really fancy me. In my first year, I got on as a sub a few times.

The following year, the beginning of the 1985–86 season marked the last year of my contract. It's like this, if I don't crack the reserves, then I'm looking at the small ads and hoping to get a real job. I had a good pre-season, everything went well, and in the first eighteen reserve games of the year, I scored fifteen times. Somebody had to notice.

One weekend, the first team got beaten 6–1 at Everton. The next Wednesday the phone rang. The club had decided to send me on loan to Port Vale. A train ticket was booked. A bed and breakfast was organised. I was to see John Rudge at four o'clock the next day. By lunchtime on Thursday, I was packed and ready to go. Then there was another phone call – don't move, come in to Highbury tomorrow.

On the Friday, I discover that Tony Woodcock is struggling. He'll have a fitness test on Saturday. Paul Mariner goes over on his ankle;

ditto for Paul. I reckon the club have a choice of playing Chrissie Whyte up front with Charlie Nicholas, or playing me. They'll go with Chrissie because of his experience. After all, we're playing Liverpool, and it's the first English League game to be beamed live all over Europe. When the squads are pinned to the wall in the gym at Highbury, I'm in the first-team squad but my name has just been pencilled in after all the typed names. I knew it.

We're lucky the game's being played at home. This is a time when Liverpool are great; they can beat ordinary teams without getting out of their pyjamas. They stroke the ball around at the back while you run and run. The League is using the adidas Tango ball and it flies around. We don't call playing at Liverpool what other people call it. We call it Chasing the Tango.

I get off at Finsbury Park on Saturdays so that I can buy the Irish papers. This day I grab an *Irish Independent* and on the sports page there's a flyer of a story – 'Hurling Star to Make Debut'. We are to meet at two o'clock in the dressing room. I shove the paper into my bag. Newspapers – what do they know?

After he's called out the team, Don Howe calls me into his office to explain why I'm in it and why I shouldn't be worried.

'No pressure,' Don says, in his little room.

I don't have time to be too nervous. Graham Rix is beside me, taking the mickey out of me, I'm wondering if everyone is watching at home, then it's time for the warm-up. No! Unbelievable! Look! I can hardly stop myself from pointing at them. At the other end of the field are Ian Rush, Ronnie Whelan, Kenny Dalglish, Mark Lawrenson, Steve Nicol.

When it starts, I'm in dreamland. Until I get into a scuffle with Steve Nicol early in the game, I'm cruising around in my own little world. I am imagining conversations I'll have later – 'Yeah, Lawrenson is taller than you'd think. Nice guy, Hansen.' Steve Nicol snaps me out of it and before I know it I've set Charlie Nicholas up to score with a simple little dink. It puts us 1–0 ahead. Later,

Paul Davis takes a shot, Grobbelaar spills it and I score. I love this game.

That's practically all I remember, apart from one lesson. A ball comes up to me, Mark Lawrenson arrives from nowhere, goes straight through me as if I'm not there and clears it upfield in one majestic movement. Today it would be a yellow, possibly a red, card. Instead, when he clears the ball, he apologises and puts out his hand to pick me up. It's a gentleman's game at the top level, I think. Total respect for each other, that's what we professionals have. Three games later at Tottenham, one of their defenders does the same, flattens me and clears. I put my hand up for him to pick me up in gentlemanly fashion and he stands on my other hand with his studs and pretends to be pulling me up. Done me a treat. I still have a little scar.

My debut is done. None of the family are over. Nobody knew I was playing until it was too late to travel. By accident, outside the ground I meet Benny O'Byrne, who lived near me in Crumlin. We have a night out in Muswell Hill in a place called Manhattan Lights.

Next morning in the papers, Brian Glanville says I was 'refreshing'. It's the fiftieth anniversary of Ted Drake scoring seven for Arsenal. Ted hit the bar to be denied his eighth. Nobody says that the new Ted Drake has arrived.

I'm up and running with the soccer players, the senior drinkers. We went to the King's Head that morning and life was a breeze. Christmas was coming. So was my first playing bonus and my first win bonus.

Roy arrived in the Irish team as a kid with no respect for authority. As Brian Glanville might say, it was refreshing. One famous story is worth retelling. In 1992, when Roy was still a kid, we went on a summer tour to America, played three games and had a good time. We had an evening flight home and some of the team decided to get in one last round of golf before leaving. We rounded up whomever we could and got the mini bus. Roy and Steve Staunton (known to us as Stan) were missing. It was no problem; we knew where to find them. Frank Gillespie, who had become a friend of the team's, ran a pub, The Blackthorn, on Broadway in that Irish part of Boston known as Southie. Roy and Stan were last seen . . .

We drove down to The Blackthorn and Kevin Moran was deputed to fetch the boys. Kevin went in but never came out. Bravely, somebody else volunteered to go in – same story. We decided that the rest of us should go in as a group. Golf? Play was abandoned.

Jack Charlton, the Irish manager, was away on one of his 'earners', those gigs that he seemed to pick up everywhere in his capacity as the Ireland manager with the Geordie accent. As was usual on those occasions, our captain, Mick McCarthy, had taken control of things.

Jack got back to the team hotel around teatime and there was Mick McCarthy and only half the team. Our flight from Logan Airport was about two hours from take-off. Mick knew where to find us, though, and he rang the bar to summon us. He and Mick Byrne went around our rooms, threw everything we had into bags and loaded up the bus. Jack was in a right fury by now and headed off to the airport in a taxi in a huff. We crept on to the bus, with Mick McCarthy having a go at the latecomers. Roy was last on board, happy as a dandy and wearing a 'kiss me quick' hat. Mick tried to reassert control by having a little go off the new boy. Mistake! Roy may have been a kid on his first trip with the team, but he took on Mick McCarthy, the World Cup captain and legend, and put him away – gone in sixty seconds. If it had been boxing, it would have been stopped.

'Aye, and look at you,' said Mick as Roy clambered on board. 'Look at the fucking state of you. You call yourself a professional footballer?'

Roy scarcely paused.

'And you call what you have a first touch?'

Roy had him. It wasn't the sort of remark a kid would make to a World Cup captain but it was a good one and it was audible to the whole squad.

What amazed me was the fact that during that long overnight flight home, Roy never seemed to have a moment when he thought, Shit, what have I done? He never lifted his backside off the seat to go to apologise to Mick or to build bridges. He never went to anyone to ask, 'What should I do?' He never asked did we think Mick would be offended. That tells you something about Roy and a side of him that I've always liked.

He was always quietly different but also he came under the influence of strong men. Brian Clough and Alex Ferguson have helped to mould him into somebody who demands the best from everything. I hear him talk about them sometimes and the total respect he has for the two of them is in every word. Roy might contradict me but I think they have had an enormous bearing on the type of man he has become.

I guess he has a point sometimes; the rest of us don't hunger for success as resolutely as he does. I know I haven't. Perhaps, as a result, Roy sees himself as being more professional than I am. I do what suits me best and maybe Roy has to go through all the circles of hell that he does, through all the strictness, the self-denial and the building of desire. I don't believe I can win a Saturday game on Tuesday morning. Roy is the opposite. He has to train on Tuesday like he's playing the most important game of his life.

He has been incredible these past few years. It takes a unique and extraordinary person to be the way he is but I think it takes a toll. He's given glimpses of it with these public shows of disillusion. I think he'd concede that being such a good player has created a Roy Keane aura, a Roy Keane myth, and it leaves him trapped inside with very few people he can really trust.

I've never been good enough to have that. I don't know how I'd react. He's hounded. I lived near him in Manchester when I played for City. I could go to bars and have a few drinks and meet fans.

I'd walk into places on my own and start up conversations. Occasionally, I went out with Roy and he'd get a non-stop stream of people bothering him, literally non-stop. His contract negotiations are in the papers for six months, day in and day out. Mine take twenty minutes. Roy becomes suspicious of people easily; one or two have let him down badly. I've not had that experience. I wouldn't want, and wouldn't be able, to live in the way he lives. I'm not sure how much he likes it either.

He likes simple things. We've both had children making their first communion recently and we've had chats about being involved in the preparations with them, the meetings we've had to go to, the fun of being with the kids. He's happier talking about his family than he is talking about anything else. He's always said that the way he plays football is fair game for criticism, but if anyone tries to get to the inner sanctum, his family, he never forgives.

I can't imagine that life, that pressure. Captain of the biggest club in the world? Adored and hated with equal intensity? Recognised everywhere? There are times, when I'm in the supermarket or having a drink in the pub or just standing on the terrace at a Munster final, when I think of Roy. Nobody is bothering me, and I'm glad I'm not him.

We went to Iran without him in November 2001 and every question for three days was a Roy Keane question. On the street, in the hotel, at the airport, people with just a few words of English would nod their heads in friendly fashion and ask, 'Where is Roy Keane?' In press conferences, it was, 'How is Roy Keane?' Sometimes it feels as if we are living in the shadow of a great mountain.

If you offered to make me a deal, to give me all the skill he has and the life he has to lead, I'd decline. I couldn't be a bird in a cage like Roy is. I understand why he pecks at the wires so much. The day Roy retires and everything is lifted from his shoulders, I think you'll see a different man. He'll lighten up again. He'll have a laugh some day about how he spent the best days of his life wound up like a coiled spring. He'll shake his head and wonder about how uptight and intense he was. I hope he will anyway.

We played Manchester United on the Saturday after my debut. It was December 1985 and United were streaking away with the League while we were patting our pockets, wondering where our form had gone. Mariner and Woodcock were both fit again. I travelled anyway.

This was the big time. I could smell it, hear it, see it. Frank Stapleton played for United. I roomed with Dave O'Leary. In the youth team, the furthest we had been was France. We stayed in a school.

On Saturday morning, I went into Manchester city centre and did some shopping. I had no idea that we were supposed to rest up. I ambled back with a new pair of trainers in a plastic bag, just in time for a pre-match talk and meal at 11.15. Don named the team and I was in it again. So I was playing against United who were nine points clear. In our last away game, we'd conceded six goals. I was shocked, and mentally prepared myself for the worst.

Most of that day is a blur but I remember Gus Caesar seeming to kick Jesper Olsen from one end of Old Trafford to the other. We got stuck in, especially Gus. It was an ugly game, looking back, the football of cavemen, but I thought I did OK. I wasn't a beacon in the darkness but I was OK. I won my headers. The game was going out all over Europe again and I was winning my headers. That was good. Europe would know!

I was playing against Kevin Moran and Billy Garton. John Gidman was full-back and Johnny Sivebaek was in the other full-back slot. I always liked playing against Kevin. He was big and as hard as nails but he was honest. You'd go for the ball with him, there'd be an almighty clash of bodies and you'd win or you'd lose. Kevin would recover quickly and smash into you again. That sort of straightforward play was always a relief.

Later, I played against Paul McGrath a few times at United. His skill and athleticism were a nightmare for me. He'd just nip in and pinch the ball off my toes. Against Kevin, I'd feel like I'd been beaten up; against Paul, it was more like having my pocket picked. (Years later, David White and I took Paul and Kurt Nielsen apart when we were playing for City and Paul was with Villa. We scored five and I remember Paul asking the referee how much time was left. I loved Paul and hearing him ask that question made my day. It was the only time I ever got anything over on him.)

That day at Old Trafford, Kevin and I were involved in the game's pivotal moment. I remember the ball breaking and chesting it down. I was waiting for Kevin to arrive and clatter me, but I got it down and smuggled it past him with just time for a shot. 'Ooooh,' said the crowd. Gary Bailey got a hand to it. 'Oooooh,' again. Billy Garton was running back to clear but he stopped, Charlie Nicholas flew in – 1–0 to the Arsenal. Kevin crucified poor Billy Garton for his hesitation. Years later, Kevin was still moaning about that goal and Billy Garton. It was the beginning of the end of United's season.

On the happy coach journey home, I thought that this life would always be easy – live games, six points out of six, QPR at home next. Then, two days after the QPR game, it was the London derby against Spurs.

That was when I came up against Paul Miller and Graham Roberts for the first time, and realised that, in terms of intensity, Liverpool and Manchester United had scarcely registered on the scale. The game finished goalless but I should have scored the winner. Late on we were pressing and the crowd were howling. I flicked one on but was late getting to the box. Graham Rix was picking himself up off the ground when it bounced out to me, and my header hit him on the back in front of an empty net. Turns out I'm not the luckiest guy in the world after all. Definitely not.

On wet days Mick Kavanagh, Paddy Hughes and I gambled. We loved it at the dogs, fancied we knew the form and the favourites.

So scientific was our approach that we ritually backed trap two in the last race every day. Our social lives at weekends depended on how trap two went during the week.

In my early days in London, Tony Donnelly, the kitman at Highbury, used to come with me to the dogs. We'd sit and talk in urgent murmurs, like two spies.

'Well?'

'Nothing. You?'

'Heard two dog.'

'Yeah? You backing it?'

'Nah.'

'See ya.'

'Good luck.'

I was establishing the parameters of a lifestyle that entertained, sustained and almost broke me right up until the time I got married. The others were lucky that it did not take over their lives. For me, if it wasn't raining and the boys were at work, and if I wasn't working in the gym, I'd be in the bookies for the first race at two o'clock and I'd leave at 5.30. I didn't bet big but I didn't earn big. Usually, I'd gamble away the next instalment of my signing-on fee before it came.

When the afternoon was done, I'd go over to the snooker hall and play cards. It was a colourful world up the stairs in the snooker hall, a place full of characters out of Damon Runyon – Tom the Ticket, Slim, Jewish John.

We'd play kaluki, a type of rummy game using two packs of cards and two joker cards. It's a great gambling game, especially if you need to lose your money quickly. You try to meld or lay down your thirteen cards by forming sets of equal rank or runs of consecutive cards. You win a hand by getting rid of all your cards like this and all the other players get penalty points depending on what they have left. Anyone who gets over a certain number of points, usually 150, is eliminated but has the chance to buy himself back

Early days.

Ever the fashion icon, the same
shirt does for a day out at Sally
Gap with Mam and Dad and
sister Gerry and for dreaming of
Croke Park out in the back
garden.

All dressed up in our Sunday best: Dad, Ambie, me on Rosaleen's knee, Mam and Gerry.

Here comes trouble.

This was how we all looked in the seventies — honest!

(Left) After winning the All-Ireland long-puck Under-12 competition in 1976. I held the trophy (below) for the next two years — a record that still stands today.

Smiles all round after we beat the Territories College team in Australia in the summer of 1983.

Just before the 1990 World Cup I was given a great send-off by the people back in Perrystown, Crumlin.

In Mam and Dad's garden.

Cutting the cake on our wedding day, 24 June 1992, after the ceremony in Killiney, Dublin.

Gillian and I together in Silks restaurant, Marbella. There is no doubt that meeting her brought a new calm to my life.

Aisling on the day of her first Communion, two days before I set off for the World Cup in 2002.

Mikey shows off his skills on the back lawn.

With Jim Bolger, who took on 'The Hats' in Ireland and improved Irish racing beyond all recognition.

Christy Roche on Cois na Tine after winning the Futurity Stakes in record time, with proud owners looking on. He was my first horse and we eventually sold him for £250,000, which helped to pay off the mortgage. After injury, we brought him back to be with us in the North-east.

Munster final day and standing on the terraces with friend and former Tipperary legend Joe Hayes.

Whatever disasters befell him, Jack Doyle always walked on the sunny side of the street. His attitude to life has been an inspiration.

Gillian with two special mascots for my charity game, Aisling and Mikey.

A crowd of over 37,000 came to the charity game and another 20,000 bought non-attendance tickets. I felt almost embarrassed by all the attention that was focused on me during that period.

in. So the pot grows bigger. Eventually, the last surviving player wins the lot.

I can remember one morning coming out of an all-night session. The Arsenal club bus to London Colney stopped just beside the snooker hall and I asked the driver to hold on for a few minutes. One of the guys I'd been playing with needed to go to the bank to draw out my winnings. He went into the bank and came out with £1,200 for me. Towards the end of the week, I had to ask the driver to do the same again. I went into the bank and came out to give it all back to the same bloke, plus another £200.

Sometimes I'd cut the cards short to get to the dogs at Harringay. Many nights I left Harringay penniless and had to walk the hour and a half back to Enfield. Sadly, instead of seeing sense, I began deluding myself by placing my bus fare home under a stone in a garden near the dog track. Even this didn't work. If I lost all my cash early, I'd nip out, retrieve the bus fare and put it on the last race. Any wonder I'm travelling to the World Cup as the squad's official optimist!

I had a row with Roy once. I grabbed him by the throat during a Cup game at Old Trafford in February 1996. It's a day that most Manchester City fans will remember solemnly.

We had a young kid called Michael Brown playing his second game for City. It was one of those frenetic derby games and Roy went over and frightened the life out of the kid – pushed him in the chest, turned on the scary piercing stare. Poor Brownie froze like a rabbit. This is the sort of thing that a referee can't easily do anything about, so I intervened. There were a few sharp words, Irish stuff that brought Dublin and Cork into it as terms of abuse. I held him off by the throat and then we were pulled away. I have no excuses except it was City versus United and for once I was up at a level of desire and intensity that might have matched Roy's. I knew then that any chance I ever had of getting close to him was gone. In terms of that game, I was fighting a losing battle.

Uwe Rosler had given us an early lead and we were playing well. United won a corner. Eric Cantona and our German defender Michael Frontzeck both jumped as the ball went yards over their heads. We all turned to clear and chase and the whistle sounded. Roy heard the shrill, grabbed the ball, ran to the referee with eyes switched to maximum glare and screamed, 'I never touched him.'

'No, Roy,' the ref said. 'It's *for* you. It's a penalty.'

He'd penalised Frontzeck for something on Cantona. Roy was baffled and embarrassed that he'd got the wrong end of the stick. We were all furious. They scored. Lee Sharpe added a second right at the end of the game. We got knocked out of the Cup over it – 1–0 up and cruising, and then mugged.

Roy dominates the pitch. In my early years at Manchester City, we used to get so close to beating United but Roy cropped up to score or make goals every time. You knew he was the only person on the field who could do it, who would have the energy to do it, the desire and the brashness to do it.

He's the same now only he's grown more dominant. Last time United visited Sunderland, young Paul Thirlwell was playing in midfield and all week you wondered what to say to the lad – don't worry, he's not as good as they make out? Each day, the poor guy is sitting there, white as a sheet, and nobody can think of anything more encouraging to say than good luck. In fact, as luck would have it, Roy didn't play. But whoever plays against him just has to get on with it. You understand that not only is Roy very good, he's always very good. Usually, the people with presence on a pitch are loud bawling centre-halves, or the centre-forwards who can score a goal out of nothing, or the midfielders whose tackling and passing dictates the rhythm of the game. Roy is all three. So what do you tell Paul Thirlwell? What do you think when Roy announces he's quitting your team? Denial is your friend.

Next morning in Saipan, skies are blue and we are twenty-three again. It's all blown over. Roy is staying. I meet him at the door to the lifts first thing.

'Well done, Roy,' I say. 'I'm really pleased you're staying.'

He didn't seem to notice me and walked straight past. At least he's staying. After talking to Michael Kennedy and Alex Ferguson it came down to a snap decision early this morning, and Roy did the right thing.

A few of us have quiet thoughts for Colin Healy. When Roy pulled out yesterday, Colin was told that he was coming. Then Roy changed his mind and Colin was told he wasn't coming. I'm soft about things like that. I can't help wondering how it must have felt for a quiet kid like Colin Healy to be rung and told to pack his bags, that he was in the World Cup squad, and then to be told an hour later that the deal was all off. Roy will share that sympathy, but he'll deal with this in his own way.

For the lads all things pass. In football, you just get on with things. Roy was going. Roy is staying. It's time to train again. We make a few jokes. Alan Kelly comes out wearing a balaclava. Roy laughs at himself. It's good again.

If anything, I never fully absorbed the implications of him going in the first place. These things happen and you assume there are people looking after it. People will be having meetings and when you wake up, he'll be staying. I move on and stop worrying about what's eating Roy Keane. He's been agitated from the word go and I'm getting used to it now. Perhaps it was because he hasn't had the opportunity to let off steam during the intensity of a match or hard training.

In an ideal world, if Roy's injury had been slightly more serious he would not have come here. David Beckham stayed home after England left last week. Roy should have done the same, or been asked if he'd like to. Instead, it's been one thing on top of another, a slow adding on of grievances – my game back in Sunderland; playing against Nigeria; the media; the facilities; many of us out drinking; the rumours circulating over the last couple of days that the *News of the World* is going to do a job on him and his family.

It's Wednesday now, hotter than ever. We trained this morning and Roy is in a good mood. In two days' time, we fly to Izumo to start the World Cup proper. We won't look back.

CHAPTER SIX

EVERY TIME WE SAY GOODBYE . . .

The torch was impromptu. The torch was unsanctioned. He informed the Boys. He informed them post torch. He stressed his pure motive.

JAMES ELLROY, *THE COLD SIX THOUSAND*

There's a story of a famous Manchester United defender from years back. In quick succession, he got found out, divorced and booted from the family home.

'So where are you staying?' asked one of the lads.

'Hotel.'

'All right is it?'

'Five star.'

'Fair enough.'

Pause.

'Have to look through the window to see four of them, though.'

In my debut season I was ten feet tall and poverty stricken. We got to the quarter-final of the League Cup and the FA Cup fifth round and got beaten by Villa in one and Luton in the other. On the weeks when I drank too much, I'd borrow money and wait till

I got a first-team game and the bonus that went with it to pay the lads back.

There were consolations. I wasn't playing every week but neither was I back doing either of the odd jobs I'd had before football. I wasn't a furniture remover. I wasn't a turkey disemboweller.

After losing both cups, the crowd at Arsenal began to turn on us. Rumours began floating about concerning Don Howe's future. Don ended them swiftly – he walked out. Steve Burtenshaw took over to the end of the season. We finished seventh.

My flat was now being shared between three of us. Paddy Hughes came from across the road in Crumlin. He was a tacker on the building sites. Mick Kavanagh came to stay for five days and stopped for three years. Mick was an asphalter. Most mornings the routine was the same. The boys thundered about at break of dawn, looking for boots and stuff, while I searched for the coolness on the other side of the pillow.

'Good luck, lads,' I'd shout. 'Don't forget your shovels.'

'Yeah! Fuck off, Quinny,' they'd call back merrily.

'Hi-ho, hi-ho, it's off to work . . .'

The door would slam and I'd settle back to sleep until training time loomed. Wet days were best. Training would be short; the lads wouldn't work if it was raining. Wet days caused me to lose most of my wages in saloon bars and bookies' offices.

At work, Don Howe had walked the plank and Steve Burtenshaw had put in his time. I was a six-foot four-inch tall striker who needed bigger shoulders and to put in some work on his floor game. The guy who had signed me was gone. The guy who had given me my debut was gone. If I had been smart, I would have been worried.

Then I got a call from Jack Charlton. Jack had been the manager of the Irish team for about three months at that stage, and was still a controversial choice. He was big, he was blunt and he was English. Worse, for the nation of Giles, O'Leary, Brady and Stapleton, he had a reputation for playing coarse football. We were happy as we were – beautiful, skilled losers.

I got the call from Jack summoning me to go and play for Ireland in a triangular tournament in Iceland. Some of the news surrounding the trip was jarring. The Liverpool players had dropped out. Dave O'Leary hadn't been picked so he'd booked a holiday. Then he was belatedly called up but he'd taken the hump and said he wasn't going to Iceland. Dave would be the first to realise that Jack could outlast anybody when it came to having the hump and keeping it.

I turned up at Heathrow on the appointed day in May and Jack, who was talking to a group of journalists at the time, broke away to say loudly to his assistant, Maurice Setters, 'We've not picked that lanky boogah, 'ave we?'

'Think we had to, Boss.'

I was a disciple immediately. However, Jack wasn't one to learn the names of his disciples. He called me Arsenal for the whole week in Iceland – Arsenal this, Arsenal that, make the bloody run, Arsenal. I decided to say nothing unless Jack began abbreviating the name out of familiarity.

We played Iceland on the Sunday and I, Arsenal, made my international debut. I played for six minutes as a replacement for John Aldridge, should have scored but didn't, and Ray Houghton tore a quick strip off me. We played Czechoslovakia two days later and I played for fifty-five minutes before being replaced by Frank Stapleton. Frank scored the winner.

We won the tournament and for me the whole thing was a wild success. First day in training, I scratched Frank Stapleton's face with my nails by accident and the other players went around saying encouraging things like, 'Frank is going to fucking kill you.' Instead, Frank muttered to me about getting my nails cut like a pro and got on with it.

I roomed with Michael Robinson. The other players had quietly warned me that he fancied himself a bit. If you ask me, I think I did well to squeeze into the room. The other absolute beginner on the trip was Liam O'Brien. Most of the time Liam and I were too shy to approach the senior players, who were a pretty formidable bunch even then. The first night we got there, Liam and I sat in the hotel lobby like two old maids until Jack strode through looking like an agitated ostrich, as usual. He ordered us to go to the pub with the rest of the team. It was depressing him looking at us in the lobby.

Flying home, I got my courage up to join a game of seven-card stud. Mick Kennedy of Portsmouth was on his first trip, too, and had got into the game. Mick was way out of his depth. I've never see anyone on such a bad run. At one stage, I went to tell him he couldn't bet right there because he couldn't possibly win. I got the sharpest dig in the ribs that I've ever experienced in football.

'If he wants to throw it away, you keep your mouth shut, sonny,' I was told.

'OK,' I said.

I got back to England for pre-season training late in July and as I was walking down a hill near my flat, a guy in a passing car shouted out the window, 'George Graham is the new manager.'

A group of us were summoned to see George later in the week. Tony Woodcock, Paul Mariner, Martin Keown, me – there was a whole line of us queuing up in the sunlit marble halls. Paul went in first, Tony next. All we could hear as we stood in the corridor was shouting and cursing. Each visit ended with a senior player storming out. Eventually, Martin goes in. He's in there for half an hour. There's more shouting. Martin won't sign a new deal. He storms out.

I'm last. I'm confident still. I've just broken into the first team, I'm now an international player, I'm a tall striker and there's a good market for tall strikers. Anyway, I'm cheap. I'm still on £175 a week with my signing-on fee coming in increments of £1,666 a year. Who in their right mind wouldn't want me?

George sits me on a little seat on the far side of his desk and looks me up and down. I explain the glorious nature of my recent achievements to him, point out the worthiness of my claim not just to be retained but to be rewarded like a grown-up. I can see he's impressed. He has an increase in mind for me, something in the low single figures. He pops up my wages by £7 a week.

Thursday in Saipan is endless. We've settled into the routine of things and this is our last day here. We train in the morning, and it's a good session with nobody grumbling. There's an end-of-term feel to it.

We haven't got everything we wanted from this epic trip to the corner of an island that's three landmasses past the middle of nowhere, but the week is over now. Time to move on.

In the afternoon, some of the lads go golfing again, a few more swim, others head to the gym on the far side of the hotel garden. A couple of us just hang around the open-air lobby of the hotel. I see Roy heading off for a walk. I have a couple of interviews to do. I'm doing World Cup diary stuff for one paper in England and one in Ireland. I'll have the talking drops in till teatime.

Why not? The atmosphere in teams nowadays has changed greatly. There aren't any card sharks any more. Years ago, you could win or lose your week's wages in a couple of hours playing cards. As a youngster, it was important to get into the card game that best suited your wage packet and your expertise; otherwise, you'd be fleeced without mercy. Now the most important thing is your selection of movies to watch on DVD, the quality of headphones you have, the diversions on your Game Boy. In my day, we made our own fun. I'm old.

*   *   *

When the 1988 European Championship qualifying games rolled around, Jack retained me in his squad. Things were happy at Arsenal and my extra £7 a week was keeping the British economy buoyant. With Ireland, we got off to an unexpectedly good start under Jack. Suddenly, back home there was a fascination with what the big Geordie might achieve.

We drew with the Belgians in Brussels. We held Scotland to a scoreless draw at Lansdowne Road. Jack kept including me in squads. Then we went to Hampden Park and Mark Lawrenson, playing in midfield, scored the only goal of the game. So we came home with an away win under our belts. Even Jack was surprised.

Six weeks later, we had to travel to Sofia to play Bulgaria at the Levski Stadium. At the time, Bulgaria were all but unbeatable at home but there was excitement and expectation building in Dublin. The match suddenly assumed an outsized importance, even to Jack. We began to prepare with an earnestness that didn't suit.

Jack and Maurice came over all Dick Dastardly and Muttley and we began scheming for our trip behind the iron curtain. For instance, Jack had a video and he was going to use it. For us at the time, this was a technological revolution on a par with the splitting of the atom.

Giddy and ribald as usual, we were corralled into a video room for the matinee showing of a previous group match between Bulgaria and Belgium. Maurice, as the younger and more in-touch man, was put in charge of the operation of the video machine. The tape was duly inserted, the screen crackled and we all sat back to watch, but there was something odd about the game. After a couple of minutes, we started to whisper among ourselves – 'Something wrong here.' 'Yeah, weird.' 'Doesn't look right.' 'Better ask Jack. Be careful, though.'

'Hey, Jack.'

'Aye.'

'How come there's nobody at the match?'

'Buggah.'

'It's an Under-21 game, isn't it, Jack?'

'Buggah. Switch it off, Maurice.'

Maurice is gently dozing in his chair. Jack is exasperated; best laid plans and all that.

'MAURICE! Switch it bloody off! I only ask you to do one bloody thing all day and you cock it up!'

The laughter accelerates Jack straight to the end of his short tether. In fact, the end of his tether is some way in the distance behind him. Jack is steaming. The more he steams, the more we laugh. The more we laugh, the redder his face gets. The more we try to suppress the laughter, the worse it gets.

A few years later, on another occasion when Jack tried to give us the run-down on our opponents, his lack of understanding of technology had a similar effect. We are expecting him to produce a clipboard, or at least a copybook or a folded page. Instead, Jack fishes out an old fag packet from his pocket, lays it on the table, flattens it out and looks at it intently, as if it's written in hieroglyphics. He scratches his head.

We're biting the backs of our hands to stop ourselves laughing, pulling our tracksuits over our faces. Our sides are hurting, our jaws are aching, some of us can't breathe.

Jack's mood is turning dangerous but suddenly, with a final squint through his specs, he breaks the code.

'Oh, fuck it. Ah, fuck. I've wrote one to eleven down here and I've wrote their strengths and their weaknesses from one to eleven, but I haven't wrote which fucking team is which.'

He's killing us. This is too much.

'Listen. There's nowt for it. I'll do this lot on the left and if I'm wrong and it's Latvia and not Austria, we won't worry because we've got Latvia in three weeks. It's not a bloody waste now, is it?'

We are in a state of paralysis, tears rolling down our cheeks. We are about to wet ourselves. Undeterred, Jack begins reading down through the list on his fag packet.

'Goalkeeper,' he says. 'Not much to do, but flaps at crosses. Right-back, classy. Left-back, show him the outside, no pace. Centre-backs, big strong lads, tendency to ball watch. Six, runs . . . six runs – eh, six runs?' Jack scratches his head, shoves the glasses up on his nose and looks again. 'Bloody hell. Either some buggah has made six good runs or the number six runs around a lot.'

We can't go on hiding it. There will be fatalities. We explode, every one of us collapsing off the chairs. We can't speak. We can't sit straight. We can't see through the tears of laughter. We are creased and crumpled and delirious. Jack is not amused.

'Fuck you lot. I've come here to try and help you. Now fuck off out of here the lot of you.'

Team meetings always have the potential for that giddiness, even now. But it was this sense of the team all in it together that Jack created that has stood us in good stead for so long.

Roy has done an interview, with *The Irish Times*. Within the squad, the interview is no big deal. We are on the home straight. We're going to Izumo tomorrow, putting it all behind us. Few of us have seen it but news of it travelled around the squad today. We rolled our eyes and wondered if Roy has had a pop, but really the aggro is behind us. Anyway, how sensational could an interview in *The Irish Times* be? It's not tabloid country.

Roy's motives? Who knows? He did a couple of interviews yesterday that were arranged long before the training-ground incidents. Maybe he's embarrassed over the way the going home thing played out from his point of view. It may have looked as if he was prepared to give up on the World Cup because of a training-ground squabble. I imagine he's just taken the opportunity to explain himself.

Mick McCarthy is off cycling again this afternoon. He is going to ride to the top of Mount Topatchau, the highest peak on the island. This Roy business has disturbed him a bit but generally he's been calm and serene for the past few days. He's been up front with the media about what happened on Tuesday and I think he uses these long rides to gather his thoughts. He's performing well under the circumstances.

It's a long listless afternoon and I spend most of it sitting in the lobby speaking into tape recorders. At one stage, Mick Byrne beckons me to a quiet corner to say that there is a problem with Roy's interview. Mick is excitable at the best of times. With so many press people around, I don't make an issue of it. Last duty of the afternoon is an interview with Philip Quinn of the *Irish Independent*. When Philip turns up, he has a downloaded copy of *The Irish Times* interview. He's pretty wound up about it but I don't really want to read it.

'Where's Mick McCarthy? Everything might change when Mick sees this,' he says. 'We might be changing your whole diary.'

We do our regular diary stuff anyway and Philip goes off to find Mick to get a response to the interview. The lads are back from golf. A few others have been to the cinema; they are drifting in now, too. I wander upstairs to have a shower and change. Before going down to dinner, Mick Byrne informs me there will be a meeting after the meal. At this stage he doesn't need to tell me why. On the way down to the dining room, I see Mick McCarthy talking to Jason McAteer near the lift. I hear Mick saying, 'Apparently, he's gone and done a fucking article.' I keep walking.

The restaurant is laid out with round tables that take eight people apiece, so we sit down in groups of seven or eight. There's a staff table and three other tables for players. The mood is light. I join an overflow table with Roy, Jason and Steve Finnan. A band is playing in the corner and the lads are clapping and singing along, waiting for Mick. Jason whispers to me that he hopes Roy will still be singing and clapping when the meeting is over. Word is that Mick is going to ask him about the interview.

We've been there for a while when Mick comes in. The band is still blasting away, playing of all things 'Stand By Me'. The lads are getting into it until, finally, Mick asks the band to leave. He stands in the middle and speaks about one or two general matters, mainly to do with moving on to Izumo in the morning. And then he unfurls Philip Quinn's copy of *The Irish Times* article.

'Roy, I want to speak to you about . . .'

Suddenly, it's gunfight at the OK Corral but Mick hasn't brought his gun. Roy goes off, rat-a-tat-tat.

'Who are you to fucking ask questions about me?' he starts. What was said then is not for me to repeat, nor is it the point.

Make me a deal. Ask me to kill somebody with a speech. Offer me a million pounds for every time I hit a nerve, open a cut or make a wound. Well, if I use Roy's speech, neither I nor any of my family will ever have to work again. It is the most articulate, the most surgical slaughtering I've ever heard. Mick McCarthy is dismantled from A to Z – his personality, his play, his style, his tactics, his contribution. On it goes.

Roy deals with Mick chronologically. He brings up the spat they had on the coach in Boston in 1992 when Roy was new to the squad. He deals with every incident and perceived slight since then.

Spineless.

Useless.

Stupid.

Gutless.

Roy is extraordinary when he gets going. The vein on his temple stands out in relief from his face. His voice goes up a few octaves into a desperate screech yet every grievance is ordered and filed neatly with an appropriate insult attached.

Incompetent.

Ignorant.

Backward.

Conman.

We're all mesmerised. For ten minutes it goes on. We sit there in a trance, blood draining from our faces. This isn't going to end with a group hug. We're not going to hear Roy saying that, apart from all that, Mick, I think you're OK.

Afterwards, people will ask everyone who was in that room what was so shocking. We came out of there like people who'd seen ghosts. We couldn't utter a word about what we'd seen and heard. I remember looking at Dr Martin Walsh and his face was glazed over; he was rigid with shock. People who weren't there may say but you've seen that sort of thing before – training-ground bust-ups, dressing-room rows.

Was it the language?

Was it the vehemence?

Was it the duration?

Was it the setting?

Was it the surprise?

It was everything, the whole enchilada – a feat of oratory, intelligence and some wit that shocked everyone.

Mick is knocked on his heels, visibly taken aback. He has no strategy for this. I think he came in here to put things to bed, to say to Roy that in future we keep things in-house and now let's move on.

At first, Mick says nothing. Then he starts trying to cut in but every time he does, another bullet whizzes past, taking off a slice of his hide as neatly as would a scalpel.

'But Roy . . .'

Pow!

'Surely, Roy . . .'

Pow!

Afterwards, I spend many hours wondering why I didn't cut in, why early in the performance I didn't say, 'C'mon, this is getting us nowhere. Let's wrap it up, let's cool down, let's just get on to Japan tomorrow.' I wonder why none of us did. I wonder why one of us didn't just stand in front of Roy and tell him he was out of order. Why didn't one of us haul him down? Fact is we were transfixed, bolted to our seats. The thing had to play itself out.

'Listen, Roy . . .'

Pow!

'Jesus.'

Finally, Mick gets off a sentence.

'Did you pick and choose your matches, Roy?'

As a response, it's not exactly Oscar Wilde. Mick won't be embroidering it on pillows when he gets old. It's not going to make Roy shrivel and die.

'I don't do fucking friendlies,' he shrieks at Mick. 'Friendlies are a waste of time.'

'OK then, what about the second Iran game?'

Later on, people will present this exchange as being a central part of the whole thing, as if, for some reason, the day before we go to the World Cup proper, Mick McCarthy opted to walk into a team meeting and dress down his best player about attendance at friendly matches over the years. It wasn't like that. This is Mick belatedly reaching for a weapon, any weapon. He's on the floor and the bullets are still coming and he throws whatever he can at Roy. Probably it was unfair, and probably it was a mistake, but the previous nine-minute contribution from Roy was all unfair and all a mistake. Nobody has cause to be judgemental about what happened in the last thirty seconds of this débâcle.

Mick brought up the Iran game because he knew many of us were surprised to wake up on that Sunday morning in Dublin and learn that Roy had gone back to Manchester without saying goodbye or good luck to any of us. We'd beaten the Iranians 2–0 on the Saturday in the first leg of our World Cup play-off, and Roy went.

I don't think there was one of us who thought he'd pulled an injury to get out of going to Tehran. We knew that Alex Ferguson had done us a huge favour by letting Roy come to Dublin in the first place. He hadn't played for Manchester United for three weeks before that. Roy got up early on the Sunday, felt his knee was not right, had a brief conference with Mick in person and Alex Ferguson on the phone, and took the next flight back to Manchester. What stunned me, what was so typical of Roy but still so shocking, was that he could leave without once looking back over his shoulder.

The conversation that morning ran:

'Roy's gone.'

'You're winding me up.'

'Swear to God.'

'Wow. Jesus. Just like that?'

And now Mick, recalling our shock that morning and perhaps trying to conscript us on to his side of the argument, dug it up again. It draws an end to the thing, anyway.

'Positive result,' screams Roy, a bit cryptically, and he's turning to go already.

'What?'

'Positive result. Fergie, someone who knows how to manage a football team, said, and you agreed, that I wouldn't go to the second leg if we got a positive result. We got a positive result.'

Silence.

'I'll fuck off, then,' Roy shouts as he gets to the door. 'I'll not go to the fucking World Cup. Now you have your excuse. It's all Roy's fault. See ye later, lads.' And he's gone.

The silence couldn't be more perfect if a death had occurred in the room. Silence eats us all. You can hear other people's breaths travelling in and out of their lungs. Mick is white as a sheet. I think he's shaking. You can hear brains whirring back into action.

Roy Keane has just signed himself out.

He's just punched the clock and left.

He's out the gate.

Oh, fuck!

I say, 'Should I go after him? Is this retrievable?' Mick shakes his head. More silence. Dean Kiely, the reserve keeper, cracks it with a joke. 'Mick, can I offer my services to fill that midfield dynamo role?'

There is an explosion of nervous laughter. Any valve is useful at this stage. We just want to be a team again, laughing and looking forward to things. Teams are great illusions. While you are part of one, you can convince yourself that you will live for each other, stop bullets for each other. You can match your ambitions with everyone else's and move forward in step together. Teams aren't designed for this sort of complexity and stress. Teams aren't built for having their most useful component remove itself when most needed.

We don't know what to do. This team doesn't know what to do. We can split into a million pieces right now. Gary Kelly stands up.

'Well, is that it?' he says. 'Is it over? Listen, lads. Are we behind this man or not?' He nods towards Mick McCarthy. 'Are we going to give him a round of applause?' Everybody claps. That's when I know this thing has fucking gone mad. Packie winds up the meeting a few seconds later with a few grave words in support of Mick. We fall out into informality.

As I say, the fabric of the greatest team in the world isn't designed for this. We fall back on other things – our own hopes, doing what is right, saving ourselves, putting the team together again. With a great stretch of water left to travel, we've just seen our most able seaman go berserk and toss himself overboard. Our reaction is self-preservation – mend the hole, pull together again.

We break into little groups, telling each other that this is going to be a hard one to get through, that this is going to be the story of the World Cup. Roy hasn't actually been sent home in the formal sense but in this room now, we all know it's over for him.

Mick is telling people that he can't have the sort of abuse he's just suffered. We know, we know. The rest of us are pretty much in shock.

This will be bigger than we can imagine, I say to a few lads. Stan is saying the same thing. BIG. Look after your own World Cup, boys. Try to think of your own future and what this tournament means to you. Think of yourself and what you came here for. Get your head back on the game. Get through it. The ship is sinking and we're asking people to think of the fun they'll have at the destination. If twenty-two of us are selfish enough, we'll be a team again.

Mick comes to Stan and me and tells us that he is having a press conference soon and he would like our support. We ask for two minutes together, and after maybe fifteen seconds of that, Alan Kelly comes over to join us. The three of us know immediately that we have to support Mick. Any options here? None.

We know it will be the end of eleven years of companionship with Roy. We know that we are being asked to do something you never think will arise in your career, publicly backing a manager against a player. Any choices?

No.

If we don't get behind him, Mick McCarthy is on the next plane home. Then we have anarchy and chaos. It's not perfect, but is there a better course of action? Emphatically, no. We look at Mick, who is still shaken and white. How the meeting didn't end in physical violence is the mystery of the thing for us now. We can't come up with an argument for defending Roy Keane.

The wilderness – how to get there in a few easy steps. We start our first season under George well. I'm cheap and he likes me. I stay in the team, play almost every game, score twelve goals. We beat Liverpool in the League Cup final.

I've skipped a bit. In the run-up to the League Cup final, George twists my arm to sign a contract. I won't sign it. I'd earn more on building sites that give you no money if you stop for rain. George says he's concerned. He can't pick someone for a Wembley final if that player is in dispute with the club. What way would that be to conduct business? 'That's fine,' I say. I have about eighteen family and friends coming over to Wembley but I'll bluff it out this time.

A few days before the match, George calls me in again. His offer goes from £300 to £350 with no signing-on fee. I cut and run. It's a raise. I stood up to him for a week or two. It's not big money but it gives me a little bit of security. Besides, I'm playing well and scoring. We'll renegotiate soon enough. I'd still be better off working on a building site but at least I'm going somewhere now.

Within twenty-four hours of signing, I have the spare time to go and work on a site. In the week of the final, George signs Alan Smith, the tall, clean-cut striker from Leicester City. Alan comes to watch us at Wembley.

Hey presto! That little bit of hardball worked! Anyone want me to cut a deal on their behalf? I've just nailed down a four-year contract on bad money and the only chance of playing will be when Alan Smith gets injured or suspended. He doesn't do either. Alan Smith is not only bulletproof, fireproof and waterproof, he's never been booked. Pat Rice cheers me up. This Smith can't be that good if he's never been injured, never been booked. But he was that good. We'd bought a six-foot four-inch centre-forward who was perfect.

The next year, I started six league games under George. I scored against Manchester United three times, but Roger Milford, the jewellery-enhanced referee, allowed just one of them. He has apologised every time I've met him since. We would have won 3–2, but we lost 2–1. I needed that hat-trick like a poker player needs aces.

Welcome to the world of serious drinking.

The press conference takes place in a little Chinese restaurant tucked away in a corner of the hotel's entrance lobby. It's a bizarre setting. We follow Mick through the lobby where a string quartet is playing. The media have been rounded up and are ready and waiting. I feel like I've entered the twilight zone. I know, walking up through the chairs, that I am putting myself in a dreadful position, but shutting up would be the chicken way out.

Mick begins by saying that he is sending Roy Keane home. This isn't quite right. Roy has walked out. At this stage, it's horrible to be here. Do we have to do a press conference so soon? Mick feels it has to be done now, taking account of the time difference at home (we are nine hours ahead). It might be an error. It might be closing doors unnecessarily. Asking us to go on stage with Mick might be clicking the lock; perhaps, perhaps, perhaps.

Right now, too much second guessing and hindsight just makes huge excuses for Roy. Right now, we're hugely disappointed in Roy. We're hurt by him. Our captain and our best player has effectively walked out on us for the second time in three days. Whatever is going on in his head, this team isn't coming first. Whatever his beef with Mick McCarthy, this isn't the time or the place. He has lost all sense of proportion. He's lost us.

Stan says a few words. He's the new captain. Sad circumstances surrounding the appointment but the perfect choice.

I'm asked don't I think that Roy is brave. Wrong time, wrong question. I say that I don't think running to the newspapers is very brave, no.

Alan Kelly says a few words. There are questions and queries. Somebody keeps asking Mick if he will be making a report of this to the FAI. We all imagine the FAI will be getting to hear of it anyway.

When the press conference ends, Stan and I agree to go straight to Roy's room. We cross the lobby and it occurs to us that we don't know where Roy's room is. There's no reason to know.

If I have a jersey I need to get signed, I'll sometimes say to myself that I won't bother Roy. Anyway, Johnny Fallon, our kitman, does a fine Roy signature if you're desperate. Getting the kitman to forge the signature of one of your team-mates is the price you pay when you start making accommodations for genius.

When Stan and I get to Roy's room, I'm half hoping he'll say, 'Fuck, lads, I've gone and done it here.' No chance. He gives off such an aura of control and self-possession. He is like steel. We are more flustered than he is.

Me: 'We've come to tell you we've just done a press conference with the manager. Just come to tell you that.'

Stan: 'What the fuck?'

Me: 'Roy, I think you were wrong.'

Stan: 'What the fuck were you thinking?'

Roy: 'I'm fine, don't worry about me. You make your own choices.'

Stan: 'What were you doing?'

Me: 'I am making my choice. I think you're the best player I've ever played with. Extraordinary. But you've gone too far. It's a huge mistake.'

Roy: 'It's no mistake on my part.'

Stan: 'What was going through your head?'

Roy: 'That's fine.'

Stan: 'What, in the name of God?'

Roy: 'Look. I think I was right. Don't worry about me. I did the right thing.'

We have little left to say. Roy is hard and in control. I tell him that I'll most likely be retiring after all this and there's a chance I will never see him again. If we ever meet, it will be an awkward, shuffling thing between two men who used to play football together. Probably this means more to me than it does to him. I don't think Roy sees the world in that way. I don't think he carries those sentiments around with him. We shake hands and Stan and I leave.

No stars in the sky tonight.

CHAPTER SEVEN

SUCCESS HAS MADE A FAILURE OF OUR HOME

I don't worry about what tomorrow brings. I fear what happened yesterday.
OLD ARAB SAYING

There's an episode in the life of Homer Simpson where Barney, Springfield's top alcoholic, and Homer are arguing.

'What did I ever do on you?' says Homer, and the cartoon switches to flashback. Barney is a young undergraduate about to do his final medical exams and Homer is pestering him to come and have a beer. 'One beer,' says Homer. 'What harm can one beer do?' Barney relents and cracks a can of Duff, his first drink. He takes one sip and he turns into the Barney who is forever welded to the seat in Moe's bar. 'Hey! I like this stuff.'

I feel like Homer Simpson.

We wander around the little duty-free area at Saipan Airport, fingering the tack and whispering to each other. The media are among us. None of us wants to get cornered for a quote. We all have stuff we want to say to each other. Between ourselves, we're blaming everyone now – the press, the FAI, Roy, Mick. And why isn't Michael Kennedy here? Michael would sort this in two minutes. We're all trying to absolve ourselves this morning.

Everything in the last twelve hours has been rushed. Nothing is composed. Nothing has been planned. It should have been a game of chess. Instead, it's Twister. We're all over the place, all a bit guilty.

Early this morning, we left the hotel quietly. Roy was alone in a room somewhere upstairs. I'm not sure that any of us apart from Mick Byrne even knocked and said goodbye this morning. We're too pissed off with him. It's too raw.

On the bus, Mick Byrne tried to jolt us back to life. Mick is hurting worse than anyone else is; he has a real friendship with Roy. Seeing the team sunder like this breaks his heart; leaving Roy behind like we've just done is cutting him up. But Mick has a role in the team, so he puts a face on and tries to cheer us up, as usual. Lately he's become a grandfather and he begins singing one of the theme songs from the programmes he watches in the morning while he's dandling his grandchild on his lap. Slowly, we join in.

On the back seat where Roy usually sits, one of the lads has stuck a little envelope with RIP on it. It's a black little joke; Roy's sort of humour. We stare out of the windows at the last any of us will ever see of Saipan Island.

Today is Friday. We will fly to Izumo and our training camp, and tomorrow we will play Hiroshima in our last friendly game before the start of the competition. In eight days' time we play Cameroon in the second game of the World Cup, our first game. In twelve hours, not one of us has wasted a thought on Cameroon.

Maybe we'll get through this, maybe not. This is as low as I've been in nineteen years of football.

I switch on the television one day and Paul Merson is on the screen. Paul is giving a press conference and he is in tears. He says he's addicted to drugs, he is addicted to gambling and he owes a lot of people a lot of money. It hits me like a sledgehammer.

A little while later, I pick up the phone and call Paul's dad. It's been a long time.

'Fred. It's Niall Quinn.'

'All right, Niall.'

'Saw Paul on the telly. Really upset for him. I was thinking of giving him a call only I don't have his number any more.'

'Listen, Niall. Part of his treatment is that he's not supposed to speak with you.'

'Oh.'

'Sorry.'

'Well, could you tell him that I'm asking for him and thinking of him.'

'Well, we're not actually supposed to mention your name to him.'

'Oh.'

Not too long after this, Tony Adams wrote a book, *Addicted*. At every junction on the road to Tony's alcoholism, I seemed to be with him, leading the way. He and I got into a public spat about some dates he had mixed up in the book, but it wasn't the point.

For me, at Highbury, the bad times were the best of times. I was young and carefree, and we were living like kings, but two of my friends were laying down the seeds of heartbreak, addiction and broken marriages. I just noticed that they were getting more games than I was. We talk about teams, about dying for each other and 110 per cent, but mostly football is me, me, me.

What happened to Tony and Paul sucks the colour out of some of the best memories. I was a good drinker and a bad gambler and being out of the team most of the time for more than two years allowed me to improve my performance in both disciplines. I brought Tony and Paul along for the ride.

Football-wise, my touch got slowly better, and I put on a little, but not enough, weight. In the end, I would escape Arsenal.

Meanwhile, I got to know the inside of every snooker hall, bookies' office and pub in north London.

We were harmless, almost comically so. Paul and I always had schemes bubbling away. We were top-class shakedown artists. One night, we were in a casino playing blackjack. Paul has it sussed. I will play first and somehow I will draw all the bad cards. I'm to bet fivers. Paul will come in, take the good cards and back them up with the big money – fifty quid a throw. We sat at a table with a guy in a cowboy hat. I won about seven out of ten hands. We were in deep. Pretty soon we were smashed. Dopes like us? Casinos bar them from leaving.

'Best be getting back to the hills, boys,' drawled Cowboy Hat.

Paul was fascinated by anything that had odds attached. I remember once he cracked it, he truly did. He purchased a mini casino, brought it aboard a long-haul flight with the team and set up shop at the emergency exit. He had the little green eyeshade and everything. I helped out. We'd made a small fortune by the time we got to Bermuda.

It was SuperBowl weekend and when we arrived Paul decided we'd take the experiment a little further. We set up as bookies for the SuperBowl, taking bets here, laying some off there. The long shots won, we made a big killing and stayed drunk for days.

Of course, there were the ones that got away. One Friday in the spring of 1986, we're soaking in our baths, eight in a row, when Merse hops out of his. Eureka! He's got a surefire thing. Seven to two on! He needs a hundred quid a head from seven seniors, all to be refunded on Monday. Can't lose. Steve Davis is playing this pub singer in the World Snooker final. A fahkin' pub singer! Some geezer called Joe Johnson. Davis cannot be beat! C'mon, roll up, roll up, roll up.

Seven wet players come up with seven hundred quid. Davis is odds-on, but get enough down on him and it's money for jam, best weekend's work a boy could do.

On Tuesday morning, Merse is saying, 'Snooker is possibly the most bent sport in the world. It's fixed for the TV. Steve Davis loses to a pub singer? C'mon.'

There's a story of a taxi journey late one night back to Paul's place. He's in the front, with Perry Groves and a couple of other lads in the back. Paul whispers, 'Hey, let's do a runner.' Bit of excitement.

The taxi gets to Paul's estate and at the first corner, Paul says to the driver, 'Pull up,' and then he shouts, 'Now!' The doors are flung open and they run about three yards but something's wrong. Perry Groves is dozing like a baby in the back seat. They make a joke of it all to the taxi driver, pretending they were sticking Perry with the fare. What a wind-up, eh mate! They give him just about every penny they have as a tip.

Later, towards the end at Arsenal, Paul is settled down a bit and my phone rings in the early hours on winter Sundays.

'Quinny.' It's just a whisper on the other end. 'It's me. Merse.'

'Merse?'

'Can't talk. Don't want her to hear me. Get your teletext on.'

'OK.'

'Get me the American Football scores. Just read them out. I can't talk.'

'OK. Dallas 21, New England 17.'

'Yes.'

'Chicago 17, Oakland 12.'

'Yes, yes, yes.'

'Philadelphia 31, New York Giants 10.'

'No, no, no. Fahk, no. Giants bastards.'

'Miami 17 . . .'

'Aw, it don't matter no more, Quinny. Cheers.'

In the end, people gave Paul credit to gamble with, more credit than he'd earn in a few years with Arsenal. They baited him with it and reeled him in. He told me once about trying to get out of a big hole he'd dug. He looked at the four big American Football matches to be played one Sunday and worked out that if any two of the four results went right for him, he'd be out of the hole. If three or all four went right, he was back ahead. He bet big on each of them – lost all four.

When I look back at the bad times at Arsenal, I remember the good times that came with them. I thought we were all on the same big slide, happy and free. If anyone had a problem, I thought it was me. In the 1987–88 season, I started six league games and Paul started seven. Tony, an old pro by now, started thirty-nine. The next year, Arsenal won the championship. I got two starts, Paul got twenty-nine and Tony thirty-six. So it went till I left Arsenal.

I'd cut loose for long periods. The Dog and Duck, the Chase Side Tavern, the Moon Under the Water, The Thatch, The George, the King's Head, the Orange Tree – they were my home patches.

I envied Paul and Tony. The long periods out of the team, the meaningless approach of each Saturday, the odd week when I'd get my hopes up, it all ate away at my soul during those years. They were out there week after week in an improving team. They lived the life in full Technicolor.

In the long run, though, I got the better half of the deal. Football didn't consume me but neither did the gambling or the drink. I played everything for laughs, took it all lightly enough. People around me were drowning; I pushed on, lost touch, got mentioned in their therapy sessions.

I watched Mick this morning as we moved. He's feeling his way back into this reality. Nothing in his plans for the World Cup can have included what happened last night. I truly believe that we were within seconds of Mick walking.

I don't know yet what way the team is breaking. When everyone goes up and chats in their room at night, the conversations can veer all over the place. I know this, though. I know a lot of the lads feel about Mick the way we young players did about Jack Charlton back in 1990. Regardless of Roy's immense contribution on the field, Mick is the guy who has got us here. Now he's got to be the guy who gets us through it.

Last night there was huge support for Mick in that room. That's perhaps where Roy misjudged the ground. Players moan and grumble all the time, but if there was anyone else in there who didn't support Mick, well, they wanted to go to the World Cup anyway. They held their peace. The next few days will be important.

When Mick was playing for Manchester City, I once tried to lay him out. He was never the quickest so it tells you something about my technique when I say that I missed.

It was early in my career and I was proving a point. I was tall, raw and built like a pipe cleaner, and Mick ran right over me in the first few minutes, just letting me know he was there. It was supposed to scare me. It did scare me.

I decided that I couldn't spend the next eighty-five minutes being scared, so the next ball that came across, I made as if to head it, then checked and aimed an elbow at Mick. It was one of your more theatrical assassination attempts. Mick got out of the way. My momentum was such that I almost elbowed my own ankle. He saw the intent, though.

Not long afterwards I was called up by Jack for the Icelandic tournament. Mick produced an article he had written for a newspaper in which he described the incident. He wrote that he'd thought a lot more of me after that. That's Mick McCarthy.

He was captain the day we won the tournament in Iceland and he was captain when we went to Italy in 1990. I've got used to his gruff authority, his dead straight belief in loyalty and the team.

Early in 1991, he was doing a gig for the Children's Hospital in Crumlin and was trying to get on *The Late Late Show*, Ireland's top TV talk programme. He'd written a book. I'd just scored for Ireland in a big game against England at Wembley and the programme would only have Mick on if I did the show, too. I went. My sisters had come to Manchester for the weekend but I went anyway. I don't know why; just something about Mick McCarthy and what he expects of people. Most of us respond to him. It was my first time on a chat show on TV. We talked and we sang 'These Boots Are Made For Walking' with Maxi. If you don't say no to Mick under circumstances like that, you never will.

I don't know where the bad seeds were sown in his relationship with Roy. They had the problem in Boston in 1992 but that was over and done with. I played against Russia in 1996 in Mick's first game as manager, when Roy got sent off, but they both seemed to handle that. Before the qualifying campaign for this World Cup, Mick went to see Roy at his home in Manchester. Mick can be abrasive but he can be very straight and they got a lot sorted then.

There was a breach later back in 1996 when Roy didn't show up for a summer tour to America, but that was many miles back down the road.

Locked in the team's vaults there's a more recent story that gets taken out and examined occasionally. In the Airport Hotel in Dublin one night, some friends of Roy's and some friends of Gary Breen's got into a boisterous argument. The crowd travelled from the bar, down the corridor where the team were sleeping. It was nothing serious, just loud. They stopped outside one door, which opened and Mick put his head out.

'Keep it down boys, will ya,' he said.

Roy turned and said, 'None of your business. Get in and shut your door.'

Mick shut the door. What else was he going to do? The deal with Roy (as it was with Paul McGrath in a different sense and in a different time) was to get him on to the pitch.

Maybe something altered in the chemistry of their relationship back then. The rest of us never took the time to notice. Much was made of a famous photo depicting Roy's reaction to Mick when he ran jubilantly on to the field when we beat Holland in qualifying for this World Cup. In the photo, Mick is delighted, his hand outstretched. Roy has just given one of his great performances but he looks baleful. He is avoiding eye contact and has offered Mick a limp shake of his hand as he strides past. That got played up quite a lot. Maybe that set the ball rolling. Who knows?

For the rest of us, there was no problem with Roy during the qualification series. He was magnificent all the way through. He was outstanding against Holland and Portugal at home. His desire to come to this World Cup was immense. You could almost feel it.

Under George Graham we became Club 18–30. We spent more time in the sun than we did in London. George would whisk us all away on club holidays at the drop of a hat – three days in Marbella, a week in Bermuda. He loved the sun. We loved the lifestyle.

One weekend we'd played on Saturday and were off to Marbella on Sunday morning. I drank through the night and got to Gatwick at 6 a.m. to find the plane was delayed. I fell to drinking again until mid afternoon when our plane took off. Finally, we got to the hotel and George summoned the team to a meeting. He was in the middle of telling the lads that we had an important game the next Sunday, live on TV. He was saying that he expected us to behave, and we could drink only in moderation, when I wandered in, glazed, went to sit down unobtrusively and missed the seat entirely. Ah, George loved me.

We'd sing, all the time – try stopping us. Whenever George was around, I'd break into 'If I Were a Rich Man', just to wind him up. Merse, though, had a style of his own.

One night in Bermuda, he and I are skint, we're both out of the team, and we're cadging drinks where we can. One by one, the lads have drifted off back to the hotel. It's getting bright. We fall in with some locals who invite us to Sunday morning at the rugby club. We're in trouble for not being back at the hotel – we're in trouble if we go back, in trouble if we stay out. We head for the rugby club. We're a bit out of our social depth when we get there, but it's eleven in the morning and the drink is flowing again. They start a sing-song – rugby songs. Then Merse stands up and sings, with me joining in behind him, 'I'll Be Back In The High Life Again'. The man, the moment, his credit rating – all captured in one song.

Tony is four days younger than I am but he was ahead of every one of our generation at Highbury in terms of his progress within the game. We got on well, played against each other at various levels for Ireland and England, and as the George Graham era progressed, we began socialising. It didn't take long for Tony to become a quasi Irishman. We'd drink with the team and often when we were done there, he'd come with me to the Irish pubs and clubs that I haunted. When Tony got married, I cut short my honeymoon to be at his wedding. By then, our era as the kings of the Holloway Road was over, but the drinking was beginning to eat into Tony's life.

We had our favourite spots. You knew the rules. If you went to these places, you didn't get out before dawn. Tony and I would have long sessions. We'd often get silly, have races up lamp-posts outside, and then crash out anywhere we could find for a couple of hours before hitting training.

When George took us away, we planned our drinking tactically. We'd hold off on rounds, like cagey stockbrokers, then we'd come in to the market and take up our options in the round system late on, just as the more senior lads were wandering off. Usually, a hard-core of Tony, Merse and I would move on to a cheaper place to start the serious drinking – invest everything in drink; buy, buy and buy some more.

We had our public spat in the newspapers about the date of an epic drinking trip to the races at Windsor. Tony remembered us as going straight from three days of drinking to get the bus for the championship-winning game at Anfield in 1989. In fact, the jaunt took place in mid-April, the game took place at the end of May – not that it was exemplary behaviour for the young professional to follow either way.

We were given a couple of days off early in the week and had no weekend game, so there were no surprises in the line-up for Windsor. Tony, Merse and I were joined by Steve Bould and we were straight into a taxi in our training gear and off to the races.

It was a perfect evening, good weather, good racing and good drinking. The four of us finagled an invite into a private box and the free drink flowed. Tony and I got separated from Steve and Merse and when, finally, it struck us to head for home, the racecourse was deserted and pitch black. We weren't in a terrific state for navigating. We walked for what seemed like miles up a dark avenue from the course until we saw a car coming in the distance. Tony waved it down and, as luck had it, the driver was a football fan; well, a Wimbledon fan, which is the next best thing. He recognised Tony and even claimed to know who I was. We had a merry drive with him.

'As a centre-half, Tone,' he asked, 'what do you make of Wimbledon's Vinnie Jones?'

Tony was diplomatic about it. 'He's crap,' he said.

'You're saying he can't play, Tone?'

'I'm saying he's doing well to make a living. He's shit.'

The driver turned to me for a second opinion. I weighed the odds. Wimbledon have so few fans the odds are good that this one knows Vinnie Jones personally.

'I think he does a job for them,' I said, 'does what's needed.'

Tony got stuck into me and we proceeded into the town of Windsor, arguing over the merits and faults of Vinnie Jones until the driver threw us out at a pub.

The night is young. We drink till closing time and it's still young. We go to a nightclub in Maidenhead. Our Arsenal tracksuits seem to be working against us now. We spend the rest of our cash on a taxi to Heathrow. There's method in this madness. Tony has a credit card. We check into the Penta Hotel and start putting the drinks on the room bill.

We wake up the next morning with very little money but the good news is that it's only Tuesday, and the sun is shining. We decide to take a tube to find somewhere nice to drink. Two stops later it's Hounslow – beautiful place to drink. We get some cash and start drinking. It's about 11 a.m.

After lunch, we decide that a really nice place to drink on a day like this would be Richmond, so we take another tube to Richmond and find a nice riverside pub just as it starts to spill rain. It's a monsoon, bless it. We are in the pub and the landlord is putting sandbags against the door to keep the water out. We're stuck.

We drink until seven or eight in Richmond by which time the rain has stopped and we head to O'Riordan's in Brentford because I think Tony would like the Guinness there. We drink in Brentford until very late and then get a taxi to my place in Enfield. At least, we mean to but we're hijacked by a Greek club called Winners, near where I live. Winners stays open till 4 a.m.

On Wednesday morning, we wake up in the flat in Enfield. Tony wonders if I want the good news or the bad news. I opt for the bad first. 'I've wet the bed.' Good? 'You're going to make money out of it.' He signs the sheet 'All the Best, Tony Adams'.

Weeks later, we're playing Wimbledon at Highbury. On the night of the game, we can hear Wimbledon arriving, with their usual disrespect for our marble halls. Next thing, our dressing-room door bursts open and Vinnie Jones is blocking the light from outside.

'Adams, you fucker, where are you?'

'Hi, Vinnie,' says Tony, who clearly has no memory of the conversation in the car a few weeks ago.

'Windsor? My best mate? Ringing any bells, Tone? I am going to rip your fucking head off tonight, Tone, and I'm going to spit down the fucking hole.'

Tony is sitting there stunned and as Vinnie spins round to leave, his eyes meet mine.

'Quinn. You're not a bad lad.'

A couple of weeks later, against Liverpool, Tony became the first Arsenal captain to lift the league trophy since 1971. He was twenty-three.

Funny how big things can hinge on the smallest development. Michael Kennedy has acted for the players as a group in brokering the deal with the FAI for the division of the players' pool and the payment of World Cup bonuses. Altogether he acts for five players within this squad, including Roy and me. Generally speaking, he is the cleverest man most of us know. Originally, he was going to be here in Saipan with us but his work intervened. He couldn't get away for this part of the trip so he said he'd come for the matches.

In an hour, the Irish squad are catching a plane in one direction, and later in the day, our captain, our best player, will take a flight in the opposite direction. We have nobody with the stature to intervene, to negotiate, to call a time-out, to knock heads together.

The FAI are an irrelevance at this moment. Things are happening to their team that they can only gape at, and all in a horribly public way. It's late at night back in Ireland now. The papers are getting ready to roll. Roy, Mick and the rest of us are going to be the only story in town and there's no white knight coming over the hill to rescue us.

Stan and I chat. The team needs protecting. It needs people out front deflecting some of this or there is a real danger that we are going to fall apart this week. The irony is that the team was going so well, not just in the sense that we were putting together results, but you could feel us filling with confidence, becoming the sort of team we plan to be.

The game against Holland was the one that gave us the belief. Jason McAteer scored the winner in front of a heaving Lansdowne Road and the Dutch finished in disarray. We had only ten men on the pitch when it ended but we knew what we were doing.

That's the mystery. Roy must have sensed the potential, and he's experienced enough to know that at international level you put up with a bit more. You are in football for yourself first of all. You take what you want for yourself, and if you don't like it at a club, there are ways of engineering a move. You only have one country. There's nowhere to walk out to and you either want to play or you don't.

This is bad? Roy knows the stories of the true bad old days, the disorganisation, the endless friendly games in somewhere like Poland arranged because somebody in the FAI had a girlfriend there. He knows how it was under Jack Charlton even. And he knows that so many great Irish players have put up with it because they only had one country to play for and they loved it. They wouldn't let something so important go. When it's your national team, you enter into each new era with enthusiasm. You believe because you have to believe.

That's what we did when Mick became manager. Mick was Jack's right-hand man and when Jack was off on an earner, Mick assumed control above Maurice Setters. If that bothered you, it bothered you, but you played.

I can remember as Mick began experimenting with three at the back, Tony Cascarino and I would be in our room grumbling like the two old codgers on *The Muppet Show*.

'What do ya think of it so far?'

'Rubbish!'

But we played till we dropped; we believed it would come right and I think it has. We've come through the toughest of qualifying groups unbeaten. We have a young team. These shouldn't be bad times.

I found out early that the best thing with Mick was to let him feel that you really want to play for him, give him everything on the field. Nothing more was needed.

✻   ✻   ✻

So Arsenal won the championship in 1989. For me, the trip to Windsor was just part of the growing distance between myself and the heart of the club.

In March the year before, during championship run-in time, I woke up one morning and realised it was Cheltenham Gold Cup day. I called in sick. Who would suspect an Irishman taking ill on Gold Cup day?

I went, had a few drinks and watched the race on the screen. Charter Party won, Richard Dunwoody on board. Go on, my son! We'd all backed him. The following morning was now in jeopardy, too. Thirty of us high rollers bellied up to the Town and Country Club in Kentish Town. In you come, lads. The proprietor, Mickey Whelan from Leitrim, gives each and every one of us a bottle of champagne on the way in. We're going to see The Pogues. The boys are in their prime. It's no night at the opera. It's brilliant, exhausting chaos.

We're the last to leave. We were invited to a pub in Highbury Corner, where Paddy Reilly of Dubliners fame is performing at midnight. OK, why not? Mickey comes too. Soon it's dawn. On the way out into the morning cold, Mickey sticks a bottle of champagne into each of my hands — breakfast and dinner. By 10.30, I was training and feeling like a dog.

The championship seemed like somebody else's business. I was still the gangly centre-forward whose play on the floor everybody felt entitled to have a cut at. I read the criticisms, from Sir Alf Ramsey to Emlyn Hughes, and began to take them to heart.

When it came to playing Liverpool in the last game of the 1989 season, I looked back and smiled at the early Chasing the Tango days. One night at Anfield, Charlie Nicholas and I were delegated to play up front. Neither of us were ranked among the world's greatest athletes and Liverpool pushed the ball around all through the first half and made fools of us. Charlie and I came off at half-time whining like puppies. It was agreed that we'd drop back to the halfway line, crowd midfield and let Liverpool do all the passing they wanted back in their own half. It worked perfectly and ever after, that's how George's teams played when they went to Liverpool. Charlie and I being wheezy was, I like to think, the great tactical innovation that changed the history of soccer!

Not long after the famous night at Anfield when Arsenal won the title, the club had a reception to present the league medals. All the players got their silver and a free camera from JVC, our sponsors. I didn't have enough appearances to qualify for either and was able to keep my hands in my pocket all night long. Paul Davis was in the same boat but the club were in negotiation with Paul for a new contract. They arranged for Paul to be presented with a medal.

We'd won the title by a whisker. Arsenal and Liverpool finished on the same goal difference. We'd scored a single goal more than they had. I didn't win Arsenal the League but a single goal was what I had scored for the season. It wasn't so much the medal as the isolation that bugged me. The league win was a graduation for a group of us who had been kids together. Tony Adams was the First Division's youngest captain; Merse was the Under-20 Player of the Year. Tony, Merse, Dave Rocastle, Martin Hayes, Micky Thomas, Gus Caesar and I had all come through as a group of friends. During the championship run, I'd travelled to most games as thirteenth man but spent practically every game watching from the bench. I felt that they also serve who sit and are ready, most of the time.

A week later, the chairman of the club sent me a silver tray. I was a kid in flatland London with an inscribed silver tray. My own kids use it now for sledding down the hill behind our house, when the snow falls in winter.

The old friendships fared scarcely any better than the tray. Teams are organisations we pass through. I don't call, I don't write, I don't even think of them that often. But on the occasion of my testimonial I got a text message out of the blue. Merse!

It meant a lot. It bolted me to the floor for a minute. Merse! It reminded me of everything I'd left behind. Yet I think I began falling out of love with Arsenal at the time of the silver tray, and when I made the break, I made it clean.

Football is not a game of sentiment. From Roy on down, it's a world of me, me, me. Mostly we're in too much of a hurry to discover the why, why, why.

CHAPTER EIGHT

JUST BECAUSE YOUR WIFE DIES DOESN'T MEAN YOUR HOUSE CAN'T BURN DOWN TOO

Beside me the Sheriff's face was as tight as his hands on the wheel, his eyes bloodshot and tired. His breath was harsh and his nostrils dilated taut and I knew just what he was feeling. Right in the back of my head was a cold spot where the bullet would land if we moved too fast or too wrong.

MICKEY SPILLANE, *TOMORROW I DIE*

Izumo is in the prefecture of Shimane and that's all we know about it. We are in the Royal Hotel in Izumo in the prefecture of Shimane somewhere in Japan. It's beautiful here — mountains in the mid-distance, paddy fields and little irrigation channels running right to the edge of the town.

The hotel bedrooms are tiny but we have one each. When Izumo went looking for a World Cup team to come and stay, they offered an entire hotel for free. We took it. We have the run of the place. We have guards on the front door. We have a wonderful training facility three minutes up the road. We have whatever we want whenever we want it. Everything is perfect. The people are lovely. The weather is fine.

Roy, I wish you were here.

We are all preoccupied with this holy war. There are welcoming receptions and parties for us but we're buzzing in and out sourpussed and with our minds elsewhere. In the lobby of the hotel there are a couple of computers for our use, with Internet access. The lads spend their free time sending emails and downloading the latest Roy stories from every paper they can find.

Here we are in this quiet hotel somewhere in the heart of rural Japan and the biggest story of the World Cup still hovers like a thundercloud over our heads. Every phone call home tells us a little more about the craziness going on there. Television and radio have switched to all Roy, all the time. The Taoiseach is involved. The country is bitterly divided. The story is news everywhere, not just in Ireland. With India and Pakistan on the verge of nuclear war, Roy is front page in the *Delhi Times*.

Soon after our arrival we went to a reception at the Izumo Dome, a huge wooden structure built specially for us with a football pitch inside and another one outside. This will be our training centre for the next week. We couldn't help but notice how absolutely perfect the pitches are – the pitches, the organisation, everything.

We were twelve hours away from getting here intact. Twelve hours! Roy, I wish you were here.

The reception in the Dome seemed to go on for ever. It went on for so long we started getting giggly. Roy would love this, lads, standing here listening to this.

We are waiting for our instincts to come through. We have a game tomorrow and we should be getting up for it. Instead, lots of our nervous energy is gone. We should put the legs up and think about playing Hiroshima tomorrow. Yet it hasn't been twenty-four hours since we had the meeting in Saipan and we are still absorbed by it. The World Cup begins in seven days and we're still asking, who did the right thing here? Who screwed up here? It's a nightmare.

On Saturday, against Hiroshima, we start poorly. We are distracted and disorganised and obviously they are keen to do well. Some of the tackles are over-enthusiastic and at one point Jason McAteer is the victim of a crude hack down that for a little while looks like ending his World Cup. At half-time I have a heated exchange with Bilong, the player concerned. He's Cameroonian and he's contrite but we're in different orbits now. We need to turn the game around in the second half to grind out a result. It's not a happy day, but in a way it's an important game for us. Tactics and fitness worked well when we concentrated. In one respect, Saipan has worked. The island was far more humid and hot than Japan is and we trained at the height of the heat every day when we were there. Today against Hiroshima, we felt we could run for ever.

Afterwards, Bilong comes to apologise. He's distressed and sincere. Not today, though, thanks. He's told to fuck off; Jason fears that he may out of the World Cup and is still very upset. We leave as Mick is giving a press conference inside. Rule number one: no Roy questions. Rule number two: no Roy questions.

A few hours after the Hiroshima game, David Connolly and I are the last two down for tea. Dave is quiet and looks miserable. I'm surprised when he comes over and asks can he have a word. I look at him quizzically and before he says anything else I know he's been talking to Michael Kennedy. I just know.

Here's a quick digression. In my early days with the Irish panel, when Dave O'Leary was out of favour, I roomed a lot with Liam Brady. I was young; to us he was a divinity. I willingly acted almost as his personal butler, fetching this and doing that. One day, late in my Arsenal career, I was playing golf with Liam when he said to me, 'Niall, I'm finishing playing football and going into this agency business.'

'That's great news, Liam.'

'So in future, I'll be able to look after your affairs for you.'

'Well, hang on a minute.'

'So you should tell Arsenal that I'm looking after you, or I can call them, let them know that I'm the man to speak to now.'

I don't have an agent. I've never thought about having an agent. I'm not sure if I want Liam as my agent. I bought some time.

'Well, let me speak to my parents about it.'

Some time later, I mentioned it to Dave O'Leary and he fished a number from his pocket. 'Give this guy a ring,' he said. It was Michael Kennedy.

Michael was a friend of Ray Wilkins. He met Dave at an Irish function in Liverpool and in the course of conversation it came up that he had handled Ray's move to Italy. It stuck in Dave's mind and next time he had to deal with Arsenal he called Michael Kennedy.

Michael doesn't handle many footballers. I was his third. He has a full and successful life outside of football but those of us he looks after, he cares for out of interest and curiosity. There's no mercenary motive. He handles everything with a sense of dignified calm and intelligence that's rare in football. He doesn't tap people up, he doesn't promise moves hither and thither, he doesn't go out and hustle for you. When the time comes for you to call him, he comes and makes a deal on your behalf, the best deal you can imagine. Those of us whom he has taken under his wing he has taught to appreciate what we are worth, and taught clubs to pay us the same. In turn, we worship him.

Dave introduced me to Michael, and Dave and I introduced Roy to Michael when Roy was still at Forest. He came into our room in the Nuremore Hotel in Monaghan one afternoon, agonising over his pending move either to Manchester United or Blackburn Rovers.

Dave said, 'Roy, ask Niall what he would do.' I said, 'I'd ring this man,' and wrote down Michael's name and number. Roy made the call and for a couple of years afterwards he'd thank us profusely. The influence he has had on all of us is immense. If he weren't the common link between Roy and me right now, this situation would be dead.

A week after Michael Kennedy took me on, I got a phone call from an upset and angry Liam. It was a small price to pay.

That was twelve years ago. Now before Dave Connolly can say anything, I know that Michael has been working in his quiet way.

'What if,' says Dave, 'what if Roy said he was sorry?'

'Mmm,' I say.

I go back upstairs and ring Michael in London. He has spoken to Roy, who is home, angry, hurt and determined. He blames us all, but in Izumo, Dave Connolly and I think that perhaps there is a way out. Michael thinks it can be done. I think we could all use our best player in the World Cup. So it begins.

I wander around the hotel, canvassing the team. It's fair to say that there is no Roy bandwagon. A few players say they'll fly home immediately if Roy comes back. The response of another group could be classified as 'aw, leave it be'. The rest say yeah great, we need him. I go to see Mick in his room to tell him what I'm thinking. He tells me straight out that he'll have nothing to do with this.

Michael Kennedy made my deal for me with Manchester City. By then, I was beginning to feel like a hostage at Arsenal. George played me occasionally, when Alan Smith needed a rest, but apart from that I was left to my own devices, wandering London at will, drinking myself silly, gambling till I was broke.

I went to Steve Burtenshaw and told him that if being at Arsenal cost me a place at the 1990 World Cup, that was it. I was quitting football. Seeing as football had almost quit me, it was no idle threat.

The first time I spoke to Michael, he mentioned to me that Dave had told him I was having a problem. He said he'd have a word with George Graham. I assumed he was just going through the motions but a few days later at training, Lee Dixon pulled me aside and said he'd heard that I was on my way to Manchester City. Lee had good contacts in Manchester and they were right. At the end of the session, George Graham summoned me for a chat.

'We've agreed a fee with Manchester City for you,' he said. 'You can go.'

I clenched my fists by my side. Arsenal was over. Manchester City!

'Beware the Ides of March,' said George darkly as I left his office. It was 15 March. Only George would have had that to hand.

I went home and rang Dave O'Leary, who told me to get in touch with Michael Kennedy again because there'd still be work to be done. Michael said he'd come to Manchester with me later in the week.

The next day was Wednesday and I had my last Arsenal duty – a golf match against St Neots Golf Club in Cambridge. I stopped off at an Irish club on the way home and hit Enfield at about 1.30 a.m. to find four messages from my new boss.

Message number one (circa 7 p.m.): 'Hi, Niall. Howard Kendall at Manchester City here. Just calling for a chat about you coming to City. Give us a call when you get in.'

Message number two (circa 9.30 p.m.): 'Hello again, Niall. Howard Kendall here. Still hoping for a chat. They tell me you like going out so I imagine you might be late. Call me. Thanks.'

Message number three (circa 11.45 p.m.): 'Niall, I know now you are most certainly in a pub somewhere but I'd appreciate a call immediately.'

Message number four (circa 12.45 a.m.): 'Look you big pisshead, I've been calling all night. If you don't bloody ring me . . .'

I wondered if he was a few Kendalls to the wind himself. I was looking forward to City. When I finally met him in Manchester, he just said, 'Bloody hell, where were you?'

So Michael did the dealing for me at City. It was an education. I was on £350 a week at Arsenal. Manchester City offered me a signing-on fee of £25,000 straight off for a three-year contract, then £800 a week for the first year, £1,000 a week for the second year and £1,200 for the final year. All this and I would probably play football, too. I was nodding like a dog on somebody's car dashboard when Michael showed me the offer.

For the chance of football, for the long shot of getting to the World Cup, I would have played at George Graham prices. Michael looked at me sadly and beckoned me to follow him into the office.

'We're not sure we like this contract,' he told the secretary.

The secretary went to see the chairman. I sat sweating. Jesus, I was in the hands of a lunatic. The secretary was back to us within five minutes. The amounts had gone to £1,000, £1,000 and £1,200. I'm in the hands of a genius. I turned to the genius, who asked those present if they would mind stepping outside the office. He needed to speak to me. They left.

'Yes, Michael?'

'Nothing, Niall. Just let them sweat.'

We spent five minutes chatting about Ireland. They came back with the offer of a car, the £25,000 signing-on fee, £1,000, £1,250 and £1,500. Michael nodded. I grabbed a pen and signed quickly in case he tortured them some more.

Michael flew to Manchester that day, bought me dinner, educated me and changed my life around. He's never taken a penny for any of it, not even his plane fare. I bought him a painting as a thank you. He sent it back with an apology, saying that his wife didn't like that painter's work. I mentioned it to her a couple of years later and she knew nothing about it.

*　　*　　*

I have the easy task and Michael has the hard task, even for him. I just have to persuade twenty-two hurt footballers and their manager. Michael has to get Roy into the starting gate.

Talking with the players here in Izumo, the central midfielders are a problem of course. They live in Roy's shadow, endure the endless comparisons, answer the questions when Roy is missing, put up with the popular misconception that they have to prove themselves to be as good as Roy. Most people have the idea that they all work under Roy's direction, that they are his supporting cast. And when they play alongside Roy, they hear the most from him about their failings. They are professionals, though. On Sunday, I talk to each of them, one by one.

Mattie Holland is a gentleman, always quiet and dignified. He's been very upset about the Roy business, upset with Roy and with how he could allow himself not just to miss the World Cup but to cause everyone else the problems that he has. He's written an article for one of the English Sunday papers and by any standards it's strong but from Mattie it reflects something of the anger he feels. He thinks that whatever grievances Roy had, the team should have come first.

Mattie is a modern professional, always available to play, always willing to play within the needs of the team. Even though he will almost definitely start the World Cup now, unless Roy comes back, he has found Roy's behaviour hard to accept. He could be rubbing his hands, viewing this as his big break. To his credit, he's hugely disappointed in Roy. He hurts for the team.

Mark Kinsella shrugs his shoulders. He's laid back. Do what you have to do is his attitude.

Lee Carsley finds it hard, all this turmoil and aggro, especially when we speak about getting Roy back. He says to me that if he did something like Roy has done, he wouldn't expect to be allowed back. What can I say to that?

In the end, all three come around. I like that about the three of them – they practise what they preach. For two days they talk about their amazement that Roy didn't put the team first. Then they put the team first and accept that Roy might be coming back and we would be a better team with him in it.

It is Sunday evening now. After twenty-four hours on the Internet and a day of speaking to their relations at home, after many hours spent in their rooms letting it all sink in, all the players have come around. I think we all appreciate that the story is bigger than us and our feelings. Even those players totally against him coming back have come round; even the diehards are behind getting Roy back. Everyone has gone full circle.

The last one left to convince is Mick. If Mick is willing to have Roy back, the players would embrace Roy.

Mick has been away today at the England–Cameroon friendly in Kobe. Stan and I call him after the game on Stan's mobile and Stan explains what we have been doing, but Mick has hardened still further.

'To be honest, Stan,' he says, 'I've met just about every coach at the World Cup here today and everyone is saying well done.'

'Sure,' says Stan gently. 'Well, just letting you know how we feel.'

'I can't have him back,' says Mick.

We're unsure what to do. Just because rival coaches congratulate you on sending home your best player doesn't make it the best course of action available. Later, when Mick gets back to our hotel, I have another talk with him.

'You're the manager for the people back home as well,' I say. 'They want to see Roy Keane play in this World Cup.'

I think the enormity of it in an Irish context is beginning to sink in. Mick's a decent man and deep down I believe he sees the sense of it but he is still hurt and stung. He shakes his head. Shit.

I know that if Michael is moving Roy, somewhere in his heart he must want to come back. It seems such a straightforward proposition. If Roy wants to come back, Michael will get the ducks in a row over there. In Japan, we need Roy. I think we all recognise that. It shouldn't be so hard to get all the ducks in a row over here.

But it is, it is. I think it would be easier if we had two Michael Kennedys, one speaking in Roy's ear, one in Mick's ear.

Do I think this can be turned around? Do I believe it? Listen, on 14 March 1990 I had started fourteen league games in three seasons. On 21 June 1990 I scored the goal against Holland that put Ireland into the second round of the World Cup in Italy. I believe it.

It was springtime and we had qualified for the finals for the first time ever. Through three years of drinking by night and kicking my heels in the reserves by day and on Saturdays, my only salvation had been the fact that Jack Charlton kept picking me in his squads.

Still, it was difficult not to notice the trend. I'd gone to the European Championship in 1988 as the youngest member of the squad and had played in three of the qualifying games on the way there. Jack kept bringing me to the games; I wasn't exactly barging my way to centre stage. I'd played in two of our eight World Cup qualifiers on the road to Italy.

Not playing for my club was a huge hindrance. I played thirty-five league games for Arsenal in the 1986–87 season and forty-eight games in total that year. After that, I was virtually redundant. In my final season, I played six times and scored twice, the goals coming in successive games against Norwich and Millwall before I was sent back to the bench. Alan Smith was having his first difficult patch in an Arsenal jersey but it was clear that George was going to see him through it.

Some of the criticism was hard to take. One of my games in that last season was against Liverpool at Anfield. Liverpool were going well at the time but it was a showcase opportunity for me. We played badly and I missed a good chance. Next day Emlyn

Hughes wrote a newspaper article suggesting that I wouldn't ever score a goal at Anfield or any other ground come to that because I shouldn't be playing in the First Division anyway. His old buddy Tommy Smith wrote that I was better suited to painting ceilings than playing. Looking back, I can't believe I took those two clowns seriously, but I did.

We went to Italy and played well for a draw in a dour match against England. Then we went to Palermo and stank the place out in a terrible scoreless draw with Egypt. I played the last six minutes.

Four days later, there was speculation that I might get a start against Holland. The speculation ran to fever pitch, at least, it did in the room I was sharing with Dave O'Leary. My six minutes was the total contribution we had made between us.

Dave gets a bad rap in the press these days and if you believed all the cuttings from the past year, you'd assume he was the devil come to earth disguised as Ned Flanders. I roomed with him for a long time and yes he was different, yes he made me tidy up, but he looked out for me. And I learned a lot, mainly how to get entertainment out of him. He bore it all well, especially in 1990 when we spent a few days in a hotel just outside Dublin before going to Italy. One of the lads, knowing Dave's obsession with tidiness, I'm not sure how to phrase this, deposited a turd under Dave's bed.

For the length of our stay, the smell drove Dave berserk. He'd open every window in the room and the door to the corridor, lie on his bed and announce he could still 'get that smell'. Also choking from 'that smell', I had to pretend I could smell nothing. I spent most of the time outside the room while Dave entertained a stream of surprise visitors whom he interrogated about whether or not they could get 'that smell'. Nobody could, of course. Nevertheless, Dave felt that a hotel of that quality shouldn't be haunted with odours of that nature.

We knocked fun out of him on occasions like that. One morning after a night's drinking, I had to call to Dave's house for a lift to

Gatwick Airport for some trip or other. It was hideously early and I could barely stand. Dave bundled me into his car and just as he was pulling away he noticed his children at the window waving to him. Now Dave had a big front garden and at the top, in front of the house, the drive looped in a circle around a big piece of grass and some sort of ornamental fountain.

'Ah look,' said Dave, and he drove around the circle once, waving at his kids – and twice, and three times, and four times. 'Look, Niall. Ah look, they're not just waving to their daddy, they're waving to you, too.'

'Well, if they want to see their daddy get puked on just keep driving around in fucking circles, Dave.'

He drove off, waving his hand out the window and shaking his head sadly. 'Niall, Niall, Niall.'

I was a disappointment to him but he looked out for me and he genuinely wanted me to get picked for that Holland game. No word came. In the dressing room before the game, Jack gave us his talk. Same old Jack. He always had one good, simple idea that would turn it, that would unsettle the other side even more than our relentless style did – push out on Lineker, smother Hagi. I think we were supposed to place a posse on Ruud Gullit but I wasn't listening. My ear was cocked for mention of my name. It didn't come. We went out for our walkabout on the field and Jack caught up with me.

'Now, Big Niall, you know what I want tonight.'

'I'm playing then?'

'Course you're playing, soft lad. Did that Maurice not tell you?'

We go a goal down after ten minutes – Gullit scores it – then we have a goal disallowed. In the second half we are making chances; well, half chances. Tony Cascarino warms up. It can only mean that I'm gone, but he comes on for John Aldridge. On seventy-one minutes, Packie Bonner hoofs a huge ball forward. I go for it with Benny Van Aerle who turns and jabs a surprisingly firm back pass to Hans Van Breukelen. It comes off the keeper's chest. I have chased in, optimistic as ever, so I stick out a long leg and deflect it home. A World Cup goal! Against the European champions! I can barely describe the feeling.

ITV interviewed me immediately afterwards. I could hear Emlyn Hughes whinnying in the background. 'Hey, Emlyn,' I call to him. 'I scored.' It didn't make any sense to most people but he knew and I knew.

I stayed in the side to play Romania. In the penalty shoot-out, Dave scored the goal that put us into the quarter-finals. Instantly, his legend was secure. Our room was a happy, odour-free paradise.

They were some of the best weeks of my life. For a lot of Irish people, that World Cup adventure seems like a landmark in their personal history. So many people can tell me precisely where, and with whom, they were when I scored against Holland or when Dave scored against Romania. And for Ireland, it represented the turning of a corner. The miserable eighties were over. Ireland had arrived in some place new. Italia 90 was one long party from beginning to glorious end. As a nation, we drank and made merry all the way from Sardinia, to Genoa, to Rome and home again to a reception party of one million people out on the streets. For a month, we just blew away the recession and all the statistics that went with it, and freed a different part of our nature.

The team captured the imagination of the country and kept it for a few weeks. It was an incredible thing and an incredible time. That's why I believe now, just about.

We have the nation's undivided attention again, like we've never had it before apparently, and we don't know what to do. A lot of the time when we are together we make jokes. Shay Given does a great impression of Roy and when he suddenly shouts for Mick Byrne in the corridor or on the bus, by reflex Mick will jump up. It's not having a go at Roy; we just have to take some of the tension out of the situation.

I'm usually the most optimistic one of the bunch but I lie awake thinking about it all for hours on end. One thing that's occurred to me in the worst moments is that, for somebody who was desperate to get here, I might have been better off not coming. It's that miserable. Of all the players except the reserve keepers, I reckon I've the least chance of playing.

Every time I stop for a few moments and wonder why Stan and I are dealing with all this, that's the thought running through my head. I wanted to come here so badly, wanted to end the years on such a high, and this is horrible. I'd prefer to be at home with the kids.

Stan and I have spoken about it all quite a few times by now. We have to put our heads together and help the lads, gauge their feelings. Despite all the shouting on the pitch, the younger players idolise Roy. He's the role model – he's the player they look up to, he's the one they are overawed by. I wish sometimes that Roy could be a fly on the wall in this hotel and understand what we feel about him deep down.

He says he has no friends here and that he doesn't like talking to other players. The lads are willing to accept that and still to like the bloke – not because of what he can do but because of the atmosphere in the squad. He's just a different part of the set-up.

I think Stan is getting to the end of his tether with all this. He'll play next Saturday and for one thing he needs to start getting his head around that. For another, the reports from Ireland have Roy and his supporters laying into Stan, Alan Kelly and me. According to the reports from some writers and on some radio programmes, we stitched Roy up. We had a meeting between ourselves and orchestrated the entire thing. We never told Roy we'd done a press conference. I stood up and led the cheering when Roy left the room.

Every kind of lie imaginable seems to be doing the rounds in the press. Stan's family are upset and he's mad. He and Alan Kelly are keen to start suing somebody, anybody, to nail the lies. I'm against that, I'm just blindly angry at the reports. To pin the blame on three players hurts and it's frustrating that people believe it.

Things are out of control now. There's no one reassuring voice putting the world back together for us. Football, which has always been a boyish pleasure, is suddenly a hard adult world. I've never taken it too seriously – even the worst days at Arsenal were followed by the best nights – but now, right at the end, this has got to me.

Roy has done an article for the *Mail on Sunday* in England. This is a setback. Rumour runs around the hotel that he has been paid £140,000 for it. True or not, the perception in the Royal Hotel in Izumo is that he's profiting from this. Apparently, I am branded a coward. Stan, Alan and I wanted Roy out because we're mediocre and resent him, and because Roy didn't come to my testimonial. I'm almost too angry to respond to that.

Then there's the 'English cunt' business. Somebody has decided that this was one of the phrases that Roy threw at Mick. It wasn't, but it's a sensitive area to start digging into. Players raised as Irish people in England were in the room that night and they know it wasn't said, but reading it now as fact they must wonder is 'English' a key part of the insult? If Mick McCarthy can be regarded as 'English', what about me? Are we all the same here or are we not?

Every knock on my door brings something new. Every phone call that comes into the hotel muddies the water a little more. Somebody says that the world outside is pro Roy. No, it's rabidly pro Mick. Somebody else says that our fans will turn their backs on us on Saturday. Children at home are crying, people are protesting, mud is flying.

We're in the Royal Hotel in Izumo in the prefecture of Shimane somewhere in Japan, slowly going mad.

CHAPTER NINE

LIFE BUT NOT AS WE KNOW IT

*For every complex problem there's a solution that is simple,
neat and wrong.*
H.L. MENCKEN

I am worth £700,000. At least, that's what Manchester City think.
The boys at training won't let me forget it. Every clanger I drop
today starts it up.

'Can you believe we've paid seventy thousand for that?'

'Seven hundred thousand I think it were.'

'Nah, you're kidding me.'

What can you do? You have to laugh because, first, there's no
harm meant and, second, £700,000 seems like a whole pile of
money when you look around you. Maine Road is a crumbling pile.
Where are the marble halls? Where are the busts of previous
managers? Where is the impeccable good taste?

Manchester City is a club with a great history. Sadly, it has no
present worthy of its own past. The reputation for exciting
flyweight football is balanced by a reputation for being tight with

money. City are attractive, loveable losers, and down the road, our friends the enemy are just beginning to stir. Manchester United are going somewhere. If City are going anywhere, it's the Second Division.

We get by on spirit and gallows humour. The joke among us is that if we could win trophies for cock-ups, we'd be world class, we'd be Real Madrid. On my first day at training, I'm thrown some type of garment that Tarzan might once have worn as a loin cloth on a bad night out. These are my shorts. Next come these horrible, horrible stretchy shiny nylon tracksuit pants. They come with those stirrups that loop under your foot. Nobody has worn tracksuits like these since 1978 I reckon, and they come with an earnest warning that I am to take care of them because at the end of the year I will have to hand them back. The reserves will be stepping out in them next year. I'm no fashion plate but there's an incentive to stay in the first team if ever there was one.

At Arsenal, if there was a hole in your sock you weren't allowed to wear it. At training, no Arsenal player could go out wearing a sock with a hole in it. Socks with holes were not the Arsenal way. No, sir.

The Manchester City I joined was a hole in the sock sort of place. It reeked of poverty and bad organisation. The club hated spending money. I remember trying to get a pair of boots from Tony Book. He winced. It was like drawing blood from a stone. If Tony had lived with the Taliban, they would have told him to lighten up a bit about the damn boots.

That was before boots manufacturers were fully convinced that having professionals wear their product was entirely a good thing. Puma gave me football boots once – two pairs for a season, rubbers and studs. I did a little better with Lotto but they went broke. (I feel no guilt. My boots can't have tipped them over.) With adidas I did better again but I'm old enough to remember the time when if you got a rip in your boots, the local cobbler would repair them.

City still lived in that skinflint world – patch it up and get on with it. But the club had heart. That's what I loved about it. It had heart and soul, and the sadness was that I was there long enough to see those things removed.

On the way down the tunnel to the pitch at Maine Road, on the left-hand side, there was a small gymnasium. The beating heart and the living history of the club were in there. Training started at 10.30 but ritually we'd come in at about nine o'clock to play head tennis in the gym, and we'd stay there for hours after training. That gym is where I licked it up about ball control.

Tony Book and Roy Bailey, our physio, were the reigning champs. They knew every nook and cranny of that place. For the uninitiated, head tennis isn't really played with the head, not exclusively anyway. It's a game of ball control and touch. The idea is to keep the ball up off the ground and lob it over to the other side; 21 points win a game, best of three games wins the match.

At Maine Road, where there might have been a net there was a taut rope about two inches thick dividing the 'court'. You'd go to head a ball near that rope and Book or Bailey would yank it upwards. Stick your head down lower and their feet might be flying. It was a tough game on all sides.

It was gladiatorial. Book and Bailey had been unbeaten for about eighteen thousand years and you had to earn the right to play them. They'd come in once a week and deign to play whoever was hot. They'd slice and dice the best we could pitch against them and then they'd strut off, cackling at us. Adrian Heath and I became obsessed with beating them. We played for hours every day and, eventually, we arranged to play them.

In that epic match, we lost the first game and won the second. Girls from the office come down to watch the third set. A moment of Manchester City history was about to be made. This was the old order being overturned. This was Bastille Day. We got to 20–19 ahead. We could hardly contain ourselves. The entire staff of the club was in the gym. This was as tense a football situation as either Adrian or I had ever been involved in – 20–19 up on Book and Bailey. Match point.

Then the lights failed. The old-timers had it to a tee. They hadn't just switched them off, they'd pulled the plugs from the fuse box. The codgers wandered off, calling back into the gloom, 'Unlucky chaps. But still unbeaten.' I loved it.

A while later Francis Lee's regime pulled the old gym out to make room for an executive lunch suite. That hurt. Kaziu Deyna used to play head tennis in there during his three-year spell with City. He was unbeatable, too. Once the gym went, well, it tells its own story.

The sad thing was that City wasn't an executive lunch kind of place. City wasn't a weekend hangout of the prawn-sandwich merchants. It was quintessential Manchester. People who get rained on all day every day, those people are Manchester City fans. They knew us, we knew them.

One punter, Gary, sat in front of Peter Swales. He was as big as any two or three of us players put together. He'd come to howl abuse at us week in and week out. It was his pleasure. He'd come on the pre-season trips. He'd come to away games. He'd talk to us. If he cornered us in the bar or lobby of the hotel, he'd be off. 'Your problem, mate, is . . .'

Once, in the Isle of Man, he showed up after Oldham had beaten us 3–0 in a pre-season friendly. He had a new Porsche with a person-alised number plate – Kippax after the famous Maine Road terrace. He came in and started telling us where we were all going wrong. I'd had enough. I nipped out and did every one of his tyres. Then I came back in and nodded yes Gary, no Gary all evening. Honestly, I felt the better for having let some air out of Gary's tyres.

At breakfast the next morning, the hotel manager crooks his finger at me. 'Mr Quinn, a word in my office when you have a moment.' There I am on video, like the main attraction on one of those world's dumbest criminal shows. I'm looking all around, making sure the coast is clear, and then with a satisfied grin, letting the air rush from each of Gary's tyres. The hotel manager enjoyed his moment but never said a word; well, not as such. After that, any time he was in the vicinity he just dropped great big hints about the whole thing for his own amusement.

I spent the first half of the first game of the new season hogging the bench. During the second half, I'm warming up to come on when suddenly from behind me, so close I can almost feel his breath on my neck, Gary is bellowing, 'Oi, Quinn, I know you let the air out of my tyres. I know it was you.' I'm a professional footballer, I'm warming up, this is a new season and all I can think of is how does he know? What will he do to me? And isn't this a great club all the same?

Then there was Helen. Helen's gimmick was that she had a bell. She'd stand right behind the opposing goalie and ring the bell all afternoon. They loved her for it. Ray Clemence called up once and officially objected. Ray was a big shot in the goalie business and he wanted the bell taken from Helen. Now then, Helen would come into the players' lounge every home game and collect money for a nearby old folks home; she was part of what the club was about. Word of Ray Clemence's complaint seeped out and half the fans turned up with bells when his team were there.

The glory boys of the late sixties and early seventies team haunted the place. They'd won everything in that golden stretch – a league title, an FA Cup, a League Cup, the Cup-Winners' Cup. The place had never got over it.

In the players' lounge at almost any club, the previous season's squad pictures are up on the walls. In the City players' lounge, there was a 1970 photograph of Tony Book hoisted on his mates' shoulders, lifting the Cup-Winners' Cup. Huge pictures of the heroes of the revolution gazed down at us – Mike Doyle, Francis Lee, Mike Summerbee, Colin Bell. Keith Curle said to us one day, 'Lads, we have to rip those down.'

'We sure do, Keith. You do it, mate. We'll back ya up.'

They were still there when I left the club.

I'd arrived at Arsenal in time to see a great club get back on its feet again. I arrived in Manchester in time to see City roll over and almost die. At least life was never dull.

I played my first game for City on 21 March 1990 – Chelsea at Maine Road, midweek. We'd won just once in the previous twelve games and we were in the bottom three with our toes tagged for the relegation morgue.

I scored after nineteen minutes, a 'Blue Moon' goal – David White picked up, he saw me standing alone, he crossed, I hammered it home. When I looked, the moon had turned to gold. It felt like such a release. I was a footballer again. I didn't know Maine Road so I ran to the Chelsea fans and celebrated in front of them. The City fans thought I was one cocky bastard and it was a bit of a love story from then on.

We played well that night. I shaved the crossbar, got a good save out of Dave Beasant and we drew one all, which was enough to float us out of the bottom three. Oh, happy man!

I speak with Michael Kennedy a couple of times a day, at least. I think it's beginning to affect Michael in the same way it is the rest of us. It eats you up. The time lag between where he is and where we are is critical; we seem to work in twelve-hour cycles. There's a little movement and we wait for the reaction, wait for the people on the other side of the world to wake up, get about their business and absorb what's happened. Then there's a response and more waiting.

At Michael's end, there is the unbearable white noise of the media in his ears all day long. Michael was born in Kerry, his family are Irish, and I think he is hearing, seeing and reading more about this than is good for him.

In the Royal Hotel, we are distracted and listless. The only moments of liberation are when we go up the road to train. For mislaying our one true star, the people of Izumo seem to have politely forgiven us. Every session is watched by a couple of thousand people at least. They smile, clap and make a fuss of us, and for those hours we feel like we are at the World Cup.

We make our way to and from the bus signing autographs, having pictures taken, being mobbed in the courteous way that only Japanese people can mob you, and that's when we lighten up and enjoy ourselves. Somebody still likes us.

The training is perfect, too, for some reason. Every time we go out and play football with each other, we feel a little frisson of defiance. This is what we do. This is how we'll show people.

Everyone is years younger when they step on to the training pitch. Nobody can get to us there. If Roy hired a plane and wrote an insult to us all in the sky, we wouldn't notice. We do the things that we know how to do. Mick and Taff shout at us. We do our stretches and our exercises, and play our games. We have our jokes, our little rows, and we wonder quietly what sort of team Mick is going to play on Saturday. Then we go back to the hotel and worry.

There is one team meeting. Mick puts on a video of Cameroon playing somebody. He says to watch it or 'whatever' and leaves the room. The word 'whatever' is our get-out clause. As soon as he leaves, we get back to wandering and worrying.

The only story vaguely competing with Roy's absence is Jason McAteer's knee. On Saturday after the game against Hiroshima, Jason reckoned the knee was kaput. Our medical staff didn't think so but it was agreed he'd have a scan on Monday. Jason stamped his good foot and got the local hospital to look at it on Sunday. The scan shows the knee is clear. I think he's embarrassed by it, but he doesn't want anything to get in the way of playing.

Mick is clearly down. Like ourselves, he takes refuge in the training-ground routine, but for the rest of the day, for him the signals are confusing. The players all back him and we tell him so, but he knows that we are chipping away at getting Roy back. The FAI back him and tell him that they do, but they, too, want Roy back.

Michael is optimistic on the phone. Roy has got a little bit off his chest in the *Mail* interview. Mick has chosen to do the same, which hasn't sat well with the Irish media, who have respected his wishes and not asked any more questions about Roy.

Roy arrived home having had plenty of time to stew over things during the long flight. He was defensive and angry. Now he appears to be softening a bit. If he is entertaining Michael, knowing that Michael is in touch with us, there is hope. If it works out, fine; if not, we have to stand behind Mick, very publicly.

The lads think I'm soft by now. The feeling is that I should have grievances with Roy for the things he's said about me in the past couple of days. I do. I don't like being called a coward but, professionally, I can't be hard-nosed about it. I'm still glad that I backed Mick and whether Roy thinks less of me for that isn't important.

I find myself thinking about that meeting in Saipan a lot. Two or three days after the event, I think I know that Roy couldn't possibly have meant it. Was he that unhappy? Was he saying that Mick was lucky to get us there? Was he making a play for control? The players have started wondering about that one. Every theory has an audience here. In the end, the more I think about it, the more I reckon we had a situation where one small thing came on top of another until it got out of hand.

Most likely Roy wasn't looking for control; maybe he thought he was being cornered. In that situation, he backs down for nobody. He doesn't give up. And he emptied the whole chamber of resentments into Mick.

I have no real resentment towards him. I reckon I know his opinion of me anyway. He'll think I'm too nice to the press because

While the inquest begins in the Liverpool defence, I'm celebrating a goal on my debut for Arsenal.

Holding off Gary Mabbutt during the first leg of the Littlewoods Cup semi-final at Highbury in 1987 when we were very lucky to get away with losing only 1–0. We turned things round and eventually won through to the final.

Celebrating our 2–1 victory over Liverpool in the League Cup final. Unfortunately, watching in the stands was Alan Smith, the newly signed striker who was to mean that I rarely got a start in the following years. Dave Rocastle (far right) was the first person to offer me advice on arriving at the club.

David O'Leary and I display the latest Arsenal silverware. David was not only one of the tidiest men in football, he was also a complete hero to me when I first arrived in London.

Welcomed to Manchester City by Howard Kendall, who rescued me from my wilderness years at Arsenal, though he must have had some doubts when he found me impossible to track down on the night he signed me.

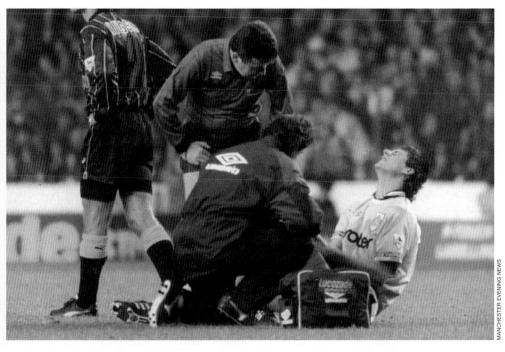

In agony after tearing my cruciate ligaments against Sheffield Wednesday in November 1993. The injury was to cost me not just an appearance in the 1994 World Cup but nearly my life.

Doing battle with 'Stan' Staunton, one of my closest friends from the Irish squad.

Squaring up to Ugo Ehiogu of Aston Villa after he caught our goalkeeper Eike Immel. I've never believed in giving defenders an easy ride.

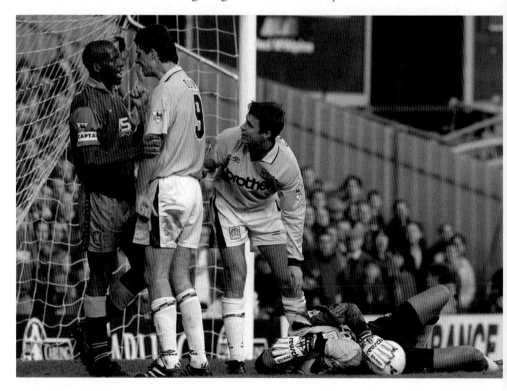

I loved my time in Manchester, even though the local derbies were never that friendly.

Joining my former manager, Peter Reid, at Sunderland in August 1996. His support and belief throughout my career was to give me a long Indian summer at the club.

Paul Stewart joins the celebrations after I score on my debut against Nottingham Forest. But after a great start, things didn't go quite so well as more cruciate troubles lay just around the corner.

Scoring a volley against Spurs at the end of October 1999. I got 14 goals in my first season back in the Premiership, a year that signalled the rebirth of Sunderland.

Back in the goalkeeper's jersey, this time against Bradford City in March 1999. There were no penalties to save this time, but I enjoy having a chance to go between the posts. I'm not so sure the defenders do.

Another goal for Kevin Phillips and me to celebrate – against Newcastle in the rain. In our first three seasons together we scored 128 League goals between us.

Winning the aerial battle with Jaap Stam of Manchester United.

Congratulating Tony Adams on reaching his 500th League appearance for Arsenal. Tony and I shared many a pint in our early days together at the club.

the press don't bother me. They've got to Roy over the years, they've abused him. He doesn't see the difference in our experiences. He thinks I don't take any of it seriously enough. Wish I could tell him I do but that's my way. I live and sleep football, I just don't show it. There's more to life.

Roy will have me down as too soft, too nice, too much of a goody goody, too damn happy with my lot. For him, I'm football's version of the Singing Nun.

I wish I'd taken time during the last eleven years we've played together to tell him about my Uncle Niall. It would illustrate the difference between us nicely.

My Uncle Niall was a fine hurler back in the 1940s and one summer he was selected to play for Tipperary in a championship game against Cork. It was a big game (every game between those two counties is a big game) and Niall made an arrangement to be picked up by team-mates at a little village in Tipp called Horse and Jockey.

He was standing there, waiting for his lift, when he spotted a red squirrel. He was fascinated by the squirrel, watched it for a few minutes, and then an idea struck him – he'd catch the squirrel and make it his pet. So he took to the fields, chasing the squirrel up trees, down trees, across meadows, and finally he caught the little thing.

By now it was past teatime. He set off back to his own village where he was met by a concerned crowd who had been 'watching the game on the wireless' waiting for mention of him.

'Sure, I didn't go,' said Niall. 'Look what I caught.'

He kept that squirrel for years, played for Tipperary again and never had a regret about that day. He had as good a perspective on life as anybody I know.

That story wouldn't surprise Roy – well, maybe the part about somebody depending on other people to get to a match. No player expects that now.

I think a lot of us, even those who resent what he's done, quietly have sympathy for Roy. He's that hard and tough, of course, that sympathy is the last thing he'd appreciate. But every second conversation reaches a point where somebody says that they can't believe a guy as smart as Roy managed to get himself into a position where he wanted to go home from the greatest tournament in the world. He's not fumbling around looking for a way back; he's building a wall around himself. Soon it will be completed and he'll let nothing more in. Generally, when you find yourself in a mess like this, something that will stay with you for the rest of your career if not your life, the moment to show remorse comes around pretty quickly. You wake up and regret is hammering in your head like a bad hangover. This, though, is Roy Keane and Mick McCarthy, possibly the two stubbornest people in the world.

I think something will happen, but it's not a rational thought.

After Chelsea, we had eight games left in that season. I scored in three of them. Suddenly we were filled with helium. We rose to fourteenth place in the twenty-team League, and if we hadn't been beaten in the penultimate game of the season by Derby, we would have finished a few places higher.

I liked my new environment. I liked the atmosphere that Howard Kendall brought to the squad. The night before my debut, he called me up in my hotel room late in the evening and said, 'I need to talk to you about the match.'

I assumed he was testing me on my drinking habits and played hard to get.

'I don't think I should. I have a game tomorrow.'

'Not if you aren't down here in five minutes, you don't.'

So we had a couple of late pints in the hotel bar and when I went back to my room I didn't feel like an employee. That was the happy secret of the City team I joined. We all felt like we were in the mess together.

When the season finished, whistling a happy tune I went off to the World Cup, and then went on to spend some time in Ireland. I came back whistling an even happier tune but the harsh truth about Manchester City was waiting for me.

Part of my deal when I signed was that the club would give me ninety nights in a hotel until I found somewhere to live. I still hadn't got a place — I'd been gazumped — but I'd moved out of the hotel to save the balance of the nights for when I came back for the new season and needed to find somewhere in earnest. I'd used the hotel nights frugally, checking out at weekends and when we went on trips.

When I got back to Manchester, and used up the remainder of my free nights, I received a hotel bill for £5,000. I'd been checked out of the place for the last two months. The club declined to pay, saying it was nothing to do with them as the ninety nights ran from the date of signing, the majority of which I'd spent in Italy at the World Cup.

Then I got a bill from Tom Garner's Motor Company for the rent of the car the club had provided. I'd collected it on the Monday after the Chelsea game but when the season ended I had no use for it until after the World Cup. Anyway, it was supposed to come as part of my contract. That was another five-grand bill and again the club didn't want to know.

In my contract in the paragraph about the car, somebody had inserted the words 'endeavour to' between the words 'will' and 'provide'. In explaining that this, basically, was all my problem, the club gave me a list of the places they'd tried to get me a car.

Then there was the signing-on fee. I signed in March and they asked me straight off if they could have a little time to pay the signing-on fee, saying that it would come in the summer. Pre-season came, the season started, autumn came and Christmas loomed. I still had two bills to argue about and no signing-on fee. It merited another knock on the door. 'Sorry, Niall,' they said. 'We weren't sure if you wanted it put into your pension or through your wages.' They'd never asked.

There was an almost childish innocence in their approach to these things. Hee hee! We got you with the car, we got you with the hotel, and now we've got you with the pension. At about that time, Ian Brightwell found out that his pension hadn't been processed at all during his time at City. I planned to end the separation of football and commerce that exists in most clubs and involve Howard Kendall. Then Howard Kendall walked out and went back to Everton.

Peter Reid, who had been Howard's assistant, took over. I gave Peter some time and then went to him with my list of grievances. He wasn't surprised. For reinforcement I had Michael Kennedy come up from London. The bills were paid, the car was taken care of and I got a pay rise. The club went through the hotel bill and refused to pay for any tea or orange juice I'd had; saved themselves ninety quid.

That was in February. I enjoyed a great year, settled in my mind, and scored a lot of goals. I was voted Player of the Year largely because of what happened in one of our last games of the season, the day I scored my eighteenth goal.

We played Derby at Maine Road and they needed a win to avoid relegation. I scored with a volley from outside the area after twenty-two minutes. You watching, Emlyn Hughes? About ten minutes later, our keeper, Tony Coton, brought down Dean Saunders on his way to goal. Tony got a red card and I went in goal for the penalty. Saunders took it. I decided before he ran up to dive low to my left. That's where he hit it.

What nobody mentioned, and nobody ever shows, is that from the resulting corner, I went out, bowled a few players over and made a Pat Jennings style one-handed catch. That pleased me more than anything.

After that it was all beer and skittles. I was spinning the ball from my kick-outs, having a whale of a time. In the second half, after David White had put us two in front, I caught and cleared from a Derby attack and then clutched my upper thigh. Down the sideline I could see Peter Reid reach for his hair and start pulling it out. Our physio Roy Bailey came sprinting down the sideline like there was a fire, bawling at me, 'What's wrong, Quinny, what's wrong?'

I contorted my face into a look of pain as if I was about to cry. 'Got a bit of mud on my shorts, Roy.'

We finished that 1990–91 season with six wins out of eight games, in fifth place.

I loved Manchester life. I'd gone to stay with Mike Prophet, a City fan but a big friend of all the United players. He owned the Amblehurst Inn. He said come for a few days and I stayed for five months. He was a lovely guy but easily exasperated. I'd arrive back at 4.30 a.m. and press the night buzzer. It was worse for him than having a new-born baby.

One night, Mike stopped the taxi as I was leaving, leaned his head in the back window and said, 'Here's the keys to the place. Don't wake me up.'

I got back at 4.30 and rang the buzzer. Mike's head appeared above me.

'It's OK, Mike. Don't worry. You don't need to come down. I have the keys, see?'

It was a happy time for me. The city was smaller than London and I was a bigger name. There was no struggle for late drinks; it was hard to avoid them. Usually, I'd go to Tommy McKenna's Ard Ri ballroom, or 'the brawlroom' as the lads called it in Moss Side. I'd be out with some of the players and then I'd make a bolt for it.

My taste in music is so tragic that somebody should have a testimonial to fund a cure. I saw all the great Irish showbands there – The Indians, Big Tom, Joe Dolan, The Conquerors. These are names to conjure with, believe me.

At Arsenal, Graham Rix and I would have our Thursday temperance nights when we'd go out and have no more than four pints, just in case we got to play on Saturday. It doesn't sound so good now but we felt we were being responsible athletes.

When I went to Manchester, I tried to continue the tradition and at first I never went out on a Thursday evening. Manchester being smaller and me being bigger, it was not a good idea to go out close to a game. There'll always be a backlash if you don't play it a little bit cleverly.

Then Mike Milligan looked me up one evening. He'd just moved to Everton but he lived in Manchester still. I'd see him around a bit with his big Irish family. He found where I was staying and called to tell me that there was a good gig on that Thursday that we should go to. At that time there was a great Irish band playing around Manchester called Toss the Feathers. They were playing at Shakers. It was tempting but I said, 'Can't, Mike. I don't ever go out on a Thursday.' Or words to that effect.

'Ah,' said Mike, 'ya will, ya will, ya will, ya will. Go on. Ya will.' Or words to that effect.

As it happened, we were to play against each other the following Saturday. Perfect excuse. 'No, Mike. We're playing against each other on Saturday. It's immoral and indecent.' Or words to that effect.

On Thursday, Mike turns up at my door.

'C'mon.'

'Nah. I don't drink on a Thursday.'

'Come out till teatime.'

'Teatime?'

'What's the harm?'

It was a great night at the Toss the Feathers gig. I was home just before the dawn, and in to training on Friday feeling like there was a rabid dog living in my head. Loads of sleep was needed on Friday night.

On Saturday, it's 2.55 and the boys are geeing each other up. I'm just leaving the home dressing room when Tony Book pulls me to one side and whispers in my ear, 'Good place that Shakers, isn't it?'

'Oh. Yeah. So I've heard.'

'Aye, they tell me it's especially good on a Thursday night.'

'Ooh, gotta go, Tony,' and I run out on to the Maine Road pitch.

Tony Book is a serious man. If Tony Book knew about Toss the Feathers, I knew I had to produce. I scored two within twenty minutes.

We come in, high-fiving each other. Tony walks past me, face like the Grim Reaper. 'You lucky bastard,' he says under his breath.

I got on to the B list celebrity circuit. Push the Pennies Over was a big thing in Manchester at the time. Pubs would collect pennies, pile them to the top of the bar, and then a penny princess accompanied by some celebrity, or else me, would push the pennies over. You'd have a pint, do the business, have another pint, get into a mini bus and be taken somewhere else to do the same thing all over again. I was top man at pushing the pennies over.

I was asked to appear on *A Question of Sport* and loved it. I bought a flat in Altrincham, and in April at the end of that first year, Gillian came over from Ireland and slowed me down a little bit, thankfully.

They were the best of times. On paper, there were no real stars at City but we'd die for each other. We stuck by each other through thick and thin. We had our fights, shook hands afterwards and played on. How close were we to becoming a really good team under Peter? He took us to fifth two seasons in a row.

In September 1991, Peter was a fraction from signing Ian Wright from Crystal Palace, but Ian signed for Arsenal. That's all we needed really. I was a twelve to fifteen goals a year man and we needed a twenty to twenty-five goals man to ride shotgun. We just needed the edge that only a poacher can provide. Chalk another one into the regrets column.

Fifth place two seasons on the trot, ninth (and unlucky) the next — we were hovering on the brink of something. We had a handful of young exciting players, an enthusiastic crowd. We were on the brink of disaster.

CHAPTER TEN

TWENTY-FOUR

Shrek: I'm beginning to see why you don't have any friends.
Donkey: That's what I like about you, Shrek. Only a true
friend would be so brutally honest.

FROM *SHREK*

My name is Niall Quinn and today is going to be the longest day of my life.

First, a confession. Yesterday Stan and I were skimming the Internet and we opened an account with Betfair.com. We placed a fiver each on a horse and he came in at 25 to 1. Dizzyinthehead he was called. We have profited during the time of the nation's grief. Perhaps it was the day before yesterday. I've been awake for so long now that Dizzyinthehead seems like a lifestyle choice. Nobody told us that there would be days like these. Days like these are not what we signed up for, not what we're trained for.

For a while now, through speaking to Michael regularly, I have managed to insulate myself from the whirlwind of rumours and fliers that have been sweeping through Izumo. Something always gets through the defences, though. Today I've been outflanked by the rumour machine.

Somehow all of us have managed to get sucked into the hype concerning an interview that Roy has done with Tommie Gorman on RTE television back home.

The pre-publicity – he'll laugh, he'll cry, he'll end the cold war – makes it clear that once we see Roy speak, there will be peace in our time and harmony among nations. The word is that Roy will be doing a one-to-one interview in the style of Princess Diana (and, originally we are told, with the same interviewer). In the course of the interview, there was going to be an apology.

Everything is buzzing. Michael Kennedy is on his way up to Roy's house. There are three separate offers of private jets, all of which are sitting on runways right now waiting for Roy to choose between them. Roy will be whisked back to Japan as soon as he utters the second syllable in sorr-eee.

I think even Michael believes that the interview will pave the way for Roy to come back. Usually, Michael is cautious and conservative about things but last time we spoke he thought that the mountain had moved. So, we take every positive sliver about the interview and feed it into our thoughts for the future.

Then we wait and wait. There will be words of contrition. Of course there will. Why talk otherwise?

This situation has to end soon. Voices are crackling on several different wavelengths, none of them communicating properly, but surely somebody will end it all, by accident even. Surely the weight of public opinion will force us all to submit. This is the way things go; something always gives. Meanwhile, I speak with Michael, Michael speaks with Roy, I speak with Stan. Mick speaks with his agent, Liam Gaskin, and with Taff and Packie. Roy speaks with Michael but not with Mick. Roy speaks with Alex Ferguson and, rumour has it, with legendary punter J.P. McManus. Everyone wants the same thing.

It says something about the status of the FAI that, effectively, they speak with nobody. Not once since this thing broke open have they sat down with the players. Not one figure has emerged from among them to become an effective channel of communication. If you're not part of the solution, you are part of the problem, and in their own peripheral way the FAI are part of the problem now.

But we are all dwarfed by what has happened. This will be big, we said. We had no idea! The major websites at home report that they have experienced heavier traffic and more hits since Roy left the coop than they did after 11 September. On the radio and TV they speak of nothing else, literally nothing else. Our families come on the phone and they have only one way to describe how big this is at home – they tell us that there's no way to describe how big this is at home. Everyone has an opinion and by now everybody has expressed it on the radio, in a vox pop, in a national survey, in an email campaign or in a bring-back-Roy protest. Everyone has an opinion and it can change from one hour to the next.

Stan and I sat up all night, just two guys in a room waiting for word. It's not a World Cup any more. It's a saga. It's a débâcle. We go out to a twenty-four-hour café and sit and talk, and wonder how it could have come to this. We can count the hours to the start of the World Cup and we are sitting up over coffees in a café in Izumo, waiting for word of what Roy Keane, our team-mate, might say in a TV interview.

We are that sidetracked, that bewildered, that dizzy in the head that we aren't even thinking straight. It somehow seems reasonable to us that Roy will apologise in public. The notion of a phone call, a private word between Roy and Mick, has been lost to us. Roy can't bring himself to speak with any one of us yet we believe that he will address the nation, beat his breast, bow his head, say he is sorry and hop on a plane to be with us. We sit and wait.

Stan is my oldest friend in the Irish team and one of the few people in football I expect still to be friends with when football finishes. Back in 1988 when we qualified for the European Championship, Jack brought an enlarged squad to Dublin for preparations before we left. Stan and I were the kids of the bunch and neither of us really expected to be picked for the squad for Germany. But you couldn't figure Jack out if you lived a hundred years. He left the hugely promising young Liverpool full-back at home and brought the gangly, inexperienced striker from Arsenal *and* five other forwards.

To celebrate qualifying for this World Cup, Stan and I took some time out in the spring, when we played Russia in a friendly in Dublin. It was one of those landmark nights in the history of our time together. The evening should have ended in the early morning with a taxi back to the team hotel and every pub in the city shut. I had the brainwave of getting the taxi driver to drive us to Heuston Station where we got on an early train to Waterford, knowing that the bar would open ten minutes after the train left the station. It did.

There was an awards dinner to attend that night, and there was a danger that Stan might win something. However, we'd been tipped off that Roy had won and a private jet would be zooming him in. We had the Waterford to Dublin train.

That lightness has gone out of things now. This World Cup, which we all looked forward to for so long, is suddenly a job. We're not boys playing football any more. We are adults and we need human resources managers and conciliation experts and lawyers.

Stan's family have been hurt and annoyed by the mud being slung around at home and as soon as Stan has seen a red light from them, he has eased off in his efforts to get Roy back. He'll do what's best for the team, though. That's been his career – team first, always.

We sit and we sit. It's just about getting bright outside. I'm tired of feeling tired. We go back to the hotel and we can hear other players moving about, fragments of their conversations. We're waiting for news of the war. Is it over? Are there casualties? Will we ever be the same again?

Suddenly, phones start ringing around the hotel. The versions coming through are garbled and varied but it seems that there has been movement, something small and positive has come out of it all.

Stan and I go for a ramble around the hotel so we can absorb the different messages. Maybe the World Cup will be starting in earnest for us tomorrow. Roy can be here in twelve, thirteen hours. We can make a joke of all this, he can do a grin-and-bear-it photo with Mick and we can get back to work.

We meet Albert Kirk and Adrian Logan from Ulster Television. Good news, we say, hoping they'll have further details to back it up. Perhaps they'll know if there was an actual apology and how it was worded. Nope, they say, he's done the opposite. He's hammered you, he's not sorry, he thinks he's right. It's 5.30 in the morning. We go back upstairs, drained and empty.

The accounts coming through from various players' families in Ireland seem more critical when we analyse them again. We're all filtering second-hand accounts of Roy's words through our own prejudices. We need to sit down and watch the interview.

I've been in my room for about an hour when I become aware of a commotion outside the front of the hotel. The media are outside, more and more of them arriving in taxis. The Japanese security people are polite but horrified. It's morning in Izumo.

Mick is asked to go out and speak to the media. He declines. Brendan McKenna, the FAI press officer, goes out. Brendan is a lovely man grappling with a horrible job with absolutely no support or back-up. It's going to be a long day for him, too.

It starts with the revelation that this morning he is the only person in Izumo who doesn't know that Roy has been doing a TV interview. Brendan is caught on the hop. Almost everyone inside and outside the hotel has been up all night. We are all stale and tired. Brendan is as fresh as a daisy. He just doesn't know anything. Tempers are short on the steps of the hotel. Brendan turns and marches back indoors.

Everyone is up and about now and we're still getting mixed verdicts from home. Some players' families say that Roy looked distressed, emotional, broken; others that he was defiant. We don't, of course, realise that our sample audience is a bit different from the population as a whole. The people close to us are watching it more critically than the rest of the people of Ireland.

Nobody has asked the RTE people here if they could beam the interview out to us. We haven't asked a player whom we trust to watch the interview in Ireland and give us a thumbs up or thumbs down. We are relying on many, many second-hand versions – he cried, he slagged everyone off, he didn't say he was sorry but he looked sorry, it was all an act, it was stage managed, it was quite moving to see, and so on and so on.

Mick gives a mini press conference on the steps of the hotel. He has been downstairs for a while, making phone calls and getting briefed in pretty much the same way that the players upstairs are getting briefed. Into dozens of microphones, he says he is aware of parts of the Roy Keane interview. Apparently, he comes across as tired and resigned. The media who watch him day in and day out say later that he seems to have softened significantly on the whole thing but that Roy's interview in itself has not been enough. Mick tells the media that 'the call has got to come'.

The wish is father to the thought. Everyone inside and outside the hotel suddenly has the impression that Roy has only to make personal contact, has only to pick up the phone and express some desire to come and play. We are that close to the perfect outcome. The nightmare will soon be over. We'll have our best player. Roy will have his air miles. Mick will have made his point.

As quickly as they arrived, the journalists disappear. It's almost eight in the morning, just before midnight at home, and they scoot back to their hotel across town to put the good news into the late editions.

Over breakfast, news of Mick's positive tone gives legs to the sunnier accounts of the Roy interview. We're still talking to people at home and we hear the bits we want to hear. Yeah, come to think of it, Roy was emotional. See! Hard to make out what he wanted but you could see the hurt. No, he doesn't say sorry but he looks in pain. We decide he must be coming.

It transpires, of course, that to see the big picture you need to have seen the TV pictures. We haven't seen the tape; Mick hasn't seen the tape. Mick doesn't even know what's in the transcript yet. He's been caught on the back foot. There's a word by word transcript on the way.

By 9.30 we are into the morning ritual of having our strappings done with Mick Byrne and Ciaran Murray. The chatter is optimistic. We are told that we will be training an hour later than planned. There will be a team meeting at 10.30. It's getting exciting now. Perhaps everything has been worth it. It will be worth stressing again at this team meeting that when Roy comes back we have to embrace him, not keep arguing. There's no point in him being back if the disruption is going to be greater than the benefit. We'll all have to move on.

We gather in a room downstairs and the meeting is short. Mick has seen the transcript and he doesn't like it. He is quite agitated, as animated and angry as we have seen him throughout this whole thing. He says that this has gone on long enough. He says that he's putting an end to it this morning. He says it's over. Roy Keane is not coming back.

'I'll leave it with you all now. I'm doing a press conference this morning, announcing it's over. You can do one of three things. You can back me, you can do nothing at all, or you can support Roy.'

He leaves the last option hanging there so that there is absolutely no doubt in any of our minds that if we take the final option, Mick will quit this morning. Going back to Saipan when he said just that at the press conference in the Chinese restaurant, this has been an underlying threat. We've pushed him as far as he can be pushed. He wants his team back.

Mick says his piece and leaves. It's another one of those defining moments. We are stunned into silence. I read Mick's words as a message to me to leave it all alone, to stop interfering; otherwise he's gone. He's had enough of the whole thing, enough of me working away on Roy, chipping away at the players.

Finally, Ian Evans says that we should consider our next step carefully, that we should talk this through. He says that the staff are right behind Mick, the eight of them have made their choice, and they leave us to it. This is probably the last time we'll do this, the last time we'll talk about it as a group of twenty-two players. Gary Kelly says let's organise things properly. I suggest that there is no point in anybody keeping quiet now; there will be nothing served by drifting silently with the majority. Three or four people can't decide for the team. Everyone will have to say what he thinks. We'll have to have it out now, once and for all. Which way do we go? Every man must make his choice.

We go around the room looking for thoughts. One by one the contributions come. Everyone agrees we have to support Mick, even Dave Connolly, who initiated the bridge building with Roy. He says, 'Yeah, it's too late in the day.' Even me.

I say that people in Ireland won't like it at first but we have to play this World Cup. If Mick McCarthy goes home today, we will be humiliated. As a team we probably won't make it to the weekend in one piece. We will be a global joke. The best we can get out of this terrible situation is to back Mick and play as well as we can.

We are three days away from our first game in the World Cup. The facial expressions in the room range from sullen to sombre.

Again, we have no option but to stick with our manager. We are bewildered.

It's a short meeting — fifteen minutes. We are unanimous but not happy. We decide at the end that we have to issue a statement, clarifying our support for Mick. The statement will be released at the end of Mick's press conference. We will give him our official backing. Case closed.

When we come out, the staff have already gone to the training ground. We climb on to the bus for the short drive. On the way, Stan, Alan Kelly, Kenny Cunningham and I make a couple of attempts at drafting a statement before we get the words we want. Kenny writes it down. It's short and stark.

> The manner of Roy's behaviour prior to his departure from Saipan, and the comments attributed to him since, have left the staff and players in no doubt that the interests of the squad are best served without Roy's presence.
>
> The players bear no malice towards Roy on a personal level and are looking forward to a successful World Cup campaign with the continued support of our loyal supporters both home and abroad.

At the training ground, I give our handwritten statement to Eddie Corcoran, the team's logistical coordinator, and ask him if he could get the statement typed up and copied for distribution at the end of Mick's press conference.

During the stretching exercises, Mick passes me and says quietly, 'Well?'

'We backed you.'

'Thanks.'

That's the best moment of the day, as good as it gets. We're in the safe house that is the training ground, we're playing football and, officially, we're all behind the manager.

Later, back at the hotel, I'm having a shower when the phone rings. It's John Givens. John, brother of my childhood idol Don, handles public relations matters for our sponsors Eircom, and he and I are old friends and also partners in a couple of business ventures. John is calling with a friendly word. Mick's press conference has been delayed so that Brendan Menton from the FAI might join him. Menton is in Korea at a FIFA meeting and is on his way here. The press conference will now be late afternoon and will go out live on the TV and radio at home. 'So just make sure the players' statement gets held back until then,' says John.

Five minutes later he calls again. 'Somebody has given the players' statement out to the media.'

Eddie Corcoran and Brendan McKenna have had the statement typed up and copied, and because nobody has told them not to, they have gone ahead and handed it out. Now it's not a statement backing up Mick's press conference; it's a shot from the darkness.

The detail of the thing makes it worse. In a fit of enthusiasm, Brendan McKenna hasn't just given out the statement, he's held a press conference. He's announced the injury news from the squad, the bits and bobs of who trained and who didn't train, he's given the details about press conferences, or the lack of them, for the remainder of the day and announced that we are due to visit a hospital in the afternoon. Then he's added that he has a statement from the players and staff, who met earlier, he's read out the statement for the cameras, and then it has been distributed. There are no words to describe what an absolute disaster this is.

The situation is this. Mick's last contact with the media was his positive press conference early this morning outside the hotel. The daily news cycle at home was due to begin a few hours later with the good news that Roy Keane should be on his way back to the World Cup soon. Since then, we have learned that early indications are that Roy's interview has swayed public opinion massively at home. Roy wants to be at the World Cup. Ireland wants Roy to be at the World Cup. That's all redundant now. It looks as if the players have killed all hope. To anyone outside of this hotel, it looks as if the team is deciding its own composition, and Mick is a lame-duck manager. Having spent days making sure we were united about Roy coming back, it looks as if we have taken the unilateral step of making sure that he never comes near us again. I wish I was anywhere but here.

I call Michael Kennedy even though it's the early hours of the morning back home. He's bemused. I explain everything that has happened. Michael tells me about the interview, and the extent of the mess we've got ourselves into becomes more apparent with every word. Michael went to bed the previous night thinking that today would be the day he finally moved Roy to the phone to make that call.

Roy has given an emotional interview. 'You're damn right it hurts,' Roy has said. He's looked back over his life in football, right back to the time when he was a kid going up to trials in Dublin, and he's spoken about everything it means to him. Those are the things that have lodged in the minds of everyone back home. Public opinion is behind Roy now. Nobody cares if Mick or ourselves have been unable to detect enough remorse while we flick through a photo-copied transcript looking for insults. One call expressing a desire to be at the World Cup is all it should take, Michael thinks.

We agree that Michael has to get to Roy before our statement does. Then there is still a chance. Michael has to explain to the man who left the World Cup because of all the cock-ups, that this setback, well – you're gonna laugh when I tell you, Roy – it's just another cock-up really. Michael has to convince Roy that despite the release of a unanimous statement from the players telling him that he can't come back, the players still want Roy back. He has to make Roy believe that all the assurances of the past few days have been genuine.

This is the morning after Roy, the most obsessively private man I know, has opened himself up on television. It's a big thing to ask of Michael. He has to convince Roy to view the players' statement in the context in which it was meant. Even that is not great – Mick McCarthy was going to pull the plug, the players were backing him. Then he has to rebuild Roy's confidence in the process. That's not so bad, is it? Is it?

Michael and I agree that it would be good to ask Roy if there is one player or staff member in the group he would like to talk to for reassurance about the whole thing.

In Izumo, before the daily players' press conference, I'll have to speak to the press, explaining the existence of the statement. I can't disown the thing because Mick and Brendan Menton will be speaking to them later in the evening. I can't go too hard on Roy because Michael feels there is still a chance.

There's a moment of reprieve in the afternoon. I call Gillian at home in Sedgefield to ask her about the interview and what she thought. She's not too bothered one way or another.

'But,' I whine, 'your husband is out here in the middle of the biggest crisis of his life.'

'And does he want to speak to his kids or not?' says Gillian.

That's why I would be broke, alcoholic and insane if I had never met Gillian. Half an hour spent talking to your kids puts life into proper perspective again for anyone.

After dinner, we visit a hospital as arranged. We're the most depressed, bedraggled and distracted group of visitors the hospital has ever had.

At 5 p.m., I sit down in the press centre in Izumo and I wish I was at home giving water and hay to the horses. There are twelve camera crews, maybe 150 journalists, and a table crammed with tape recorders, radio mikes and mini disc recorders. It's not personal but the room is filled with hostility and passion. Before we begin, a couple of journalists tell me that this is going to be hot and heavy. The reaction at home is immense. Great.

'I've come here to explain the statement that you received from the players earlier on today. I'm probably best explaining the sequence of events . . .' I explain about the illusion we had this morning of Mick offering an olive branch. I explain that we had a meeting at which Mick effectively ended any chance of Roy Keane appearing in the World Cup finals. I explain about the disappointment we as a team felt that Roy hadn't apologised. I explain how I've been pestering Mick for days. I explain most of what I can about the meeting this morning. I explain that we are hurt as a team. I explain that we just want to get on with the World Cup.

I apologise for the premature release of the press statement. I say that it will make more sense after Mick's press conference later. I explain that, originally, the people of Ireland persuaded the team that the door should be left open for Roy.

Questions anyone . . . ?

Q: 'Was it Roy Keane or Mick? Did it come down to that?'

A: 'You wouldn't be too far away.'

Q: 'What was the key issue that made you reject this plea from Roy to get back into the team?'

A: 'After you've spoken to Mick you'll see we had no alternative.'

Q: 'This is going to go down badly in Ireland, you know that?'

A: 'Can I give you the chain of events in the last seventy-two hours . . .'

And so on . . .

Q: 'Were you concerned because Mick was losing the popularity contest?'

Q: 'Shouldn't you be beyond the blame game at this stage?'

Q: 'What do you say to the Irish fans who will be watching on Saturday?'

Q: 'Is this player power?'

Q: 'Shouldn't Mick see the bigger picture too?'

Q: 'Is it possible that Mick McCarthy's career could be shortened by these events?'

I'm beginning to detect the passion that people at home have about this. The room is hot. The atmosphere is sour. People want Roy back. I try to explain how it's been. 'I'm a senior player. I'm drained. I'm shattered . . . the younger players can't take any more of this . . . we've three days to get this right . . .' But they want Roy back.

Then Paul Kimmage from the *Sunday Independent* puts his hand up and says, 'One of your team-mates said the exact opposite last night. He said fuck the people back home.'

This knocks me sideways. It drops on me out of the clear blue sky. John Givens draws the press conference to an end. It lasted thirty minutes. I feel like I have died a slow and painful death. Somebody said 'fuck the people back home'?

I take the van back to the hotel on my own, in a slight state of shock. I'm by myself in a van in rural Japan, I've just done a massively hostile press conference on my own and this is the World Cup. How did life get so serious so late in my career?

I need a three-hour walk to clear my head. Instead, I do a short interview with Gabriel Egan from RTE. My head is in a mess. I'm not sure what I'm thinking. There's a message to call Michael Kennedy. Michael says it's still on. He's spoken to Roy. There is still a chance. It's alive.

I've just spent thirty minutes in a media centre explaining, first, how I went behind the manager's back and persuaded the players to want Roy back and, second, why now, the day after his interview, we don't want him back because we are backing Mick 100 per cent. I've zigged; now I must zag.

I finish speaking with Michael and head straight to Mick's room, hoping to catch him before he goes to do his press conference. Packie Bonner is there talking to Mick, reinforcing that he's right not to be bringing Roy back. Packie is straight and bullish and brave about these things. It's down the line with him, black or white.

I try the familiar arguments – the team is bigger than two people, we don't play for ourselves, Mick doesn't manage for himself, the people at home are the ones we represent, making this gesture will protect Mick, we need Mick, we need Roy. There are football arguments, political arguments, social arguments, and there's a huge wall of hurt. We argue for almost forty minutes.

Packie agrees, eventually. Fair play for him; it takes a big man to allow his mind to be changed. We are tired, overwrought. Mick cries. I cry. It's not easy. It is not fucking easy.

Finally, Mick says he will do his press conference, then he will come back and will wait for the call.

Mick's press conference begins at 8 p.m. and ends eleven minutes later. It is a disaster. Brendan Menton, trying to keep the process alive, scuppers the conference when it becomes clear that for the first time in a week, Mick has a message he wants to get across. Mick wants to reassert that he is in charge. Brendan wants him to say nothing. They come across as a Punch and Judy show.

Mick is told of my version of this morning's meeting – back me or I'm off.

Mick: 'Is that right? Well, I didn't give them an ultimatum, nor a recommendation. If the players wanted the situation reversed, I would go with them. I would back them.'

Brendan: 'We are not interested in exacerbating this situation.'

Mick: 'I think there are some issues to be answered of course, Brendan.'

Brendan: 'I think this is not the time.'

Mick: 'No?'

Brendan: 'I think the important thing is preparation for this game.'

Q: 'Mick, did you accuse Roy of feigning injury? Did that start it?'

Mick: 'No. He lost his temper from the first second I spoke.'

Q: 'He lost his temper?'

Brendan: 'The association doesn't want to revisit this. The timing of it . . . resurrecting itself . . . I think Mick has said what he has to say.'

Mick: 'I think the question was in terms of picking and choosing games actually, but it was about friendly games and playing in friendlies. He said, no I don't play in them any more. They are for other people. Yes, the Iran game was mentioned, in terms of picking and choosing games. I'm not going to go down that line.'

And Brendan Menton ends the press conference.

Mick comes back and we speak briefly. He says it didn't go well. He goes to his room to wait for the call, which I have promised him will come.

I don't know how Mick must feel. His day has lurched from bad to worse to disastrous. On the steps this morning, he let in a little bit of light before he had seen the transcript. The premature release of our statement made him look weak and peripheral. I explained at length in a press conference how Mick ended Roy's World Cup. Three hours later at his own press conference, Mick has scarcely managed to get a word in. Now he's waiting for a call from Roy Keane while the media are down the road writing Mick McCarthy obituaries. Practically anything Roy says on the phone will force Mick to have him back. Roy just has to tell the world that he made that call. He has won.

Mick is a proud man and a lot has been asked of him today. He knows that by tomorrow the Irish media will be howling for his head. Every one of us has made mistakes this week. We've all made them today. This evening, though, Mick's room must be a bleak place to be. He deserves better.

With Mick upstairs, Taff Evans has a word with the team downstairs. Is everyone sure? Are we all going into this wholeheartedly? Does anyone want to back out now? We all say yes, it's been a long day, let's have him back, let's get on with it.

I feel great again. Our side of the bargain is fulfilled. Michael just has to get Roy to lift the phone. Michael promises me that we will stay in touch every hour. We do that for a couple of hours, clarifying this and that about travel and jets. Then there is a gap and when Michael rings again it's 3.30 in the morning in Izumo.

'It's over, Niall,' he says. 'We're going to issue a statement. Roy is not going to apologise.'

It's all played out. Roy throws the last card on to the table:

I do not consider that the best interests of Irish football will be served by my returning to the World Cup. The damage has been done.

In the interests of all genuine supporters of Irish football, the time has now arrived when I should bring a conclusion to the continuing speculation with regard to my participation in the World Cup, and for the players to concentrate fully on their preparations for the competition, free from all further distractions.

He wishes us the best.

It's Tuesday night. We have two days left in Izumo. On Friday, we fly to Niigata for our first game, which takes place on Saturday. We have just two clear days for preparation because our captain went off at the deep end because he wasn't happy with our preparation.

I'm at rock bottom now. Feelings have run higher and higher all through this day. Now I just know that this is not right, this is all badly wrong. I've made mistakes, every one has made mistakes, but only the smallest movement was necessary to put them right – one hard swallow, one short call.

We all talk about how we'd do anything to play for our country, for the honour, the privilege and the glory, how we'd die for the green jersey. Well, we wouldn't, not all of us. We know that now.

CHAPTER ELEVEN

THE PERFECT STORM

W.C. Fields: Remember the time I knocked down Waterfront Nell?
Bartender: Why, you didn't knock her down, I did.
W.C. Fields: Well, I started kicking her first.
FROM *MY LITTLE CHICKADEE*

Football does things to the people who live it. Football takes them away from their homes at fifteen or sixteen years of age, tells them that they are special and they are going to be rich and famous, and then football lets their personalities develop shut off from the real world. When you are a footballer, you grow up competing, listening to dressing-room humour, being flattered and cursed in equal measure. You grow up in largely male company. Your work is a game. Maybe you don't grow up at all.

It fascinates me. For Roy, professional football and huge acclaim arrived like an explosion in his head, and it seems to me that the last half of his career has been spent battening down the hatches, taking the wildness out of the ride. He's more controlled than he used to be. He doesn't drink any more, he doesn't go out. He is intensely private. That's how experience has changed him.

The game has hardly touched Damien Duff. He's not hard. He has no ego. If there was a World Cup for snoozing, he'd be Ronaldo. No, he'd be Damien Duff. That's world class as it is.

When I was at Arsenal as a kid, a lot of people there didn't like Dave O'Leary. He had the club in the palm of his hand and other players resented that. I used to marvel at him. How did a youngster who came over from Glasnevin in Dublin when he was fifteen years old pull it off? Why wasn't he like all the rest of us? Yes, Dave was obsessively tidy, fastidious about all aspects of his life, but he was a one-off. Character had overcome environment. Some didn't like him because he was different. They still don't. I found him amusing and interesting, mostly.

What still surprises me is that the game accommodates so many diverse personalities and that, by and large, we all rub along together all right. When we left Dublin a couple of weeks ago, we ranged from Duffer, who is so laid back that we have to check for a pulse each day, to Roy, who is a twitching, twenty-four hour a day obsessive.

It's not often you get the obsessive personality with the talent to match. They are usually difficult cases, hard on themselves and hard on everyone around them. Every team should have one, except when things turn sour.

When I listened to Roy uncorking himself in Saipan, it stirred up an old ghost. It was from my Manchester City days, one of those driven midfield types who needed to have the first word, the middle word and the last word in any argument – Steve McMahon.

I remember him for an incident that happened ten years ago and brought out the worst in both of us. More importantly, the postscript to it seemed to signal the beginning of the end of the good times at City.

You wonder in football when you look back, what makes loyalty. It's not fans or media or club traditions. It's the people you meet. I met Peter Reid early in my time at Manchester City. We went to see Van Morrison play during the first week I was in Manchester. Peter turned up wearing a Crombie coat and a pork-pie hat. I loved the guy. He's sharp, he's loyal and he's witty in that diamond scouse way. I often think that if Peter came in one morning with bird droppings all over his collar, I'd say nothing because by the time he'd finished with me he'd be making the rest of us feel bad for not having the same.

Steve McMahon and Peter were never going to gel. Steve came to us as one of those franchise players who had done everything elsewhere already. The idea was that he would do it again with us in tow. He'd made 204 league appearances for Liverpool in the dynastic era, and when the mileage clock tipped past thirty, City went against their nature and laid down big money for him.

We all felt that Steve was going to be a great signing. He had that strength about him still, but when he arrived I wondered if he missed playing for Liverpool. I felt he didn't seem as geared up for it as had been the Steve McMahon we had all seen charging around leading Liverpool to titles. However, because he expected to win trophies, he could make the players at City feel bad about themselves, because we didn't have the same expectations. The worst thing was that there was no comeback. He'd done what he'd done, he'd won everything. There was resentment of him among the home-bred players. He was too intense for us. The happy-go-lucky atmosphere in our squad didn't appeal to him.

We went to Penola in Italy for one of those long-slog pre-season tours that clubs undertake every summer. There's no excitement about them, no decent games, just hard work and good intentions. Our tour coincided with the Olympic Games in Barcelona and we were there on the day that Michael Carruth won a boxing gold medal for Ireland.

The world being a small place, I'd been at school for three years at primary level with Michael and his two brothers. They had their classes in the pre-fab hut opposite mine and we'd play together at lunchtime every day. They were green snot and red hair; I was green snot and black hair. The Carruths were two years behind me but they were tough.

On the day, I stayed in to watch Michael's fight and I was touched to see him win Ireland's first gold medal since 1956. It was lump in the throat time. I caught up with the lads later and it was beer on the lump in the throat time. The merriment was well under way. A boxing ring had been set up in the middle of the square for some reason, and Sam Ellis, our coach, and the rest of the boys decreed that we were to have our own Olympics. What followed was a spectacle. It was lads with drink taken, standing in the sunshine slapping at each other. Somebody was acting as towel man; somebody was the umpire. It was football comedy.

Unfortunately it didn't stay that way. The fighting also made its way into the toilets in the corner of the square when Steve McMahon and I got into a squabble. I think I'm more sober than he is but, drunk or sober, I'm not much use at fighting. 'Behave,' I say. But things won't stop that easily.

Sam Ellis comes in and pushes the two of us out the back away from any prying eyes. Sam is a man's man but he's no Don King.

'Go on then, settle it,' Sam says, helpfully.

Steve's been drinking; he's had a head start on me in that regard. He's looking at me but I'm not certain that he's seeing me. This is good. If I was to have a fight plan for a bout with Steve McMahon, it would include him being almost too drunk to stand up.

It would also include me running away, but I've got Don King behind me. Steve gets his fists up and throws a few punches my way. I'm not used to this. My only tactic at this stage is to hope that my head will meet his knuckle and shock him into submission. I can feel the little rush of breeze past my ears as each punch misses. Perhaps Steve's own momentum will make him fall over. I'll get Sam to take a photo of me with my foot on Steve's chest and one arm raised in the air. I'll go back to the lads and tell it all as a funny story.

Eventually, I try a punch. One punch. Can't hurt to try to hit him back, can it? Sam is commentating. Steve forgets to duck, or even to sway.

'Ooh and a sweeping right-hander from the big lad,' says Sam.

'Uurrrnnnf,' says Steve.

I connect with his nose and there's a dull crunching sound. I'm not used to punching people and Steve's not in a condition to take a punch. His skin comes apart, splitting his nose from top to bottom.

'Over and out,' roars Sam. 'He's outta here.'

Steve's not quite 'outta here' but the big fight is over – first round, busted snout. There'll be no post-bout interviews. I feel guilty straightaway. I know it's wrong, professionally and in every other way. Not only is it wrong but it is probably going to get me into trouble. Football clubs don't like their big signings to go around boxing, or splitting each other's noses. There is going to be hassle when Peter Reid finds out, and then there's going to be war when Gillian gets to hear about it. Why couldn't Steve just have hit my nose? Sam props a shoulder under Steve and begins to drag him home, like a beaten gladiator. At least it's over.

Rick Holden had joined the club from Oldham that day. He'd signed the papers and flown to Italy to be with us. He's in the little square when I walk back. Ahead of me, Steve McMahon, the super-star from Liverpool and the club skipper, is being dragged home by the coach, with a river of blood flowing from his nose. Welcome to Manchester City, Rick.

'What's going on there, Quinny?' says Rick.

'You don't want to know, Rick,' I reply. 'This is the club you're joining.'

'Phew.'

After Steve McMahon exits stage left, Rick and I ramble off in search of entertainment and refreshment. My shirt is ripped and a bit blood splattered, not a look that bouncers generally like, and the heat is beating down, so I abandon the offending item. We wind up in some sort of dance bar and, keen to show Rick that we're just a wholesome, family type of club, I engage in some frenetic dancing. Probably it scares him half to death. By now, I'm wearing just a pair of cut-off jeans and I'm hardly aware that there is a group of hardcore City fans watching. These are the sort of lunatics who travel to our pre-season away games, and this is the kind of spectacle they live for. I don't realise they're there until I'm treated to the first performance of the song that will follow me till the end of my career, and will probably serve as my epitaph.

> Niall Quinn's disco pants are the best,
> They go up from his arse to his chest,
> They are better than Adam and the Ants,
> Niall Quinn's disco pants.

There it was, my punishment for hitting Steve McMahon. This was 1992. Ten years later, that ditty still trails after me like a stray dog. It followed me up to Sunderland where somebody turned it into a record. Once I was inveigled by John Inverdale into singing it on TV. For my sins I did it and I cringe when I think of it.

Suddenly horribly conscious of my disco pants and grotesque dancing style, I abandon the night fever and sit down to chat with Rick. Poor Rick. He is beginning to get the wide-eyed look of a pretty girl who's just stepped inside the haunted mansion in a horror movie. I'm persuading him that we are a normal, happy club when Steve McMahon walks into the pub and gets his own back, hitting me hard on the back of the head. I collapse on to Rick.

I find my senses and, forgetting all about how this must appear to Rick Holden, I chase Steve out of the pub. Rick comes after me, putting on his sheriff's badge and looking determined to make the peace. When he comes out the fight is going well. Steve is on top of me about to kill me. I had a surprise manoeuvre up my sleeve, I'm sure — pretending to be dead already, perhaps.

I am just about to turn the tables when Rick wrestles Steve off me. I should thank Rick for saving my life, buy him a drink and continue our conversation. I really should. But Steve goes running down a back street and I follow him in a fury. Catching him is a surprise. This is the first time in my life I've ever caught somebody. I'm not sure what to do so I push him. He gives way more easily than I expected, much more easily. In fact, he goes backwards through the plate-glass window of a tailor's shop.

For a second I think I've killed him. All the falling glass must have sliced an artery, lopped off a limb, spiked his brain. He's lying there in a pile of toppled tailor's dummies and I'm staring at him, seeing headlines: 'Quinn Murders Club Captain. "No More Mr Nice Guy," says beanpole striker'. Rick has caught up with us. He, too, is staring at Steve and we're both thinking, Is he dead?

No, miraculously he's not. I am when Gillian finds out, though. I don't know if I communicate this thought to Steve telepathically but instantly we are both sober. All three of us are sober and frightened.

Steve gets up and walks off. I go back to the pub and tell the landlord that I will be paying for a window in the back street because, well, since we left the premises in such dignified circumstances a few minutes ago, we've had a little, ahem, accident. I write down my name and hotel number. I'll pay in the morning. In every way, I'll pay in the morning.

I go back to the hotel and slink straight off to bed. It's a short night. At 7.30 in the morning the phone is shrieking. Peter Reid is shrieking, too — 'Get your fucking arse down to my fucking room now.'

I had a vague feeling that I was in the right but it was the sort of feeling that needed teasing out by someone with a sympathetic ear. Peter is no shrink, not at 7.30. There'll be no couch to lie on as I talk it through.

When I get there, he's already started on Steve. Steve starts arguing but, realising he's heading for a reef, he changes tack. 'Sorry,' he says. 'I was drunk. I don't really remember.'

I sit with my mouth shut — goody-two-shoes, that's me.

'Well, you must remember something,' Peter says, tenderly. 'You smashed a fucking plate-glass window. I'd remember that.'

'Mmm, yeah,' says Steve. 'Did I? Sorry. I'll pay for that.'

I continue sitting with my mouth zipped shut. So far so good. Finally, Peter dismisses the two of us from his room. Steve and I hit the corridor and burst out laughing as soon as the door is closed. We're rolling our eyes at each other, half embarrassed, mainly relieved. This could have been worse.

The man with the window rings me an hour later. Obligingly, I put him in touch with my new friend Steve McMahon who pays him three hundred quid.

By breakfast, I'd become a hero among the young lads — Quinny the Macca Slayer. I came down for the Cornflakes, walked in and the players dropped their spoons and started up with the theme from *Rocky*. Jesus, if Gillian hears about this she'll make ashtrays out of my kneecaps.

The twist is in the postscript. I came home from that trip a couple of days early — got a hamstring tweak and was sent back to Manchester for a scan. When the team came home, Sam Ellis and Steve McMahon were late for the flight. They were playing cards in the departure lounge and misheard the flight announcements. The plane was held up for twenty minutes. When Sam and Steve got on the plane, all the lads clapped good-humouredly, but this little story appeared in a Sunday paper at the weekend.

Soon it was clear that the club wanted Sam out. Sam had been a good henchman for Peter. He did the hard stuff, the coal-face stuff, when dealing with the business suits. He was the buffer and they didn't like it. Peter and the club were on a collision course from then on. Peter was given an ultimatum later that year — Sam goes or the two of you go. The following August, after a night-marish start to the new season, Peter went. Of course, the cameras followed us around. Coming from training, a microphone was pushed in my face and I denounced the decision. Later that evening, I was watching the local news and there I was, laying into the board. The piece cut to Steve. 'Well, that's football,' he said.

One punch, but no regrets.

It's day one of life after Roy. We train and, as usual, it's a release. We're boys again, boys on the verge of a World Cup, boys thumping footballs around with excited commentaries running through our heads. We're disappointed but life is football again and football is uncomplicated.

The days have sped past. If there is any silver lining to the cloud we've all lived under, it's that. The World Cup is right in front of us now. We haven't approached it from a long way out. We just looked out today and there it was. We have been distracted rather than nervous, anxious rather than bored, and we've learned to love our football again.

We have a couple of days before we fly to Niigata to start the tournament. Izumo is beautiful and friendly and we'll never see it again. That'll be fine, too.

Everyone has regrets that they'll pack away and take out when the World Cup is over, even some members of the media. I have three letters in my bag from various organisations apologising for aspects of their coverage over the past few days. One is from Sky News who blithely reported that Damien Duff and Robbie Keane were on the brink of going home. There has been some crazy stuff, a universe of rumours and lies during the whole Roy Keane affair. I'm not sure where they came from but somebody has been putting them out, things that just never happened. It all rankles, the whole lot of it, and until we start playing matches it will continue to do so.

We're not perfect. We've all made mistakes from Mick on down. Most of us know that the set-up at international level will never be like it is at Manchester United. A football association run in large part by well-meaning amateurs will never be exactly like the biggest soccer club in the world. That's part of the deal. There are compensations, such as the honour, the pride and the joy.

Over the years, nobody seems to have been indulged more than Roy, from the missed friendlies to being allowed sometimes to come in for training later in the week than the rest of us. There's also having his own room, not communicating with management like the rest of us do, incidents such as the trouble in the airport hotel with Gary Breen's friends being swept under the carpet. Sometimes we benefited from the efforts that were made to keep him happy, to bring us up to the standards he expects at his club and that he thought we should have with our country. We got the better training ground he asked for in Dublin, we got the better hotels, we got first-class seats when we travel.

Things never got to be perfect but they came close. To walk away when he did? To refuse to come back? To decline even to lift a telephone? To accuse some of us of the things he has accused us of? Self-indulgence.

It's odd being here now. The local news media and television are absolutely incomprehensible to us. We can't tell if there is a mounting sense of excitement about the World Cup or not. We've had a diet of Roy news for a week. Slowly, we're putting ourselves back together.

By the time I came to leave Manchester City the club was a pile of little splinters on the ground. When Howard Kendall was allowed to go you feared for the place. After Peter Reid was forced out you could hear the foundations creaking and cracking.

I loved the place still but had the feeling that it would break my heart. I wondered if perhaps I should get out before it fell in on top of me. Brian Horton was the new manager and although we were never quite enemies, we were never quite pals either. Just before Christmas, Howard Kendall threw me an escape line — come to Everton, be our big man up front.

I liked the idea. Football isn't merely football, though. It's politics, too, and by now the politics of the terraces was beginning to terrify Peter Swales, the Manchester City chairman. To lose a player, a goalscorer, at that particular time would have caused further revolt. I found myself being persuaded to stay.

Peter Swales got Max Browne, a mutual friend whom I knew from golfing outings, to talk me into staying at City. Max did a good job. For me, things don't have to be perfect. Then Peter moved in armed with a new five-year contract and a deal that at the time seemed crazily generous. It was the generosity of a desperate man. Peter gave me a new contract, including a signing-on fee of three-quarters of a million pounds spread over five years, and he almost doubled my wages! I called Michael Kennedy who commented wryly that I had outgrown him.

So, overwhelmed by flattery and money, I said I'd stay. It was getting on towards the end of 1993. Within a few months, Peter Swales was gone, Francis Lee had taken over and I had different worries.

Franny Lee swept into the Manchester City chairman's office as the fans' favourite. He looked like an unlikely revolutionary, small, paunchy and opinionated. He'd been an icon at the club since his days as a tricky winger in the sixties and he'd made a decent-sized pile of money in business since he'd left football. He arrived promising to get the best from both ends of the broom. I felt his time in charge was a disaster.

Top players proved too expensive. The game had changed more than he could have imagined and was on the verge of changing even more violently. He seemed to want to be hands-on in every aspect of the club's existence, which meant that he couldn't leave the manager to manage. One day, to our shock, he came into the dressing room and gave the teamtalk with Brian Horton standing in the corner looking embarrassed and humiliated.

By the time he arrived, my own life had changed completely and I was a spectator for the events that brought him back to prominence. In fact, I was lucky to have a life, lucky to be still filling a grandstand seat.

When I decided to stay at City I had a lot to look forward to. I had a good contract and was still owed my signing-on fees. I loved Manchester. I had the 1994 World Cup coming up. In November, Ireland had travelled to Windsor Park and famously Alan McLoughlin had volleyed an equaliser that was enough to qualify us for our second successive World Cup. I'd started every one of our twelve qualifiers and we had this new kid Roy Keane who'd moved from Forest to Manchester United the month before we qualified. He was the real thing. He'd given us a bit of pep. Kevin Moran and I had called in to see him and welcome him to Manchester when he arrived – great night. It held out the prospect of friendship, I thought. Life was good.

Within two weeks of qualifying for the World Cup, City are playing Sheffield Wednesday at home. It's not going well. We end up losing the game by three goals to one. In the second half, I go for a ball, chest it and go to turn, but my studs stick in the ground and I fall over. One of their players is standing behind me and the referee, Dermot Gallagher, awards me a free kick.

'Dopey Irish fucker,' he says. 'He did it himself.'

Dermot wags his finger at him. 'Hey, less of the dopey Irish stuff, son . . .' Dermot Gallagher. He should have guessed. Dopey.

I get treatment and try to play on – I even hit the post with a header – but when I run, I fall over and remain in pain for maybe ten or twelve seconds before I try to get going again.

On the Monday of the next week, I found myself in a clinic in Bolton. Tony Banks, the Manchester City surgeon, was keeping me waiting. He had the results of the orthoscope. I assumed it was good news. It was like watching the Oscars, waiting for the envelope to be opened. His nurse smiled at me.

'Don't worry,' she said with a thin smile.

What does that mean? I thought. Don't worry – that smile, those words? Why say that to somebody who has just twisted his knee out of shape a bit? I'm hoping to play against Forest tomorrow night. I spent last night in the middle of the scrum in front of the stage at a Sawdoctors gig. What's up? Don't worry? I wasn't worrying, till now.

Mr Banks comes out with a big brown envelope, X-rays and charts. Usually he's a jovial guy but he's wearing his gravedigger's face. One word swims before me – cruciate. I've done my cruciate. No, my cruciate has done me. It's busted – snapped, knackered, ruined, bollocksed, wrecked. It's betrayed me. It's done the dirty. It's sold me down the river. It's screwed me over.

In the theatre, the luvvies forbid themselves to say the word 'Macbeth'. It curses everyone, apparently. The dread word in soccer dressing-rooms is cruciate. I've done my cruciate. I am dead.

Right now Gazza is struggling with one. Paul Lake is struggling with one. A lot of people I know have had to quit. The word is that the taller you are, the harder it is to come back. Something to do with leverage. Thanks. I'm a beanpole and I'm gone. You do your cruciate and your friends are soon coming by to shake your hand and say how sorry they are for your troubles. We are gathered here today to bury the career of Niall Quinn . . .

Mr Banks is telling me about my cruciate, what it's for – *what it was for, don't you mean?* – what can be done – *a simple, tasteful ceremony perhaps?* – where to go – *back to the real world? Down the job centre?* – the new surgical techniques – *so they don't just shoot you?*

One sentence seems amplified above all others. Does he shout it? 'I'm sorry, Niall, but you'll have to forget about the World Cup.'

Of course. Yes, I'll forget about it. We'll have that small dignified ceremony to say farewell to my career and I'll get on with life, forget about the World Cup, watch cricket. Perhaps it's for the best. Cheers.

Brian Horton is one who feels I'll never be the same. For him, I'm just a dead man walking, or hobbling.

Gillian drives me home from Mr Banks' clinic and I ask her if we can call into Maine Road on the way. I had to break the bad news and I want to get the sympathy of fellow professionals and hear their hopeful words. When Brian Horton hears that I have the curse of the cruciate, he gives up on me there and then. I'm bad luck to be around.

'I'll handle the press on this,' he says.

It was 29 November. I didn't see or hear from Brian Horton again until April. Alan Shearer called, though. Kevin Moran at Blackburn had a word in his ear and, even though I don't know Alan Shearer at all, he picked up the phone and rang me. If you get your knee sliced open by just one man this year, he said, make sure it's this man. If you put your entire career in the hands of just one man, he said, make sure it's this man – Mr Dandy. Comedy name, serious man.

CHAPTER TWELVE

MOVITA, ME

It was a wonderful time for me. Every day, besides the cables and flowers, he sent my mother chocolates and things. He really was very very nice — very romantic, I thought.
MOVITA, FROM *FIGHTING FOR LOVE* BY MICHAEL TAUB

I knew Gillian Roe was the woman for me when I picked up a piece of hairy bacon from the floor in the Manhattan at 3.30 in the morning and took a bite out of it. She took the rasher off me and ate the other half. Jaysus, I thought, I've never gone out with a girl who'd do that on the first date. The rest is history.

Unless you've lived a certain type of life you won't know the Manhattan (or Auntie May's), the little all-night place jammed between the top of Harcourt Street and the Charlemont Flats in Dublin. It's where you go in town if you have too much drink taken and need a last meal before you face the dawn. It's where you'll find other kindred spirits who have been roughed up by the night by too much drink or something worse. It's where you'll get the food that will rest heavy in your stomach till the following weekend. Probably it's not first-date territory.

The first time I met Gillian was on a Republic of Ireland photo shoot. She was doing a modelling gig for Ballygowan Water, who ironically were one of the team's sponsors back in the good old days. We were shooting in Dalymount Park in Dublin, about the last place you'd associate with sparkling spring water or romance. We were on our way to the World Cup finals in Italy a little while later and we were all pretty full of ourselves.

I'm not saying that my wife is beautiful (she is) but among twenty footballers she stood out as the pick of the bunch. I made a point of saying a shy hello, and that was it – back to England and my monastic life.

Not long after the World Cup, Dave O'Leary and I were doing another corporate gig, this time for Opel, the Irish team's main sponsors. We were at the Motor Show in Dublin, meeting and greeting. Two models were involved and one of them was Gillian.

Dave, avuncular as ever, did the work for Opel, giving me the odd indulgent glance and wink as I went a-wooing. I didn't let him down. I bowled Gillian over with the most incredible chat-up lines any woman had ever heard, really marvellous, sparkling stuff that gave her just a hint of the wonder of me – sensitive me, romantic me, lover of little animals me. Later we'd get to the rasher on the floor at four in the morning me.

Finally, as a reward for persistence, she agreed to have a drink with thirsty me that evening. Smooth operator me, I postponed my flight back to Manchester straightaway, marched her across the road to the nearest pub, the Horse Show House, and road-tested her capacity for drink. It was not great to be honest but I extorted a promise from her to stay till we got something to eat. I then successfully removed her from the Horse Show House and got her to Bad Bob's in town, which was one of the few places in Dublin where you could get a late drink to avoid having to put your date on the last bus home. From there we moved on to the Manhattan, which is the sort of place you'd imagine exists only in songs sung by The Pogues.

It was getting bright when I called a taxi and took Gillian home. I gave her a Cary Grant peck on the cheek and took the taxi straight to the airport. I had football to play! Life couldn't be all rashers and dames. I'd be hard to get from now on.

In Manchester, I went straight to the hotel. I had some time to put down before training so immediately I began trying to call Gillian. I tried and tried without any success. Damn. Cary Grant never gets slipped the wrong number.

As it transpired, Gillian's grandmother had passed away while we were on the crawl around town. It was a bad time for Gillian and a bad time for her family but I felt a small piece of guilty relief when I at last established that the number was genuine and that I could make contact. Soon we were having three- and four-hour conversations on the phone and I began to hope that some day Gillian's family would cease to associate me with mourning and grief.

So to the surgeon, Mr David Dandy. If he opens my knee for me, Manchester City won't be pleased — Mr Banks is their man — but it's my knee. I've had it all my life. And for some reason I trust Alan Shearer. He seems like the kind of person who'd be cagey about his knees.

From home, I ring Mr Dandy's clinic in Cambridge and speak to his secretary. I can speak to Mr Dandy for two minutes at five minutes past five. This impresses me. He must be up to his elbows in knees, a top knee man.

At five minutes past five we speak for two minutes. He's a precise man. He tells me to come to see him at five past five the next day.

The club didn't need to know about this. I hoped that what they didn't know wouldn't hurt me. I went to the ground and found my X-rays and report in the physio room. Next day, I caught the trans-Pennine train south. It took most of the day to get from Manchester to Cambridge. Just before five, I hobbled into Mr Dandy's on my crutches.

At five past five, Mr Dandy looks at my X-rays. He's interested. He'll do me in the morning or he'll do me in two weeks' time. I must choose.

Only Gillian knows I'm here. I have travelled with some X-rays and a medical report, nothing else. Now, now now. Make it better now, or in the morning. Do it as quickly as possible. Slice me.

I hobble out, buy a toothbrush, come back and am shown to a bed. Gulp. I phone home. Listen, I'm going to stay here for the night and have a man cut my knee open in the morning. No worries. How are you? By the way, don't tell anyone from the club that their star striker is having his knee done.

The job is started before 7 a.m. and I'm groggy till lunchtime. Then I'm groggy and sore. It dawns on me that Manchester City have to know sometime. For some reason, in fact, they have to know right away, before these drugs wear off. I call Eamon Salmon, the physio, and tell him in as chirpy a voice as I can muster that I've just had my knee done.

I'd never heard a man have a coronary down the phoneline before. Eamon goes into denial. He says I'm winding him up. He tells me that he will be sacked. He goes back to his coronary.

'I'm feeling fine, thanks,' I say. Then I apologise, explain my rationale. Eamon is not convinced.

Six days later I'm at home but not out of the woods. Within hours, I become weak and my knee is screamingly sore. A pounding, pounding pain makes it feel as if my knee is going to explode. I ring Roy Bailey, whom Manchester City have just sacked. Give me something for the pain, Roy; anything for the pain. I think that if I smother the pain it will go away, the whole problem will just stop being a problem. I can't smother it. After twenty-four hours I pass out from it.

I'm rushed to hospital. I'm doped up and drowsy but I know

when I'm admitted that I have to wear my tail between my legs. I'm back in the domain of the Manchester City surgeon, Mr Banks. Nice man. He doesn't seem to hold a grudge. He operates on me throughout the night. I have septicaemia. It's nothing to do with Mr Dandy; it can happen to anyone. I've lost lots and lots of blood.

This is November and I'm in hospital till Christmas Eve, when I'm well enough to do a runner.

I have come close to dying, but that's a secret. Gillian is seven months pregnant. The winter is brutal. We are moving house and she has to do it all alone. The medical people decide she has enough on her plate just looking at her husband evaporating before her eyes; no need to tell her that he might be gone entirely soon.

Gillian always had a way with words. She was eighteen when she first came over for a weekend. We were playing Everton and some friends of mine, Alan Salt and his wife, Helen, went to the airport to meet her and look after her until the game was over. We all met in the players' lounge afterwards. Adrian Heath and his wife, Jane, were there, too. There was a loose plan to go for a meal together. During one of those awkward pauses that can occur when nobody really knows the new person in the group, somebody asked Gillian if she'd been shopping.

'No,' she said. 'I was shagged this morning. Could hardly get out of bed.' There was a stony silence; people glancing at each other uneasily. In England, shagged doesn't mean very tired.

We carried on with weekend visits through till the spring and as the season was drawing to a close, Gillian made the commitment to come over to England. It meant giving up her career as a model and the comfortable life she had built for herself at just eighteen. She had her own house and her phone seldom stopped ringing with modelling assignments and acting jobs. Thankfully, I convinced her that her future lay in England with a dissolute footballer who liked Irish showbands.

She left a lot behind emotionally and careerwise and arrived in

Manchester with a small trove of cash she had saved over her time in Dublin. That was her next surprise. Mr Right had drunk and gambled all his own money away. Gillian's nest egg got thrown in as grist to the mill. In three months I had redistributed her wealth among bookies and publicans in the Manchester area.

I don't know why she stayed. Football hampers you in growing up and for as long as I could remember I had always suited myself when it came to living my own life. I had never lived with anyone before and it never even occurred to me to change my habits. After tea I'd announce grandly that I was off to the pub. Because I was in love, I'd kindly ask Gillian if she had any plans herself, tell her to take care and I'd see her at about three in the morning.

Soon when I asked if she had any plans, she'd say things like, 'Yeah, there's this guy I used to model with and he wants to take me to dinner. I thought I'd go.' So I'd stretch, imagine myself to be tired and announce that, you know what, I might just stay in tonight.

And so Gillian hauled me back from the slope. When I look back over my life, or through the pages of this book, so many people I've known, played with and cared for have become victims of the things I enjoyed doing. These stories are littered with alcoholics, gamblers and people who just couldn't face life straight. And I was off to join them. I was on the edge of that slippery slope – no sense of responsibility, no sense of myself, no idea of where I was going. If I had answered one of those questionnaires that alcoholics respond to when they are on the way out of denial, I would probably have ticked the same boxes as Tony Adams did. But I never got to that level of self-awareness back then, and when I did, Gillian had already saved me. She came along and anchored my personal life. The drifting ended.

With dramatic events such as Manchester City falling apart, my first cruciate injury, going broke – I'd have drunk myself to death if she hadn't been there to nurse me through them. For nearly three years, as a kid out of the team at Arsenal, I had drunk, I had buried the bitterness with good times. I lived like one of those characters from *Withnail and I.* I stopped just short of drinking lighter fluid. Another setback of that magnitude would have tipped me into dependency.

People often describe me as being well balanced. Well, it's Gillian who provides the equilibrium. Left to my own devices, I'm just a man behaving badly.

We said when Gillian first came over that we'd wait for a couple of years before getting married. I was indisciplined there, too; I couldn't wait. We took part in a festival of weddings in the summer of 1992. Gillian and I were married, with my old friend Dave Whelan as best man, in the parish of Killiney in Dublin on a lovely summer's day. It couldn't have been better. Dave and Brenda married at about that time, too, with me as best man. And Gillian and I cut short our honeymoon to get to Tony Adams' wedding to Jane.

Life just kept getting better after that. I developed some idea of how the adult world really works, some idea of when I should be home and how I should be at home. I learned how to share a life.

Sometimes the lessons have been hard. At home for a while we had an antique doorbell, the sort of thing you glance at every now and then and visualise taking to *The Antiques Road Show.* You can see yourself nodding sombrely as you learn that you have the most valuable antique doorbell in the history of the world while your mind is screaming how much will they give me, how much, how much?

One night I forgot my keys. It's around four in the morning and I'm thinking of *The Antiques Road Show* as I ring the bell. Lovely sonorous sound, I'm thinking, and ring it again; has to be worth a few quid, has to be. Didn't seem to be waking Gillian, though. She's turned a deaf ear to the bell, left me there to stew. After a while, my ringing becomes more frantic. Self-pity is setting in. Hey, I'm out here. I jam my thumb against the bell. Finally, Gillian comes down. Victory!

But no. She puts the bolts on the door. Defeat! I hear her footsteps fading away. I should take my whipping, know when I'm beaten. Instead, I ring the bell again – and again and again.

This time I think I'm definitely winning. She comes down the hallway, unbolts the door and throws it open to find me swaying dangerously and grinning cheesily. Howya love? She pulls the antique bell off the wall and crashes it down over my head. Thing has never worked since.

Gillian has been coming to the hospital in the evenings, looking at me and bursting into tears. She is frazzled, with pregnancy, with the sixty minutes it takes to get here, with the move, with simply being away from home.

I am just fading away. I lose three and a half stone in three weeks. I've been comforted by sister morphine, triple doses of sister morphine all the way through. Something always shields me.

I know the life of the drug addict. I get my morphine every four hours and I love its warm, flooding relief. Slowly it leaves me and I begin hurting for more. With three-quarters of an hour to go before my next shots, I am desperate. I call the nurse. 'Give me my morphine. You're fucking hiding it. Give it to me.' I don't know who I am any more. Pain and morphine own me.

I get drugs; Gillian gets the shitty end of the stick. When the worst is over, the hospital tell her that, frankly, it's been touch and go – not for my career but for me. She brings food every day, hoping I'll force something down – soups, Irish stew. Nothing works. I'm floating in a morphine world. She has the real world to deal with and the dark, cold Manchester nights.

I don't eat a thing for twenty-six days. I don't go to the toilet for twenty-six days. My Adam's apple sticks out so much you could hang your coat on it. I'm all ribs and elbows. I look like a dozen coathangers stuck inside a sock and, call Malcolm Macdonald, my arse has disappeared.

Gary Flitcroft comes in one day for some physio. I'm in a chair, being hoisted into a pool. I catch him looking at me. He's wincing. We have a short conversation. He can't look at me. I'm grotesque. I tell myself that the next time he sees me, I'll be halfway normal looking.

The day I got out was the day I realised how bad I had been. I went to put my trousers on and they fell straight down to the floor without touching the sides of my legs. I had pipe cleaners for legs, turkey wattle hanging where once there was muscle. I weighed eleven stone seven pounds and a strong wind would crumple me.

Mr Banks, the bad news man who holds no grudges, has an interesting history. He was once a weightlifter, tough and good with it. He tells me to go to a gym in Wythenshawe. It's a rough place but it's all free weights and honest sweat – no leotarded secretaries sipping Evian as they perch on their exercise bikes while queuing for the sunbed.

The first weights exercise I had to do in my emaciated state was with a sweeping brush. For God's sake, you wouldn't see me behind the brush if we were both queuing for a bus. After that, I give blood, sweat and tears for months. Tony Banks came with me some days and we worked out together. Glynn from the gym gave me a lot of his time, devising programmes for me, pushing me and encouraging me.

Paul Lake was going through the same thing as I was, working his way back from a knee injury. One day he said he'd come to the gym. Lakey was an obsessive worker but his knee wouldn't stand up once it quit on him. He tried till it broke his heart. At Wythenshawe, we did a three-part session with Glynn. He worked us really hard; we were sweating blood almost. Next day I called Lakey. He said he wasn't going any more. It was too much. He had Glynn and me down as lunatics. I knew then that I was flying. Lakey was fitter, stronger and more enduring than me. Thanks, Paul.

I ate liver. I ate kidneys. I ate organs of some sort for breakfast, dinner and tea. I drank shakes that contained 5,000 calories a hit. Early on, I swam. After a while I did football exercises. As often as I could, I went to the gym, sometimes three times a day.

At home I became a bastard to live with. Nobody has ever felt more sorry for himself or been more self-absorbed. Gillian got the sharp end of it. Her only respite was that I was out so much, busy looking after number one.

Gillian's family are horse people. Her uncle, Johnny Roe, was a champion jockey in Ireland for many years and once upon a time he won the Guineas in England. Johnny had success in big races all over the world and from childhood Gillian has had a love of horses. But her dad, Mick, had seen what riding took out of Johnny, at the high points and the low points, and Gillian was gently steered away from the race game. She's an accomplished horsewoman, though.

When we took our first flat in Altrincham, there happened to be a stables close by. Gillian began wandering up there in her spare time and the old love returned. Ironically, she also worked at Francis Lee's racing stable, just before he took over at City. Horses are part of the glue that keeps our lives together now. Gillian takes football and all its little soap operas with a pinch of salt. Horses we are both passionate about. When football is finished, that is what we will work at.

We've already had considerable success with breeding. In June 1993, I was away in Latvia with the national team and when we got back to Dublin, Gillian insisted on meeting me in town. I had an inkling to go out with the team that night but Gillian was more strident than usual. I assumed I was in trouble and had best get the sentencing over with. We met in a bar called Buck Whales and when I asked what was up, she handed me two little mittens and some woolly baby shoes. 'You'll be needing these,' she said. So Aisling and Michael joined us and life changed for the better.

Most of the time I'm the third child in the family. I've come to appreciate that everything in my head is already contained with room to spare inside Gillian's head, even the smallest things.

When Alex Rae was at Sunderland, his wife, Linda, kept such good tabs on him that he used to refer to her jokingly as Gentile, after the tight-marking Italian defender. Alex was drinking big time while he was in the north-east but he has since turned himself and his career around. He and I would seek each other out for long sessions from time to time, and when we'd go on the tear, we'd stick to the back streets of Durham, out of harm's way and remote from prying eyes. We were just starting one afternoon when Gillian walked into the pub pushing our younger child Michael in the pram. 'This is for you,' she said. 'I'm going shopping.' There's no need for the close marking of a veteran Italian defender when you have instincts like that.

On another occasion, a little wiser now, Alex and I went out again. It was like drinking on the FBI Witness Protection Programme. We kept away from the towns altogether and found a pub in a secluded part of the middle of nowhere – just us and the barman. We ordered our first pint and as the foamy heads were settling the phone rang behind the bar. Alex started laughing.

'That'll be Gillian,' he said.

The barman picked up the phone, turned to me and said, 'It's your wife.' I know a wind-up when I see one. Alex was setting me up.

'Yeah, good one, Alex. Give it here. Hello.'

I heard Gillian's voice saying, 'If you don't have your sorry arse back in the house in half an hour, there will be no one here when you do roll in.'

In my regular pubs in Sedgefield and Seaham, people would shout out, 'It's Quinny's wife!' just about any time the telephone rang. It became such a habit with them that one night the shout went up as usual when Gillian was sitting on the stool next to me. She flashed an evil eye around the place.

She's always two steps ahead of me. She knows what's best. She put up with the worst of me when I was injured and badgered me back to health. The club had given up on me. I'd gone and got my own operation and now I could make or break myself on my own.

The team played a relegation game in April 1994. Brian Horton got in touch that day for the first time in five months. Tony Book and David Moss had been to see me the first day I went into hospital in Bolton. Roy Bailey, the physio who had been sacked by then, called round to my house. That was it from City.

By April, I'd worked and worked. I'd been in the coal mine for the previous four months and I was ready to hit the surface again. I weighed sixteen stone, I had muscles on my muscles, I was fit again. The World Cup was a solid possibility for me.

Francis Lee wouldn't listen. He was old school. He believed cruciates are injuries from which you never come back, not properly. He'd probably have liked to sell me, to get my cursed leg out of his club. I was desperate. Jack Charlton was desperate. Jack wanted a presence up front.

I got Mr Banks to write me a letter clearing me to play in the World Cup. Mr Dandy wrote one, too. The verdict was that not only was I fit, but the quicker I got playing again the better. However, Francis Lee thought he knew better.

No argument worked. The World Cup would make me a better player. If City wanted to sell me, the World Cup would provide me with a showcase, push up my value. Damn it, I was a fit, responsible professional and I had a right to play for my country.

Jack never pushed it as hard as I'd hoped. Frannie Lee was an old England team-mate and they shared the same beliefs about cruciate injuries.

Finally, and most frustratingly, I was given permission to train with the team in America but not to play or be part of the squad. Ireland ended up having to play Tommy Coyne up front on his own. On a flight from New York to Orlando after the Italy match in the Giants' Stadium, Tommy collapsed from exhaustion and dehydration.

I was angry for a long time afterwards. I travelled to the World Cup and worked for RTE television, and some days I could hear the studio feed coming down the line. Joe Kinnear would be saying, 'What's Franny Lee doing? It's a mystery, innit?'

It still is a mystery to me. I felt sorry for myself and I felt sorry for Gillian, who had put up with so much. She bore the brunt of the disappointments I suffered and she did most of the heavy carrying while I was walking back up the hill to full health.

She even got the worst of it at the World Cup. While I was at the Irish training centre one day, a journalist from an Irish Sunday paper called to the hotel room with some cock and bull story about having been robbed and could he come in. Gillian was looking after Aisling who was four months old at the time and wasn't inclined to entertain him. He was pushy, though. Soon he had his foot in the door and he was making with the smarmy questions – does Niall like playing away? What is his favourite position? The whole experience upset and angered her. For a while, she was determined to sue and I think we've both had regrets ever since that we didn't.

So my involvement in the 1994 World Cup campaign was slightly odd and off kilter from the start. We had a players' pool that year. Players have less interest in the pool these days because the amount of money is too small. From the 2002 World Cup, with bonuses and endorsements, the Irish team will get about 50,000 euros each after tax. Mick McCarthy's stuff doesn't go in; neither did Jack Charlton's; neither, this time, did Roy Keane's. We spoke about giving Roy's share of the pool to Colin Healy who will, I'm sure, serve the country for a long time to come.

It's almost too embarrassing to think about, let alone to say out loud, but few players put themselves out too much for 50,000 euros. Back in 1994, though, the wages were smaller and, comparatively, the pool was worth a lot to players. We grabbed everything, we hustled, we pimped ourselves, we were hungry. Nobody had much money. To our shame, with bakery workers on strike and locked outside the gates, we even did a deal with Gateaux. As the son of a bakery worker, I never quite got over the guilt of that.

I was almost the face of that Irish World Cup even though I couldn't play. I was in Ireland every week doing something or other on behalf of the team. Nobody else had a busted cruciate; nobody else was available like I was.

I even got into trouble. Before we qualified I'd signed a contract with Lucozade to do an ad. Once we qualified, the pool became operational. Coca-Cola had paid for exclusivity as the soft-drinks sponsor. Lucozade thought they'd bought some of the action through my deal. We had a day of legals in Dublin. Michael Kennedy represented me. The players' representatives had a legal rep, the players' pool had a legal rep and so did the FAI, Coca-Cola and Lucozade.

We planned to argue that the players' pool should have informed me. We knew that Lucozade weren't going to charge the players; they wanted the ad to go ahead and for Coca-Cola to pull out. Michael cast his eyes over all the contracts and within a minute spotted the way out in the Coca-Cola contract, which was made on the contingency of qualification and hadn't been updated. Lucozade didn't realise this; Michael made sure that Coke did and suggested a deal — we get the Lucozade ad out for a period and give the money to the pool. Michael Kennedy rides to the rescue again. The day was saved. Nobody had to pay costs. I think the money in question was £30,000 and the ad ended up being shown just a couple of times during the World Cup.

What amazed me was how it mirrored my situation at Manchester City. Once there was a problem, all you could see were people running for cover. The blame got lumped on to the players. That's how football works. At the end of the day, it's still a feudal system and the blame piles up at the bottom more often than not. Nobody took control for us in 1994 when we ran into trouble. Nobody took control last week in Saipan or this week in Izumo.

Tomorrow we move to Niigata. We'll train on the pitch at the Big Swan Stadium. The place will be all liveried out in World Cup colours. We'll be able to smell the excitement of the competition. Afterwards, we'll fly to Chiba, just outside Tokyo, to be joined next week by our families.

We've been away since 17 May and it's not even June yet but I feel as if I have lived a lifetime. I'm looking forward to the football but I'm not expecting to play any of it. In my heart, I'm looking forward to seeing Gillian, Aisling and Michael just as much. This long goodbye to football has hurt too much already.

CHAPTER THIRTEEN

EVERY STORY ENDS

*Do you think, oh sublime ancient, said I, that there will ever
be good conditions for the Gaels or will we have nothing
forever but hardship, famine, nocturnal rain and Seacattishness?
—We'll have it all, said he, and day-rain with it.*
FLANN O'BRIEN, *THE POOR MOUTH*

We've dug the hole and we've gone down so deep that we can hardly
see the sky. It's time to start climbing out again.

All the little things add up and when you look back, it's the sum
of the little things that has made the big moments happen.

We're in Niigata on a beautiful summer's afternoon. The Big
Swan Stadium sweeps up all around us in gorgeous curves. It feels
like the first day of our World Cup. We're in a different city with
a game tomorrow and something new to think about.

Mick is talking to the players. This is where he is most at home
– on a pitch or a training ground, in a dressing room. Mick isn't
good with subtleties, those little nuances that occur within a squad.
He assumes we're here because we want to be here. He assumes we
want to win, to do our best. He assumes we're all on the same page.
If we aren't, he doesn't have a whole lot of time to devote to figuring

out why. I think that's what most of us like about him. He has his blind spots and he makes his errors, and he's made some in the past couple of weeks, but despite everything that has rained down on him, he's here and he's the same straightforward guy. He's the one who will lead us out of the hole.

None of us are especially close to him. Even as a player, in the old team, he was separate; we always knew that he was Jack's enforcer. We're not close but we know he's straight and over the years we've all had reasons to be grateful to him for one thing or another.

Early in Mick's career as Irish manager, we went to America on a summer tour. The occasion of our departure was marked by Roy's sudden withdrawal from the squad. Roy seemed to need a rest but he didn't come straight out and say so. Mick still had the impression that Roy was coming to America. That was at the time when Mick still expected a simple phone call from the man he had named as captain. The jigs and the reels that followed included Mick taking a phone call from somebody pretending to be Roy and believing the hoaxster when he said he was on his way. It was a public humiliation for a young manager.

Still, America, Mexico and Bolivia awaited us. On 12 June we went to the Giants' Stadium, scene of the national team's World Cup triumph over Italy two years previously. This time the opponents were Mexico, who'd beaten Ireland later on in the 1994 tournament. Jack had got into some silly name calling with the Mexicans over who was more used to the oppressive heat of Orlando, and there was still some spice left from that.

This game was no prettier than the 1994 one. Liam Daish got himself sent off. On the sideline I got agitated, stepped over the line and was shown a red card. I followed Liam down the tunnel to the dressing room.

'Mick's sent you to tell me to come and sit on the bench, hasn't he?' said Liam.

'Nah. I've been sent off too.'

'Jesus!'

Soon, as we were sitting there in the cool of the dressing room, there came the clatter of studs down the tunnel. 'Shit,' we thought. 'Mick.' Sure enough, Mick came in. We got our tackle in first.

'He was a shit ref, Mick. Wasn't our fault. Bad decision.'

'Yeah. Tell me about it,' said Mick. 'He's just sent me off.' He sat down and laughed, and he looked less strained then than he usually did. It was football, the richness of it and the daftness of it; it's in Mick's blood.

It's been a long hard haul for Mick from those uncertain beginnings to this World Cup. He's had to weed out old team-mates, most of whom were suffering from the usual footballing delusion that everyone was getting past it except them.

Two years ago, we were within a minute of qualifying for the European Championship in Skopje, Macedonia, leading by a goal as the game went into injury time. We conceded a corner, gave away a free header and had to play Turkey in a play-off instead. It ended badly and Mick got mauled in the press – one free header and he took the entire rap.

Then there's been Roy and the allowances that have to be made plus the difficulty of going about your work knowing that your best player doesn't rate you.

So here we are in Niigata, having our last kickabout before the World Cup, a stadium like something from a dream wrapped all around us. Mick looks ten years younger. He loses the lines on his face when he steps on to a pitch. I feel a bit more chipper myself actually. This could still be a great experience. Maybe this isn't an ending, maybe it's a beginning that I have gatecrashed.

The Manchester City and Jack Charlton eras wound down at about the same time.

The 1994 World Cup started well for Ireland and sped downhill from there. The summit was the 1–0 victory over Italy in the Giants' Stadium. Ground level was reached quickly with a tame, error-ridden, second-round exit against Holland in Orlando. It was over. The team were forced to endure an embarrassing civic reception in the Phoenix Park in Dublin. Everyone cringed and went home.

I was still stewing over not being allowed play. I went back to Manchester City and was asked to play in a pre-season friendly against Chester three days later.

Jack seemed to me by now to be softer and more indulgent. At the World Cup, he treated Gary Kelly, Phil Babb and Jason McAteer like favourite nephews. Now, faced with the challenge of building a new team around them, I'm not sure he had the same appetite as at the beginning. Yet he stayed on. Nobody suggested that he do otherwise.

At that time, somebody should probably have put Manchester City out of their misery – just pulled the plug and started again.

One night Franny Lee called me. C'mon over to my place, he said. The sad thing is that I actually liked the guy, still do. He has something about him that's charming even when he's letting you down. He told me that Aston Villa had come shopping for me. He told me not to feel bad that a club like Manchester City were willing to say goodbye to me. I told him I'd get over it. Good, good, said Franny. Then he told me that I wouldn't be getting my signing-on fees. I told him I didn't think I'd get over that. And if I didn't get over it, neither would Michael Kennedy. If Michael couldn't get over it, well, there'd be no transfer.

Amazingly, that's how we left it. I'd arrived home with this great store of bitterness still heaped inside me about the World Cup and now this. I decided I'd force my way into Franny Lee's life. I'd make him rate me. So I forced my way into his team, scored five in nine matches, played some of the best football I've ever played and established a decent working relationship with Brian Horton. It never struck me that Franny saw me as an accounting problem, that he didn't want to pay my wage.

We stayed up that year. At the end of the season I was back playing for Ireland in the European Championship qualifiers. In the spring we played Portugal at Lansdowne Road and Stan scored the winner as we beat them 1–0. I'm not sure I've ever had a better game in an Irish jersey.

Other people noticed, apparently. That summer, Sporting Lisbon came looking for me. Michael and I travelled to Portugal. I liked Lisbon, the city and the club. I had the impression that their manager didn't like me much but that could change later. I'd had that problem before.

Sometimes you have to see how top-level football operates to believe it. When we got to Lisbon, Manchester City had agreed a fee for me. We just had to agree personal terms. We sat down and, hey presto, the money being offered was exactly the same as I was getting at Manchester City. I am suspicious that the club have disclosed my current wage to the people to whom they were trying to sell me. It put me in a weaker negotiating position and made the proposition easier to walk away from despite Portugal's attractive tax rate.

What I had going for me back home was the fact that City still owed me four-fifths of my signing-on fee. That was big money for me, frightening money for Franny Lee. Either way, I couldn't really lose. I could sit it out with City and let them pay me by lump sum every year or I could move to the sun and get it all at once. On the one hand, if Gillian and I were ever going to make a move, now would be the time to spend a few years away. On the other hand, we were happy in Manchester . . . There was a lot to think about.

I passed my medical, and Michael and I were sitting around, chewing over all this, when we received a message from a local solicitor acting for Manchester City. Instructions from Francis Lee, a new brainwave – he wants me to waive all my signing-on fees.

Franny Lee won't pay. I'll stay. Honestly, the money, even that much money, didn't mean a whole lot. It was the idea of being messed around, this notion of being treated as part of the slave trade. If you or your business make a promise to somebody, you need to keep it.

So City paid me £6,000 a week for another year during which time they refused to believe in me and mostly refused to play me. We'd just finished seventeenth, losing two and drawing one of our last three games and just staying up. You can't try the patience of your fans much more than that. The next year we'd pull it off, though, with relegation, scoring just thirty-three goals all season.

And with relegation in the bag, City took £400,000 less for me from Sunderland than they would have received from Sporting Lisbon. That's how Manchester City was back then, just a means of accumulating frequent-flyer miles on trips from the frying pan to the fire and back.

That final season was one long shambles. I was staying, foolishly determined to make everyone at Maine Road love me again. I vowed that I'd score goals, I'd work on my own up front, I'd make balloon animals at kiddies' parties. Anything.

Alan Ball had by now replaced Brian Horton, a man with a World Cup winner's medal spending his middle years wading through the misery that was our club. I felt sorry for both Ball and Horton. Manchester City got in on them like rising damp and ate them away.

Ball was another old England chum of Franny Lee's. Alan and I never made it on to each other's Christmas card lists and I hardly made it on to many of Alan's squad lists. Good players left, or got pushed out – Terry Phelan, Gary Flitcroft, Tony Coton, Steve Lomas. I was next, had to be; me or Keith Curle. We felt as though the Grim Reaper was following us about with a scythe most of the time. We got ready to go out through the revolving door as a queue of cut-price foreign players were coming in.

I began to feel that when we played badly it was my fault, and when we played well it was nothing to do with me. It became very clear that I was among those who weren't wanted. Alan Ball hung it in dazzling neon. He sent droppograms. He shouted it from the rooftops. He was as subtle as a Christmas tree. I was asked to train with the reserves for much of the winter of 1995. It's a strange feeling to be cold-shouldered by a club you love. I'd hear Alan Ball croking away with the new players he'd bought and I'd watch them work and know that they were just shifting the deckchairs about on the *Titanic*. City were sinking.

We got to the end of the season, plagued with injuries, uncertainty, division. We were being sucked towards that plughole. Alan Ball was even being forced to play me. In the field of opportunity it's ploughing time again, I thought.

I was a workhorse. I played on my own up front and ran my legs off. I did it because I am a professional, because even if they don't like me they pay me and because City is a club with fans that deserve good things. I played, not for Alan Ball, but for my own reasons. I was still an outsider at my own club.

I regret the roads I haven't gone down. I could have gone to Everton. Brian Little offered to bring me to Villa. The move to Sporting Lisbon hung in front of me like a mirage. I stayed because of money and a principle attached to money. Now I'm thinking that maybe life's too short to be miserable over anything to do with money.

Ireland brought relief, as usual. We were at the end of an era and we behaved that way. Mick had retired and Jack didn't have an in-house enforcer. He hadn't the will to bark at us and bollock us any more, either; or if he did, we hadn't the legs to respond. We were an old team and people had sussed our little bag of tricks.

Not long after I came back from Lisbon, we played two European Championship qualifying games. We were declining, but qualification was still in our grasp. We drew with Liechtenstein on 3 June 1995. I remember the day for being the last I saw of Jack's wrath. I played badly and my only excuse was that I wasn't alone. We were to play Austria eight days later.

We came back from Liechtenstein and headed to Limerick where Jack was basing the team as a thank you for having been given an honorary degree by the local university. Denis Irwin, Alan Kernaghan and I kicked the week off by going to watch Clare beat Cork in the Munster Hurling championship. It was one of those historic days; the Clare defender Seanie McMahon dislocated his shoulder but stayed on the field to play his part in setting up the winning point. Even my Tipperary blood was stirred into celebration.

Jack allowed us free rein for a while in Limerick. We were allowed out the first couple of nights. Then Jack headed off up country on one of his famous earners, and to watch Northern Ireland play. The trouble with the team at that stage was that it wasn't just two or three sneaking out for a drink, it was most of us.

One day after training, I realised how lax some of us had become. Our drinking was so bad that even I couldn't take any more and I decided that I'd better go for a game of golf or I'd be in the pub all day again. I came back and had a shower and went around the hotel but I couldn't get a four ball together. Everyone was gone. So I said sod that for a good intention, took a taxi to the Henry Cecil pub at three in the afternoon and got sharp words for being late.

People knock that one trip but we were like that for years to some extent or other. We always got by and mostly we felt it bonded us like a club team. Against Austria we weren't too bad for eighty minutes; we just ran out of juice in the last ten.

Usually, Jack or Maurice Setters would take training but on one occasion that week Maurice had to go to a gig with Jack and they left Jack's son John in charge. Poor guy. It would have been easier for him to be minding mice at a crossroads.

We did the daily training from habit, and because some of us had alcohol to run out of our systems. By the time we were finished we were a little giddy, though. On the bus on the way back somebody asks mischievously what time the curfew is set for tonight. It's late in the week and we know that we shouldn't be out anywhere

Mark Wright and I go for the ball in the 1988 European Championships. It was a famous day for the Republic as we beat England 1–0 thanks to a Ray Houghton goal.

Jack Charlton, the man who started things rolling for Ireland. He may have struggled to remember names but he created a team ethos which has held us in good stead ever since. We're waiting nervously for the result of Spain v Denmark to see if we've qualified for the 1994 World Cup. I was to do my first cruciate a week later and missed the World Cup as a result.

Scoring the equaliser against Holland in the 1990 World Cup, the goal that put us through to the second round of the tournament. It was only now that I finally began to feel an established part of the set-up.

Beating Paolo Maldini in the quarter-final of Italia 90. It was Ireland's first ever appearance in the World Cup finals.

David Seaman is beaten as I score our goal against England in March 1991 in the European Championship qualifier at Wembley.

June 1996 and Mick McCarthy gives me the honour of captaining my country for the first time, against Croatia. The game was drawn 2–2 and I got the goal that saved us from defeat.

Scoring the goal against Cyprus in October 2001, my thirty-fifth birthday, that took me past Frank Stapleton's record as Ireland's all-time leading goal scorer. It was our final group game in the World Cup qualifiers, and after the play-offs we were on our way to Japan. Little did we know what that would mean...

Roy Keane pushes his way through the crowds at Dublin airport prior to Ireland's departure for Saipan and the World Cup.

The training facilities in Saipan were not to Roy Keane's liking, nor was the attitude of the goalkeepers when they wouldn't play in a five-a-side game at the end of a heavy training session.

Training with some local children in the Izumo dome. The hotel and training facilities here were excellent – everything ran smoothly. If only Roy had stayed long enough to find out.

The press conference I
gave following Roy
Keane's departure turned
into a complete
nightmare. I wished I'd
never been at the World
Cup at this point.

I'd thought I might just be going
along as the optimistic cheerleader,
so I was glad to get into the action
against Germany.

Mattie Holland and I applaud the
Irish fans after our 3–0 victory
over Saudi Arabia put us through
to the second round.

Robbie Keane, Steve Staunton, Damien Duff, Kevin Kilbane and I relax in the Sanggok-Dong sports ground in Seoul, looking back on a job well done so far.

Action from the second-round game against Spain. It was to be my last in an Ireland shirt.

The end. Mick McCarthy consoles me after we'd lost against Spain in the penalty shoot-out. Though it may look as if the emotions of the previous weeks have drained everything from me, the real pain is knowing I should have taken a penalty for him.

at all. But some of us intend to be going out half an hour after we come back from training. John is alert. He knows us.

'My father says nobody out tonight or there'll be trouble.' We start laughing. 'I'll be telling him.'

Of course, somebody says what we're thinking – 'Well, he can't send all of us home!'

By two in the afternoon, we're showered, lunched, changed and milling around the lobby dressed like we're heading for a nightclub, which we will be eventually. We're waiting on a fleet of taxis when John Charlton comes down and makes a half-hearted attempt to keep us sane.

'Look lads,' he pleads, 'try not to have more than six pints.' There's a big cheer and off we tear.

I roomed with Liam O'Brien that week. One morning we'd just come in and gone to bed when Mick Byrne knocked on the door.

'Liam, you've to ring your mother immediately.'

Liam dials home and I can hear his end of the conversation – 'No . . . no . . . aw no . . .' I'm thinking there's a tragedy at home and it's sobering me up. Liam hangs up the phone.

'What's wrong, Liam?'

He's as white as a sheet but he says nothing. He just makes sure the phone is right on the hook and falls straight asleep.

Minutes later, Mick Byrne comes clucking in with the newspapers. Liam's brother is all over the front pages. Liam wakes up, looks at the stories, shakes his head sadly, says the word gobshite again and again, and falls back to sleep.

Crazy week. The journey back up to Dublin for the Austria game capped it. We stayed in on the last night in Limerick, suddenly worried about the weekend. The FAI punished us for our excesses during the week by hiring the oldest bus in Ireland to take us back to Dublin. It was the inverse of that movie *Speed*. If it had gone above forty miles an hour it would have blown up. So we set off, slowly, and when we reached the outskirts of the city, Jack announced that he'd promised some people in Ballyfermot that the team would go and visit them for a charity gig.

OK, Jack. The bus chugged off to Ballyfermot with us all in our tracksuits but when we arrived at the community centre, they weren't expecting us at all. The messages had got mixed up and there was nothing on. A crowd gathered to look at us, of course. Gangs of Dublin kids on the ponies they keep in the fields gathered around the bus, taking the mickey out of us. We wandered into the community centre anyway, to stretch our legs and have a laugh. I remember, when we drove away, the kids on their ponies racing along beside the bus, helter skelter, and some of the English-born lads shooting mystified glances at each other.

We were supposed to be going to Lansdowne Road for the traditional training session that takes place the night before every game. We had to get there before dark and we left Ballyfermot behind schedule but Jack threw us another surprise. We had to go to Harry Ramsden's.

'What's going on there, Jack?' we asked. 'We're having our tea there?'

We all shuffled into Harry Ramsden's. Jack is a shareholder. Packie or Paul or somebody cut a ribbon and officially opened the place. So the night before the game, after a week of drink, I settled down to fish and chips.

Gary Kelly took the Harry Ramsden Challenge and ate a fish about a yard long and a mountain of chips and anything else they challenged him with. He thought there'd be a certificate but he got a free dessert instead, which he duly ate.

Jack herded us out pronto. Twenty minutes later, it's dusk at Lansdowne Road and we're all waddling about the pitch, groaning, full of fish and chips and trying to do a training session the night before this must-win game. We're burping and farting and creased over with laughter. Our main thought was it's been a happy era and it's ending soon. Back at the hotel, we played cards for a while until somebody ordered us off to bed.

Next night, at 1–0 up we were looking good. Ray Houghton gave us a lead after about sixty-five minutes and all we had to do was defend it but instead we died. Polster scored two, Ogris got one. I remember the names. From a position of having beaten Portugal that spring to set ourselves up for a cruise to the European finals, we were suddenly in freefall. We'd won four and drawn one of our opening games. We finished by dropping two points away to Liechtenstein, losing to Austria both home and away, and losing badly to Portugal in Lisbon. We would have to go into a play-off against Holland.

Sometimes you don't need a weatherman to know which way the wind blows. It was all over for Jack.

We went to Anfield in the middle of December for the play-off. I was suspended. We lost 2–0. Sometimes I still get a guilt trip about it all, especially that week in Limerick. I look back and think that we should have stayed in, should have knuckled down, but then I think that maybe Jack should have stayed, too, that things have their own life span and that team's was at an end. The genie was out of the bag. The balance we once had was gone.

For one of the first squads I was ever in, I remember Jack put on a curfew of midnight. I came back at about four, collected my key at the desk and whispered, 'Am I the last one in?'

The porter waved his hand at the row of keys behind him. 'No,' he said, 'you're the first.'

Our group survived that way for a long time. We looked at England's international players being pilloried by the tabloids for having a couple of drinks and we laughed. We had our way of doing things and we got by. In fact, we thrived.

We found our way to the strangest places – blind date nights in Carrickmacross, long sessions in Mulligan's of Poolbeg Street, drinking Limerick dry.

I remember later that year we were down to play Austria away on a Wednesday at the start of September. The All Ireland final was on the previous Sunday and Jack hadn't brought us in till the Sunday evening.

On the Saturday, using a contact at Coca-Cola, we fixed up a golf outing to Mount Juliet in Kilkenny. Maybe ten of the squad flew in early and went down to play. We had a fine day and all was well till we got near Dublin on the way back. I got out of the coach at the Poitin Stil pub on the dual carriageway into Dublin.

I had tickets for the game the next day and I knew there'd be a good session with hurling people in the Poitin Stil. Clare were playing in the final the next afternoon and Denis Irwin, Alan Kernaghan and I had seen them beat Cork earlier in the campaign. Denis was a fine hurler and we played against each other in Croke Park once. Hearing why I was getting off the bus, Denis said yeah he'd go to the game, too, so we both jumped out and, with our golf clubs, made our way across the lanes of traffic to the long night that followed.

Many drinks and three hours' sleep later, we were ambushed by Sunday morning. We had to head into town to collect our tickets in the Palace Bar in Fleet Street. That was another fine spot for drinking on an All Ireland day. We picked up the tickets and headed to the match.

Clare made the breakthrough that year and it was one of those great hurling occasions. I remember just being so pleased to be there, not least because we'd been at that earlier game in Cork, taking the mick out of Denis who could have hurled for Cork if he'd stuck with it.

After the game we went to meet Kevin Moran and a crowd in Mulligan's. George O'Connor, the great Wexford hurler, was there, and the broadcaster Dessie Cahill, and my friend and hero Nicky English, one of the greatest Tipperary hurlers ever. That is company you can't get away from. We were there till about 1.30 in the morning and then Denis and I made a stab at getting to the hotel to join the team. Kevin, retired by then, decided to come with us.

We poured ourselves into a taxi, which brought us up O'Connell Street, around Parnell Square and off to the northside of the city. Suddenly, we had a brainwave just as we left Parnell Square. Stop the cab! We screeched to a halt just outside Barry's Hotel. If you know the National in Kilburn and the Galtymore in Cricklewood, well, Barry's Hotel is their first cousin – a piece of fifties Ireland with showbands, glitterballs and nurses' dances on Thursday nights.

That night, Declan Nerney was playing. The lads were waltzing and jiving with old women. We did the jitterbug and the hucklebuck. We performed the locomotion. Eventually, my legs gave out. I could drink no more. I could stand no more. I could walk no more. I was on my back and Denis and Kevin were swaying somewhere above me laughing their heads off. The next morning we caught the plane to Austria early. I was in the horrors all the way, with every roll, every bump.

Was it professional? No. Do I regret it? Not really. There are only so many chances in a lifetime to watch Clare win an All Ireland and go drinking with Kevin Moran in the same day. Kevin was such an influence on us all. He'd wheel and deal all day and then close the briefcase and clap his hands and we'd be off following him. He is one of those characters who cross your path too rarely in life.

We lost badly on the Wednesday. It was a team in its death throes. A while later, Jack was manoeuvred out through the exit door. Enter Mick.

Shortly after he took the Ireland job, Mick came to City on the day we got relegated. I think, as a former City player, he just wanted to be there. We played Liverpool that day, drew 2–2; we'd needed to win to stay up. It was another shambles. A wrong message was sent on to the pitch with five minutes to go. I'd already come off. I had a radio and knew that Southampton were winning elsewhere, so we needed to score. Alan Ball had a conflicting message and he was telling the lads to hold the ball up. I had to run down the side-line and scream at Steve Lomas that we needed another goal. It made Alan Ball look bad, I suppose, but when you are bringing a great club down a division, you can't worry about vanity.

Afterwards, Mick sought me out, told me to keep going, encouraged me on a bad day. He didn't have to do that. He could have just slipped away. He was genuine, not going through the motions. When I joined Sunderland and did my other cruciate, I knew I had an international manager who would stick by me.

So we were relegated and it was time to say goodbye to Maine Road. I was peripheral to it all, a face from the past haunting the team as they struggled. City were keener than ever to offload me. However, by now I was a feature in 'where are they now?' quizzes. The only team interested in finding out weren't English. They weren't European. They weren't even South American. Selangor, the 'red giants' of Malaysia, wanted me.

If I wanted to play football, I had to persuade myself to want Selangor. I'd have to step on to a plane and go to see them because my career was in tatters. So we set off – Gillian, who was pregnant with Michael at the time, and me. First impressions were good. Selangor said to book ourselves first-class flights to Malaysia and they would reimburse us later. We hopped from Manchester to Gatwick to Malaysia.

A club official greeted us at the airport and gave us a quick tutorial in Malaysian etiquette. We were to bow to the president of the club etc etc.

There was bowing, there were warm greetings, there was talking, there was politics as usual. I discovered that Selangor had already announced that I had signed for them. Malaysia was on the verge of elections and the president of the club was standing as a candidate locally. I must have been his coup, his vote-getting gimmick. Selangor have a history of signing English league players from time to time. Chris Kiwomya, Tony Cottee and Dave Rocastle all played there at some time or another, but I think I'm the only one who would have been signed as a vote getter.

When I arrived, we hadn't even discussed the move. We were at the getting-to-know-you stage but Selangor waved all my worries away. They felt that I could learn to love them quickly. They had a massive stadium, the Shah Alem, with an 80,000 capacity and were regular trophy winners.

My worries included the fact that there was no Professional Footballers' Association in Malaysia. If money matters went wrong, you had no redress. The word from other players was that in this league if you had a bad game, you might not get paid.

I came up with a cunning plan. I told Selangor that I would need the bulk of my money sent to Ireland straightaway. No problem, they said. How much? All this time there was a chain of faxes humming between Malaysia and Michael Kennedy so I suppose they found me easy to deal with by comparison. I decided to ask for more than they could afford. At worst it would be a bargaining position; at best it would be a polite way out of the situation. I mentioned a figure. OK, they said.

We were dumbfounded. What's happening here? Are these people really going to put one million pounds into a bank account in Dublin?

Then it turned bad. Gillian tried to ask a question and was told, in so many words, to shut up. She was four months pregnant at the time, though they did not know this, and burst into tears. I've always felt the Malaysians got away lightly. An argument started. I was offended, shocked. Gillian was in tears. They all began shouting. We wanted to go home.

The chaos and the elections imprisoned us. There was more at stake than our feelings. Selangor were to play Middlesbrough the next day. Boro had just beaten the Malaysian national team 8–0 and Selangor were going to restore some pride. The press were waiting outside, ready to file their good news stories; not just sporting press but the political writers, too.

I was told that I had no choice but to play in this game against Boro, even if I wasn't going to sign. Relations were bad now. They were insisting that I had to play. The situation was a little out of control. I pointed out that I had no boots or kit with me, and stressed again that I just wanted to go home with Gillian.

Everybody around us was excited and angry. What do you do? Gillian was in shreds. There was nobody to appeal to for common sense. We felt frightened and a long way from home.

Eventually, I rang Manchester City and spoke to Colin Barlow, the executive director, to ask him what the position was about playing for this Malaysian team I hadn't even signed for. It was the middle of the night in Manchester. Colin's response was predictable. He asked me if I was mad.

At best, at very best, he couldn't give me permission to play until the next day but even then, I was still Manchester City property. There were insurance issues and all manner of complications. I was getting desperate. Gillian had been crying for hours and I was beginning to worry that there might be a danger of losing the baby if there was any more upset. I explained this to Colin and told him that I felt almost as if we were being held prisoner in an office at the club. I don't know how all this came across but eventually I was faxed permission to play in the game.

My plan was to sweet talk Selangor all the way back to the airport. Everything would be happy and perfect until such time as they put us on the return flight and we could pull the plug.

The game was a bizarre experience. Curtis Fleming was playing for Boro. 'What the hell are you doing here?' he said. I could hardly begin to explain.

Steve Vickers came by. 'You're not going to be putting in an effort today, I hope,' he said.

In the dressing room before the game, an English player whom I'd never met before asked me for a quiet word. Whatever you do, don't sign, he said. He told me he was getting out in a couple of weeks because things were so bad. We felt like a couple of prisoners whispering in the exercise yard.

During the team-talk the manager talked tactics and the team sat split into its various religious groups – Christians here, Muslims there, Hindus in the corner – and me. Suddenly, the Muslims were called to prayer. Apparently, this is a common event during team-talks. The manager just continued speaking to the rest of the players over the chanting.

Gillian went to the game. She sat in the stand with the man who had driven us around since we arrived, a lovely man with whom we felt safe. The worst sadness to come out of the whole venture was when we heard that he had been killed in a crash a couple of weeks later.

I intended to play badly in my borrowed boots, but how can you? A game of football is a game of football and it grips you every time. We won 2–1 and I scored the winner. Delirious supporters hoisted me on to their shoulders and carried me off the pitch. The pride of Malaysia had been restored. I was given a trophy as big as a house.

Selangor were under pressure now. Accidentally, I'd become a hero. They offered me more money, and then some more. It would be winging its way to Dublin immediately. I smiled at everyone, did much bowing, and said that I needed to be back in England to sort a few things out and that I'd be back soon. Thus Gillian and I escaped.

After that, the faxes started coming. The money in the Bank of Ireland eventually reached one million pounds. My greed found a voice for itself and began nagging at me. It couldn't compete with the memories of Gillian in Malaysia, though. We'd had happy times in Manchester with little money or no money. Why embrace misery now? It's been a law of my life – something always comes up.

A little while later, Sunderland signed me. To the football world, it looked like a journeyman's move, an end of career shift down the ladder and off into the oblivion of retirement. My luck held, though. The best years were still to come.

CHAPTER FOURTEEN

STARTER'S ORDERS

Owner to trainer: All you do is give me bad news about my horse. Can't you think of anything positive to say?
Trainer to owner: Well, you've got partners.
WILLIAM MURRAY, *THE WRONG HORSE*

Throughout the setbacks of the past few weeks, the one happy place where we have been able to escape the pressures has been the training ground. It's not spoken about but training is sharp, crisp and purposeful, and when we are out there everything else floats away. I see how hard the keepers are working and I'm astonished and a little bit inspired.

At training, we have drawn crowds every day who treat our practice like it's a real game. We've drawn a little buzz of excitement from them. They'll be watching us today.

The bus journey from city centre to the ground is old style. We're no sooner sitting down than the songs begin and Mick Byrne is up at the front trying to do somersault flips. People don't understand about Mick. They hear stories about how he makes us laugh and how he leads the singing and assume he is some kind of superfan we have incorporated into the system. We have confidence in him because he is a physio who knows his stuff. Over the years, many of us have gone back to our clubs in England and had them intro-duce Mick Byrne remedies. He's been that far ahead. He mends us physically and he mends us spiritually. Today he makes us laugh, as usual.

We are whisked in at the stadium, swallowed by the stadium almost. There are lots of fans outside waving and we're encouraged. Among the darker rumours doing the rounds we've heard that all the sympathy is running with Roy, that people have been cancelling their World Cup trips, that we have alienated the fans, who have been such a part of these journeys over the years.

The dressing room is a massive echoing space that dwarfs anything we've seen at Premier League level. Walking into a place like that makes the spine tingle; this is the World Cup after all. Each locker is big enough for a small family to live in. There are security men everywhere, FIFA people milling about in blazers, walkie-talkies and accreditation badges and zone passes. There are thirty of us, the squad plus eight staff. The place still looks empty when the door is closed and we are left alone.

Our jerseys are hanging on pegs — one to five, then seven to twenty-three. I fail to notice if a space has been left between numbers five and seven. My squad number is seventeen. Number sixteen is Dean Kiely, a reserve keeper. The keepers sit together and do what-ever it is that keepers do. I remember at Manchester City years ago, the great and then veteran keeper John Burridge was listening to his walkman one evening on the coach when we were playing a game of hearts. Somebody was out of the game and we needed another so Budgie had his arm twisted to join. The player who'd left the game went and picked up Budgie's earphones to hear what sort of sounds the guy had been listening to. It was a homemade motiva-tional tape — 'John Burridge, best keeper in the world. Bar none. Peter Shilton? Don't make me laugh! Ray Clemence? You're taking the piss now, mate . . .' and so on. Different breed, separate tribe. Dean goes off to be with his people.

I sit beside Richard Dunne who is number fifteen. He's not playing, either, but you can feel his sense of awe. He's just looking around, taking it all in. He and Robbie Keane grew up together in Tallaght. They've roomed together on trips with youth teams and Under-20 sides and here they are.

An hour and a half before the game, we walk out on to the pitch to sample the atmosphere. Whoa! We can't speak. A huge segment of the ground is full already with Irish fans and tricolours. A great rumbling, rolling roar of welcome greets us. Some of the lads have tears in their eyes; there's a lump in every throat. If I speak, I'll start to cry. We just wave. We point to people we know. We read the banners and listen to the mass singing of 'You'll Never Walk Alone'. A huge cloud is lifted from us.

Back in the dressing room, we are up, excited. It's interesting to see how people react, now we're here on the cusp of it. Dean Kiely is usually quiet but today he is very vociferous. He's going around from person to person stirring them up. Some people are getting rubs, some are meditating. I have a couple of blisters that I'm getting looked at. Other lads are getting strapped. We are busy with football business.

I sneak a look at Robbie and Damien. They are sitting beside each other. The great players have an aura of destiny about them. Those of us who have watched those two since they were precocious teenagers have longed to see them on this stage. This is where they should thrive. This is where we'll know the truth about them. Today could be the start of the rest of their superstar lives. There's nothing showing on their faces; both are quiet.

Mattie Holland is doing a lot of talking. You want to speak about professionalism in this team, start with Mattie Holland. He's talking things through quietly with everyone, clearing the haze, getting minds on to the football, clarifying everyone's job.

Some of the jokers are a little pale today; some of the quiet guys are filling the silence.

We never mention Roy Keane, not intentionally. This game of football is what we are here for. There's no more looking back. We are living in the present tense of the World Cup. Roy is past tense.

In the build-up, with the minutes ticking down to the moment when the knock on the door will come and we will be asked to go out on to the field, Mick speaks to us. He talks about how we have to think about the way we play, about our natural flowing game, how we have to pass and create. He tells us to try not to think of each individual situation too much, to keep moving as a team. Taff has plenty to say to the guys at the back. Stan has a general word.

Gary Kelly has a word, too. Gary has grown into a leader of this team and he has been picked today because of it. He has been sharp in training all through but he has been instrumental in putting us back together, in lifting us. I'm quietly pleased for him that he has been rewarded with a starting place.

We go out on to the field and the anthems are played. Those of us on the subs' bench put our arms around each other's shoulders and sing it out. Stan calls the starting eleven into a huddle. The handshaking gets done. Gary Breen is so wound up that he can't listen to what Stan has to say.

The game starts and the lads immediately forget what Mick has told them. Cameroon are African champions and they are big, athletic and confident. They are giving us trouble everywhere. Geremi their winger is punishing us down the left. They have two big strong central midfielders who come at us again and again.

We hold them for the first half-hour and begin to think that they have huffed and puffed themselves out. Shay Given makes a few saves that would be wonderful for anyone else but have become routine for Shay. If we can get back into the dressing room having held them scoreless, we'll figure out the second half then.

Six minutes before half-time they score. It's a mess of a goal with people being beaten and players getting pulled out of position. The scorer is Patrick Mboma who has been on loan with us at Sunderland for the past few months. Of all people, Patrick should have had no surprises left for us, but he controls and slots home after lovely work from his strike partner Etu. Almost immediately after scoring, he controls and volleys a cross from Geremi but puts it over the bar this time. We are struggling. At half-time we come into that huge dressing room and look at each other. What's going on?

Mick posts two words on a big clipboard – no regrets. That's the theme. Let's go out and do what we do best. He makes a tactical change, taking off Jason McAteer, bringing on Steve Finnan at full-back and moving Gary Kelly up to the right side of midfield. Jason has had a miserable half. He says his knee wasn't right. The second half doesn't start too well, either. About five minutes into the half, Mick tells me we are going for it. We aren't getting at them at all, and I have to go on. I'm delighted. While I'm getting ready, Ian Harte makes a mistake but fortunately Geremi mishits his shot slightly. Mick shouts at me to hurry it up.

Shay kicks the ball out from Geremi's wide and we equalise straight from the move. Kevin Kilbane crosses, their defence clears poorly, and Matt Holland sweeps in a lovely half volley, another for his scrapbook of stunning goals.

I sit back down again. I have the feeling that I might get on if we have to try to win the game in the last ten minutes. There'll be nothing doing before that.

We are marauding now. This big strong African team, who were muscling us out of it earlier on, are being brushed aside. Kevin Kilbane has pushed up and is having a wonderful game now that he isn't having to come back and fetch the ball in defensive positions. Ian Harte is more adventurous than before and their five-man midfield is beginning to look cramped and rigid.

Mattie Holland is manoeuvring and engineering; the two boys up front are ducking and diving. I never get on. We take one all; we settle for that, happily, greeting the final whistle with joy. The party is about to get going, I'm grabbing a couple of players to hug, when I feel a big hand on my shoulder – drugs test, please. Richard Dunne and I, and two Cameroon players, go off for a urine and a blood test.

They hand me a beaker, bring me into a cubicle and say now fill it. The tester's eyes are sixteen inches from the point of action. I'm frozen. Finally, I close my eyes, put my arm against the wall, pretend I'm in a pub toilet and get a trickle going – just make it.

By the time I get back to the dressing room, everyone is on the coach. Johnny Fallon, our kitman, is the only one left. Eamon Dunphy is writing Roy's autobiography and has become his most ardent supporter and mouthpiece. We don't know if it's true or not but apparently he's been on television wearing a tie in the Cameroon colours. It sounds hilarious. When I get to the bus, there's more. Eamon has said that Ian Harte got cramp in the second half and that this proved our training has been inadequate. We've just played the strongest team in Africa off the park in the final half-hour. I look around at the lads. Suddenly, it's all too funny. I realise that whatever modicum of impact Eamon's words ever had on the team is gone now. He's a figure of fun for us. We roll towards the airport. We have a chance now. That's all we wanted. It's on to Tokyo.

Stan, sitting beside me on the plane, says that the past three weeks or so have just disappeared. When we get off the plane at Narita Airport, Germany are 6–0 up on Saudi Arabia in the day's other group game. By the time we get to the New Otami Hotel in Chiba, a concrete wasteland just outside the city, Germany have won 8–0. We look at each other and laugh again. A one-all draw doesn't look so glossy now. Welcome to the World Cup. It's game on.

The first time I snapped a cruciate the world became a lonely place quicker than you could turn off the light in a room. In 1993, very few people made it back from cruciate injuries. The second time, it was just depression. I'd played seven games for Sunderland. I'd been a flop. I knew exactly what lay ahead.

Peter Reid had made me the club's record signing. It seems strange to think that now. Record signing! Peter has always believed in me, sometimes more than I have myself. I'm not sure why. I'm just glad and grateful.

I remember playing Peter when he was with Everton, the year they won the League. Wayne Clarke scored for them when John Lukic made a mistake. Arsenal were top at the time and looking good. It was my first full year under George. Everton went on a run from then and won the League. We crumbled and finished fourth, I think.

Peter went to QPR and I played against him again. Trevor Francis was in charge and there was talk that they were interested in me, but eighteen months or so later Manchester City came in. Peter was player-coach at City when I arrived. He ran into me on the first day, took me aside and said he remembered playing against me for QPR when I was at Arsenal.

'You battered us that day,' he said.

'Yeah?'

'I went in and told Trevor Francis to sign you, and he wouldn't.'

Anytime I've met Trevor Francis since then, he has said he thinks he was mad not to sign me – nice to hear but not the point. It proved something to me about Peter's sincerity, his basic decency. He's been a pleasure to be around all these years. The player you remember is the manager he became, hard-working and honest.

I've had one decent row with him down through the years. I got sent off against Boro when I was playing at Manchester City. We'd played at Ayresome Park, a bleak place at the worst of times. It was dank and foggy and hard. Early on, Paul Lake was the victim of a bad tackle. Paul was just back from another gruelling reha-bilitation and we'd done a lot of the work together.

When I got to him, he was in agony. I could see his knee coming out of the side of his leg. It was just a horrible sight. I called the physio on and because of the nature of the injury, and because I knew what Paul had been going through, I was a little wound up about it.

A few minutes later, we had a corner kick. The ball was cleared and I chased after it. Paul Wilkinson had dropped back to mark me and he tripped me. Splat, I went face down in the mud. I don't have a trip-wire temper or anything like it, but I was mad. I pushed him with an open hand, high on the chest.

We wound up losing. I knew Peter wasn't pleased. He'd lost Paul Lake and now I'd got myself sent off.

Back in Manchester, we were dropped off at a services area on the M60. We had to walk across a footbridge to get to our cars. Peter was about thirty yards behind me. There were people about but suddenly he shouted after me, 'By the way, you're fined two weeks' wages.' I called back to him that he could shove it.

I thought Steve Lodge, the referee, was wrong to send me off, still do. I told Peter so but he didn't care. I told him again; no change. Two weeks' wages hurt bad. For four weeks I couldn't kick a ball. I was blaming him and he was blaming me. I sulked for a month. Then I scored a goal and we were great pals again. It's in and out, up and down.

When I hit a dry run at City, he was under pressure to drop me but he didn't. Up the road, Mark Hughes had hit a dry run with United and he'd been dropped. Still Peter stuck with me.

So when he signed me from City not long after the nightmarish experience in Malaysia, it just added to the amount I owed the man. I went to Sunderland determined to make the move something more than a stepping-stone to retirement.

Early returns were all right. I came on as sub against Leicester, but then Steve Lodge, the same referee who'd sent me off against Boro, disallowed a goal. I played in the win against Forest at the City Ground and scored two. So far so good.

I had the feeling that I was winning over the Roker Park scep-
tics. Then came a game against West Ham at home and it was
live on TV, which always amplifies things, especially if you are a
striker. Score and they show it again and again in slow motion
till even you can't believe you were that good. Miss and . . . well,
I missed a sitter in the second half, which would have won the
game. So it was back to square one. I played badly again in our
next away game and by the time Coventry came to Roker Park I
had a lot to prove.

During the first half, Liam Daish challenges me from behind,
not hard but just enough to topple me. Again my studs are caught
in the ground as I go down and I snap my other cruciate.

It had to be Liam. We'd got sent off together in New York that
summer. I'd roomed with him a couple of times on trips. His dad
was a sailor and as a result Liam has a big repertoire of sailing songs;
makes him good company on a night out. Now he's getting a yellow
card and I'm rolling in agony on the ground. He's leaning over me
shouting furiously, 'C'mon, you cheat. Get up, you big cheat.'

I'm not paying any attention. I know that it's serious. The sensation was slightly different from when I did the other leg and for a
while I cling to the hope that this time it's a cartilage problem. I'm
carried to the sideline and try to stand but it goes again. I'm
stretchered down the tunnel. The first door on the left is the treatment room. It's nearly half-time and soon I hear the clacking of
studs down the concrete path to the dressing rooms. Suddenly, Liam
comes bursting in and gives me more. 'You cheating bastard,' he
shouts. I'm in too much agony to respond. Somebody drags him
out.

I went for a scan and by the Monday it was confirmed – another
cruciate.

Two quick thoughts. The last words that Mr Dandy had said to
me were, 'See you when you do the next one.' And I remember
thinking, Heh heh, I bet Daishy will be sorry when he hears this!

A week or two later, Liam Daish did his own cruciate. He never made it back. The injury finished him. I haven't seen him since.

I've been lucky to live out my boyhood dreams. Playing in the World Cup was one; playing in Croke Park was another. Now, as I get older, I return to horses.

When I was a kid, my dad brought me racing often. We never missed a meeting at the old Phoenix Park course. We went to Leopardstown, sometimes to Fairyhouse. I loved the colour, the sense of excitement, the idea of betting and the feel of being around horses. The first bet I can remember placing was on the Grand National. I backed L'Escargot to win in 1975, a shilling each way.

They didn't make cards with horses on them for young boys to collect but I knew them all anyway – Captain Christy, Pendil, The Dickler, Tied Cottage. I knew as much about those horses as I did about Pele, Gerd Müller, Johan Cruyff and co.

As a kid, I never discriminated when it came to heroes. I knew the faces of League of Ireland players as well as I knew their more fashionable counterparts in England. Turlough O'Connor and Brendan Bradley were big names to me. When English players came to Irish clubs for some easy money late in their careers, I took it as validation for our League. Why wouldn't they want to play at those great venues? Bobby Charlton played for Waterford, Terry Venables joined St Pats, even George Best arrived in Cork.

More exciting was the traffic going the other way. I remember Paddy Roche and Gerry Daly heading off to Manchester United. Gerry Ryan, who had been to the same school as myself, went to Derby not too long afterwards.

I had my hurling heroes, of course. Chunky O'Brien of the Kilkenny side of that era was one. I called a horse after him years later. We used to go and watch Tipp but from 1972 on, well, they were dead in the water. Limerick won an All Ireland in 1973 and I loved that team. I got Pat Hartigan's autograph one day at the

All Ireland sevens in Glenalbyn; got Joe McKenna's and Richie Bennis's, too.

On holiday in Kerry once, we called to the door of the legendary Gaelic footballer Mick O'Connell. He chatted for a while and signed my copybook. Then we drove from his place in Valentia over to Waterville where we found another Kerry legend, Mick O'Dwyer, working under a car. I remember asking him to sign my book and he came out from under the car and went in to wash his hands so he wouldn't smudge it.

Limerick haven't won an All Ireland title since then. Tipperary came back from the dead and I had to abandon my worship of Kilkenny icons. Kerry football had a short recession. Teams come and go but racing goes on for ever, timelessly. Nothing changes. Jockeys' silks aren't subject to fashion. The traditions of the race-course don't change, even the ones that bother me such as the required deference of great jockeys to know-nothing owners. Horses are something you can always come back to.

Back in the early seventies, Vincent O'Brien was winning in England. To have an Irish trainer sweep all the big races as Vincent did was a huge thing for Irish people at a time when national confidence wasn't high. I remember Lester Piggott riding for Vincent, and Pat Eddery. Grundy, The Minstrel – those horses streaked across my imagination.

There was something comforting about racing. When I first got into the Arsenal team, I sent away to join a racehorse-owning syndicate. It was a simple operation. There were fifty people in the syndicate, it cost nothing to join and £8 a week to stay in. The syndicate had one horse, a mare called Sirdar Girl. I sent off my £8 religiously. Sirdar Girl ran once and had to be put down. So that was it. I shelved the fantasy.

I never thought about that aspect of the racing business again until I won the Texaco Award for soccer in 1991. At the reception in Dublin, I ended up sitting next to the trainer Jim Bolger. Jim had won the horse-racing award that year for his achievements with St Jovite. I love talking about racing. I just sit and gather all the little crumbs of knowledge that you get when you speak with some-body who knows more about the game than you do. Jim and I stayed chatting till the early hours, Jim drinking his water, me drinking pints. By the next morning, I'd bought a horse. It wasn't the Guinness; it was the old excitement. It all came back as I was talking.

Gillian and I hadn't a lot of money – it was during the early days with Manchester City – and I was in deeper than I should have been. A horse! My first thought was how do I get my lies right?

I went home and kept the fact that we now owned a horse to myself. I'm not sure how I expected to keep it a secret for ever but it seemed like the wisest move at the time. I kept it up for quite a while.

Sam Ellis, who was coaching at City, helped me out of a hole and bought half the horse from me. Not long afterwards, the horse's training started and I got Marguerite, who is still working in Jim Bolger's place, to send all the bills to Maine Road so Gillian wouldn't find out. I was beginning to feel as if I was cheating on Gillian, with a horse.

Naturally, the cheques we had to write began to get bigger and the calls about his progress became more frequent. I changed my story. Now I was fronting for Sam. Sam really owned the horse but was afraid to tell his wife. Brilliant!

This was late autumn going into winter. By March, my lies were so convoluted I could hardly keep track of them myself. The horse, Cois na Tine, was running on St Patrick's weekend and City had no game. My lie wasn't just eating me up, it was ruining the whole reason for having a horse in the first place. There's no point in having one if you never get to see it. Anyway, if the horse was ever any good, there'd be no way of keeping it a secret. I came clean – Gillian, I've been seeing a horse. Our horse!

All hell broke out. We came to a compromise. Gillian would come to the race. If the horse was a dud, we'd sell it immediately. If it went well, we'd keep it. I was banking on Gillian falling in love with the horse.

We spent the day in Jim Bolger's private box, feeling a long way out of our depth. We couldn't eat for nerves. We were brought down to the stables to see the horse, and watched him being led into the parade ring where we met the jockey, Christy Roche. I couldn't believe the dreadful hat-tipping stuff. We were two professional sportsmen and I was getting 'Hello, Mr Quinn' from this wonderful athlete who brings more bravery to his trade in an afternoon than a footballer does in a season. Christy said he'd be going for it. We were glad to hear it.

I was white with fright by the time we got back to the box. We went out to the balcony to watch the race about five minutes before the off and just stood there impatiently, too embarrassed to go back in. Cois na Tine started slowly but Christy got the horse going. The businessman Michael Smurfit and his wife were there, too, and Gillian began roaring Cois na Tine on, punching Michael Smurfit in the back as she did so. Our horse won.

We were presented with a trophy by the American ambassador, Jean Kennedy Smith. Gillian was hooked.

Cois na Tine ran again ten weeks later at Naas. We were in Barbados on a special bargain holiday we'd picked up. Gillian was three or four months pregnant and not feeling the best. To my delight, the hotel was, for some reason, full of jockeys – Steve Smith Eccles, Richard Dunwoody, Graham McCourt. I remember telling them that I had a horse running that day.

'Another victim!' they said.

'No, this is a good horse.'

'Don't be stupid, man. Get rid of it. It'll eat up every penny you have.'

I went upstairs to listen to the race. Jim's brother Paddy held a phone up for the commentary to be broadcast down the line to Barbados. The horse won by six or seven lengths. I danced down the stairs like Fred Astaire to tell the lads. Gillian had a celebratory Disprin.

With two races and two wins, I was feeling pretty pleased with myself. Somewhere down the road, when it all ends, horses will be my transition into middle age. The real world? They'll never take me alive!

When I have thought about it at all, I have planned out this World Cup with us losing to Germany. In my mind's eye, I don't see us beating them. Maybe it's the era I grew up in. I wasn't reared to think of Ireland getting results against Germany. They fulfil all the clichés – ordered, efficient, hard-working.

They have had a disastrous qualifying campaign on the way here and although people say they are finished and they are toothless, I know they are stung. I've been watching World Cups since I was a kid and I know that sometimes the Germans don't send great teams but they always send good teams.

It seems they have discovered a decent forward. Miroslav Klose scored a hat-trick of headers against Saudi Arabia and now he's the tournament's leading scorer. Oddly enough, he is one of our best hopes now. They'll be pleased with themselves about how much they won in the air against Saudi Arabia and they might fancy trying the same thing against us.

As for ourselves, we sit around the hotel and quietly speculate who'll play against Germany. I didn't get to play in the first game but I'm slightly encouraged to know that I was close to it, that I was in Mick's thoughts as part of Plan B.

Against Cameroon, none of us foresaw the way Mick made the changes. We are bowled over by young Steven Reid who came on with about a quarter of an hour left and looked strong and confident. He thumped one long-range free kick that the Cameroon goalie just tipped over the bar; otherwise we'd have had a goal of the tournament contender.

The most critical press reaction has been about Ian Harte. None of us really see why. Ian had a tough first half but after that things changed. So we have done a protection job on Ian at training. Before he came here, Inter Milan made an enquiry about him and it has ruffled him a bit. We don't want people messing with his head now. If one part of us is hit, we're all hit, so we gee him up in training, we keep talking to him.

What people don't see with Ian is the contribution he makes when we attack. His diagonal passes are perhaps our best attacking weapon. He sets the team up from the halfway line, knocking good balls for players to run on to.

For most critics, he's not physical enough. I can see him developing into a player with the skills of Roberto Carlos but at the moment he's not in that neighbourhood in terms of reading and strength.

When we play practice games, I know Ian will never hurt me. With any other defender, if I want to get a header I know he'll bury himself into me. Ian is too nice, which is a pity because I think he's capable of being world class. Now the media are calling for him to be dropped but we know he never will be.

He's a funny guy. I see Mick or Taff saying something to him about defending and two minutes later he'll have curled a thirty-yard free into the net and forgotten everything.

We thought the press would be talking about Jason. He had a poor game and he's down on himself, blaming the knee injury he picked up in the friendly against Hiroshima. What Jason needs is constant encouragement. He responds well when people believe in him and tell him that they do. Cut him dead, as Blackburn Rovers did for a while, and he just withers.

So we're keeping Hartey and Jason happy and it's dawning on us that since we haven't beaten Cameroon, we now need a result against Germany.

I think before the Roy business, most of us thought it would break down differently. We'd beat Cameroon, lose to Germany, beat Saudi Arabia. Now we've got to worry that maybe Germany will beat all of us and it will come down to how many goals ourselves and Cameroon can put past the Saudis.

I know one thing. My hunger to be part of the action is growing every day.

The day after the Cameroon game, our first day in Chiba, Mick took those of us who hadn't played down to the training ground, a trip of about a couple of miles up the coast. We had the hardest session of the whole trip. It lasted almost three hours. He killed us.

Mostly it was one on one. Mick would throw a ball at me and there would be a defender behind me. I'd have to use all my strength to keep the defender from getting the ball and then I'd have to turn and take him on. A session can last three or four minutes a go. I was marking Kenny Cunningham and Andy O'Brien alternately and they were like leeches on my back. I went back to the hotel, got my ice on and fell asleep without even a shower. Next thing I knew, Kevin Kilbane was waking me for tea.

I have to get on to the pitch against Germany – can't do another of Mick's special sessions for the subs.

CHAPTER FIFTEEN

TWO LEGS BAD

And Dutch is dead on his feet and all the rooms they smell like diesel and you take on the dreams of the ones who have slept here.

TOM WAITS, *9TH AND HENNEPIN*

We're an easy access team, user friendly, open all hours. By the time the German game rolls around the punters are practically living with us in the New Otami Hotel. This contact between the team and the fans has always been one of the positive aspects of playing for Ireland. The fans treat us an extension of the holiday experience. We're like a theme park to them. They watch us train and scoot back to the hotel to greet us as we get off the bus. When we come back from matches, they'll be up for a sing-song with us.

Our families are here and our hosts have built a tented Irish village at the back of the hotel. It's home from home.

We do our tactical training every day and at the back of our minds is the feeling that we might be able to force something from the German game on Wednesday. When we train, we simulate other sides. Sometimes Mick will make a full-back gallop forward, leaving gaps for our midfielders to exploit. Sometimes he'll play with six guys going forward at us, pretending to be the opposition attacking. We cope with the situations but in our secret moments we wonder what it all means in terms of who will play.

We are hoping that the Germans will play Carsten Jancker and Miroslav Klose up front against us instead of using the more sprightly Oliver Neuville. Jancker and Klose are big men and the temptation for the Germans will be to play the game at altitude although Jancker is very limited and he can't jump. Klose has had things easy so far in this World Cup. Stan, who in my view, up until five years ago couldn't really head the ball (in fairness, he was a left-back), has taught himself how to be a tough centre-half. He'll have poor Jancker for breakfast. Gary Breen is having a fine tournament. I fancy us to contain them.

For us, there's been a sudden and exciting change of pace. The World Cup has exploded. There is football on the television all the time and watching it is a dislocating experience. It's as if the World Cup is taking place somewhere else. But on Wednesday night, we will be appearing in it again. Occasionally, we see preview packages of our upcoming game. Mattie's goal against Cameroon crops up, Steven Reid's free kick. In a five-second trailer we look world class.

There is a mini media storm the day before the game because we change our minds about spending that night in Ibaraki, where the game is to be played, and opt to drive down on matchday instead. It's seventy minutes away, tops. Kick-off is at 8.30 in the evening. Staying in Chiba allows us to train. But by now, some journalists have to include the words 'farce' and 'shambles' in their reports. It's all quiet on the Roy front and the daily dispatches from training must need the odd bit of spice. We're happy and comfortable.

Before we leave for Ibaraki, we have a team meal and a little ceremony. This evening will be Stan's one hundredth game in an Irish jersey. He's well into record territory but to play Germany in the World Cup finals on the occasion of your one hundredth cap, well, Stan isn't one to make a fuss but you can tell that sometime down the road he'll look back on today and smile.

The team has had a collection and Gillian and my mother went out this morning and bought him a watch. At the end of the meal, the youngest player in the squad, Steven Reid, presents Stan with the watch and makes a speech.

It's a good, happy moment. It's not just a celebration for Stan's one hundred caps, or because this is his third World Cup and he's the only Irish player ever to have done that, or even recognition of the fact that he has played in every game Ireland have ever played in World Cup finals. It's for all those things but it's also for his contribution this time. He has been outstanding on and off the pitch for us here.

Of the three senior players, Alan Kelly, Stan and me, who have been dragged into the centre of the Roy fuss and all the allegations that followed it, Stan was the only one who knew he'd be playing, that he'd be needed on the pitch from the start. When you get to our age, it's tough enough to get yourself right for big games without worrying about how the other twenty-one players are managing and without having to soothe your family at home when they're upset by the things that a former team-mate is saying about you.

Stan is an old-school professional. He doesn't talk about the team outside the team. He's not happy unless he's playing. He started this World Cup qualifying campaign out of the team and seemingly with no way back in. Now he's captain and one of our players of the tournament. He'll quit when this is over but he'll quit right at the top.

He's funny, too. Stan is one of the oldest graduates of the card school. He plays hearts with Kenny Cunningham, Dave Connolly and Dean Kiely. The way hearts works is that the person who is coming last drops out and a fifth player has to come in. More often than not it's Dave who drops out and he always gets in a little jab as he goes. Stan can drop him with a one-liner like nobody else can.

Stan manages it all with his usual gruff humour. We love the old guy!

In Sunderland, I suppose because they scarcely knew me, Nigel Carnell, the physio, let me do my own thing when it came to getting better. This time round a local renowned surgeon called Mr Weeber operated on me, doing a perfect job, but months afterwards, for some unaccountable reason, I was still not right. I'd been going to a gym in Durham five nights a week, working out with Gordon Ellis, another club physio. He did the full rehab with me but it looked as though it was a waste of his time and mine.

My knee wasn't playing ball. There was no sign of it getting better. The crowd at Sunderland had given up on me. They'd put money on me and I'd pulled up lame. Only Peter Reid believed that I'd pull through and play again.

I needed to believe it. If I had to give up, my financial situation was not great. Insurance wise, well I wasn't properly insured. My pension had accrued to the extent that the bills would be paid at home and the house paid for, but I had another house half built in Kildare. Sunderland had to pay me six months' wages if I finished and I hadn't gone there on great money. I'd nothing else laid away. I wasn't yet thirty years old, I hadn't made a lot of money, I hadn't won a lot of things. It had been a good time, though, and if I could have asked for one more thing, it would have been a little bit more time.

Another lucky break is what I needed, another go at it. If I could get back and wring a season's worth of good times out of it, I'd appreciate it all the more. But my knee wasn't cooperating. So I pushed the button. Gordon Taylor sent me the requisite forms and a note wishing me well. It seemed all over.

However, I played in the first home game of the new season, 1997–98, against Manchester City and scored. We won. I went with Ireland to play Latvia and it went all right. But the next Saturday I was poor and it was the same the next week.

Our fourth game of the season is against Norwich and I'm not up to it. I am desperate not to play but Peter wants me to. I tell him that I'll try but I can't run. My leg is gone. During the match, I'm put through one on one with their keeper and find that I have no power in my leg. I just trickle the ball to him. I can feel the hostility in the stadium. I'm booed off the field. It's an empty, hollowed-out feeling. If football is going to end this way, I'd prefer to quit now.

Afterwards, I'm making my way to the car with Aisling and Gillian, down and not good company, when I get spat at. He's a nasty piece of work who comes towards me and spits at me. There's an instinct, just for a second, to go for him physically but a player can't win in that sort of situation. 'Footballer Attacks Fan' is always going to be the headline; 'The Shit Hit The Fan' they'll say. We get into the car and sit there for a while, frozen.

We played Oxford a few days later. We won but I got subbed and as I went off the Sunderland crowd cheered. I couldn't run, couldn't do anything rigorous. My knee was tattered – no power, lots of pain. The crowd were on my back all the time.

I had another orthoscope on the Monday but nothing showed up. In desperation, Neil Medcalfe, our new physio, sent me down to Yorkshire to see a Mr Bollan. He prodded and poked and said he wanted to open my knee there and then. Why? I had my retirement forms. I had a job with an Irish newspaper lined up. I was resigned to life after football. But when Mr Bollan said he wanted to get his scalpel busy right then, hope rose irresistibly. OK, once more. Open it up. I'm nothing if not an optimist.

His hunch was right. I was suffering from something away from the cruciate. Mr Weeber had done a great job on that, but unconnected to that, two bones had fused together. Mr Bollan unstuck them the next day and put me in plaster for four weeks. When the plaster came off, I started to run. Wow! I'm like a foal. I'm running!

When it came to my first game back, against Forest at home, the mood towards me had changed. People had read in the papers that I was fighting my way back and they gave me a decent reception even though I hadn't played since I was booed off the last time. Here they were, cheering me on as if it had never happened, or as if one of us had been drunk at the time. I was only on for the last three or four minutes but I laid on the equaliser and nearly scored. I was quietly pleased.

A few weeks later we went down to QPR. I hit the bar three times, had two goals disallowed and got the winner near the end. I wanted the game to go on for ever. Bobby Saxton, our coach, said to me afterwards that no centre-forward in Europe had played as well as I had for the team that day. I don't know how he knew, but I loved hearing those words.

The thrill hadn't gone. This surprise Indian summer at the end of my career would keep getting sweeter and sweeter. At home to Port Vale the next month, I scored the best goal I've ever scored, had one of those moments of redemption that stay for ever. Somehow (Mr Bollan hadn't been able to give me great pace) I beat the offside trap and was one on one with the keeper. I got to the ball first, twenty-five yards from goal, and for some reason I just chipped him – one touch and I ran to the crowd before the ball had even gone past the keeper. I just knew. All the faces are staring at me in horror at the embarrassment I'm about to bring on myself, and I'm standing there with my arms in the air, grinning like a Cheshire cat, until the ball hits the net and the place goes wild.

That's the secret life of footballers. You can play in a couple of World Cups and on a handful of really big occasions, and the moment you'll treasure is a goal against Port Vale when all the storylines and all the skills intersected at just the right point.

Sunderland has been a joy ever since. Kevin Phillips scored thirty-five goals that year. I got seventeen, which meant we scored over fifty between us even though I'd missed good chunks of the year.

We've been through things as a club and a community. Peter Reid saved the club from oblivion in 1995. Promotion came in 1996. Never trust the good times though. We went down in 1997. Then in 1998 our hearts were broken. We finished third in the first division.

After a bad start Peter had gambled. About two months into the season we'd lost 4–0 at Reading. We were twelfth and we were sinking. Peter's job was doing likewise. Suddenly he threw in Kevin Phillips, Jody Craddock and Darren Holloway. Our wingers Allan Johnston and Nicky Summerbee came to life. Peter was rewarded with adventurous displays and hatfuls of goals. The crowd loved it. Suddenly Peter was the messiah again.

We couldn't quite catch up though. Small things killed us. Two-nil up against QPR and Mike Sheron scored two late goals against us. We finished a point behind Boro, who went up automatically. That hurt. We had more points finishing in third place than we had the last time Sunderland won the division.

Coming third meant we were into a semi-final play-off against Sheffield United, who had finished sixteen points behind us. Try getting yourself motivated for that. We were flat and bitter and it was a struggle. The play-offs are purgatory. Fate delayed. We lost 2–1 at Bramall Lane and then came back and squeaked a 2–0 home win.

And so we had to meet Charlton at Wembley. A high noon sort of deal. Play to the death. One left standing.

Football is a game of hyperbole and exaggeration. We all buy into it. Most defeats can be turned into tragedies. Near misses can be disasters. Big crowds can be real pressure cookers. Mostly it's just football puffing itself; you can smell the marketing and the media off it.

Few things matter more though than the promotion play-offs. The end of an epic season, the promised land of the Premiership waiting just across the river. Swim or be drowned.

Back then promotion meant anything between ten and twenty million pounds to the club. It meant the difference between Premiership contracts and first division contracts to us players. It meant the difference between going to Old Trafford and going to Gresty Road to our fans.

The play-off. It's about prestige and pride and getting the reward you've worked all season for. It's about getting your shot at the big leagues. Win and you have at worst a season in dreamland. Lose and you feel the cold reality every Saturday till the following summer. Most things you play for at the end of the season are just icing on the cake. The play-off final is the whole cake.

The play-offs are about beating your own psyche. The third-placed team, as we were, are always in the toughest position. The teams who finish fourth through to sixth have won a play-off place. The team in third has lost an automatic promotion place. In our case to Boro! In the eleven seasons of play-offs before 1997–98 only one third-placed team had come through the play-offs. It's about picking yourself up, dusting yourself down and gritting your teeth. You have to keep on, keeping on.

So Charlton Athletic at Wembley. May 1998. It was all on the line. They played Robbie Williams as we walked out: 'Let Me Entertain You'. It missed the point. We'd be happy to win with a first-minute fluke. Screw the entertainment. Sunderland people believe though. They are born again. The region has been in carnival. The only way is up. Back where we belong.

Gillian and Aisling have come down to London for the weekend. They are in Trafalgar Square with the Sunderland fans jumping in and out of the fountains like merry loons. Aisling splashing about with her Sunderland jersey on. The night before the game and all of Sunderland moved down south and lived it up. We brought a party atmosphere which lasted all the way to Wembley.

We walked out as raging favourites. Why not? We've finished a couple of points in front of Charlton and we have scarcely put a foot wrong since Christmas. Perhaps Robbie Williams is right, perhaps we'll do this in style, perhaps that's the only way we can play, perhaps this is our stage.

What followed was a game for the ages.

Clive Mendonca put Charlton ahead. Clive is from Sunderland. He stood in Roker Park right through his youth. Today though he just swerves past Jody Craddock and sticks it. Bam!

In the second half I equalise. I stoop for a header and it goes in. Scoring at Wembley, you can't do it often enough. We're off. Soon afterwards Kevin Phillips scores. It's like flicking a switch. The stadium turns to delirium. We're going up. Kevin has just broken Brian Clough's post-war scoring record for the club. This is Kevin's thirty-fifth goal. We can feel ourselves being lifted into the Premiership.

The game just keeps getting faster and more frenetic though. Charlton can't understand that we have beaten them. This is our day. Mendonca scores again. So do I. We're screaming it at them now: THIS IS OUR DAY.

Five minutes from time they bundle another goal. Richard Rufus. First time he has ever scored for the only club he's ever played for. He has to do it now. Our keeper Lionel Perez has a rush of blood to his peroxide noggin. Rufus has just to head a corner into an empty net. Three goals each now.

Into extra time and the craziness it brings. Quickly Nicky Summerbee makes it 4–3 for us. Our day. Then Mendonca finishes his hat-trick and they take all the momentum back again.

Penalties!

A whole season comes down to penalties. Let Me Entertain You? Some poor sap is going to be fed to the lions now when he misses a penalty. This is too big a decision to be settled by penalties, surely.

There should be a replay, a referendum, a tele-poll. Anything but this.

Is there any wonder we don't fancy it. Our penalty takers, Lee Clark, Kevin Phillips and Darren Holloway have all come off during the game. We have to draft three new penalty takers. I have never taken one in my life. I keep quiet. I find I'm not the only one. I decide to go sixth, knowing that it will never get that far.

We got five names together: Summerbee, Johnston, Ball, Makin, Rae. Charlton's kickers scored all five.

We matched them all the way.

Suddenly they are 6–5 ahead. So, smart boy, the cunning plan has backfired. I actually have to go sixth. I have to take one kick for twenty million quid at Wembley. For all the people who splashed in the Trafalgar Square fountains and every follower that loves this club.

Strange thing. As I walk from the centre of the pitch to the penalty spot I don't feel anything. Everything is blocked out. I'm calm. I'm in a dream.

I take my run up and Sasa Ilic dives when I'm still a full three yards away from the ball. It's as if we are moving underwater. He dives one way and I have all the time in the world to switch my thoughts and roll the ball into the other corner. It feels so odd. I expect the referee to order a retake.

We are tied 6–6 now. As I walk back I can feel the tension in the place channelling through me. This is Wembley. A shoot-out. The fear hits me retrospectively. I get a chill through the body. What if I had missed it? I turn around and the ball hits the net; Charlton are 7–6 ahead.

Michael Gray goes up as our seventh penalty taker. Tenth in line if you add the three lads, Clark, Phillips and Holloway, who should have taken kicks but were off by now. Michael does what every player is told. He picks his corner and he sticks to it.

He doesn't hit it with conviction though. Ilic has the underwater experience I've just had. He sees it, dives and saves.

The fat lady sings.

What can I say, what can anyone say? Mickey Gray is from Sunderland. He went to the same school as Clive Mendonca. He stayed here in Sunderland though, and wore the red and white stripes. Now there is a huge scrum of Sunderland jerseys around him. The players are offering condolences and consolation. Peter Reid has been first to him. We stand in a knot. Tears and curses and the clicking of photographers trying to catch Mickey Gray's face.

After the game we go to the players' lounge. While we are there, Charlton come in wearing cream suits with red roses in the lapels and big smiles on their faces. We are raggle taggle and tearstained. Mickey Gray is still in pieces, resisting all sympathy. They look like winners. We feel like losers.

Aftermath. We made our way to the coach quickly. I climbed on board with Bobby Saxton. Some of the wives asked if they could travel with their husbands and mix the populations of the two coach parties up a little. Peter said it would be OK if Bobby Saxton said it was OK. As we came out the women were pushing June, Bobby's wife, forward to ask him if it would be all right. Bobby listened to the request but said no. In fact, he chased her off, scattering all the wives.

'The footballers' bus is sacred,' growled Bobby. End of story.

Mickey was still lost to the world. No give in him. We hit the motorway in complete silence. It was Bobby Saxton who came out with the quote that started Mickey on his journey back from the depths.

The club had recently received a letter of complaint from a night-club owner saying that Mickey had tried the do-you-know-who-I-am routine. So Saxton broke the tension in old footballer fashion.

'Hey, Mickey! At least next time you go there, and you say "Hey, do you know who I am?" they'll say "Yeah, aren't you the twat that missed that penalty?"'

Mickey laughed. That's the way teams pull back together. That's why footballers' buses are sacred.

We stopped in a hotel on the AI near Peterborough and Richard Ord, who had been left off both the team and the bench that day, showed us something about his inner strength. A lone voice. He started us into a sing-song and got us back into some kind of frame of mind. There is more to our lives, more than the game just gone by. There's next season, the next game. You move on.

I got home eventually, early the next morning. Strangest thing. Sunderland fans came to my door crying, something which had never happened before. Three generations of the one family came and left again, all of them crying. They just turned and went, never saw them before or since.

You move on. Mickey Gray got soccer highlights, dyed his hair that whitey-yellow. He never hid. He became an England player. He bounced back with heart and conviction. A month after Wembley we had a young blind kid came up to see us. He knew us all by our speech and when Mickey spoke he said, 'Hey Mickey, I could have hit that penalty harder than you did.'

We'd turned a corner. It was open season after that. Open season and a new fixture list waiting for us.

The next season we cruised the First Division. I got twenty-one goals in all competitions; Kevin got twenty-five. Once in the Premier League, all we heard was people saying that we were about to be found out. That season I got fourteen league goals, Kevin got thirty and won the Golden Boot award as Europe's top scorer. It kept going. The following season Kev got a total of eighteen, I got eight.

Sunderland has been a love affair. I love the people. The north-east reminds me of home. People like knowing your business but they know where the borders are. They have values and we have given them a team that reflects that.

It helps that I feel the same things as they do about Margaret Thatcher and what she did to this region. Whenever I leave this place, I won't be remembered like Charlie Hurley is remembered but I will remember it all like Charlie remembers it. When I speak to him, he talks of what he left behind up here, what he still misses. I know what he means.

And there's Peter Reid. Peter came here late in the season in 1995 and was given seven games to save Sunderland from relegation to the Second Division. He did it and he's still here. He brought me here and he stopped me from quitting at a time when I was desperate to quit. He showed belief beyond the call of any manager. He kept playing me even when I wasn't fit. Peter saw in me at 80 per cent fitness more than other people have seen in me when I'm 100 per cent fit.

Peter has made my career enjoyable, successful and lengthier than it might have been. I love his approach to life and to football. He knows his players. With me, he doesn't mind if occasionally I'm not in great shape the day after the night before. He's given me confidence in my football, enough to overcome any fears and tensions. Peter almost gets upset now if nobody has reported seeing me out drinking in Durham or somewhere. He wants to know where I've been and what's wrong.

I've seen him change and mellow. He used to lose his temper more often than he does now in the dressing room. You learn that if you give him everything you have, all the commitment, the effort and the desire, he'll take a bullet for you. If he sees you going through the motions, he'll go through you. If he is under pressure, he'll savage you. He has a temper.

I can detect it now. I see the tension gathering on his face and I know when he'll break into a rant. This is when my knowledge of football grounds is great and invaluable. I am the Ancient Mariner of dressing rooms. I know the ones that have pillars and recesses. Unfortunately, there are none at Derby's new ground like there were at the Baseball Ground, but there are pillars at Chelsea and Leeds. I tuck in behind one and when Peter gets to the end of his tether, I sit there smiling to myself, content that Peter isn't eyeballing me.

These last few years have been an incredible bonus, financially and psychologically. I know my image and live within it. I act pious and humble most of the time but the ego loves it here. I love this place, these people, the bond we have. I love being recognised, being well known without being a star. The best has come at the end.

The game's well under way. We're flapping our wings but we're just not flying today. Germany have set themselves out just as we wanted them to, we're confident and eager, yet in the first half they score with just about their only real chance. It's not that they've been bad, we just have this sense that we've let them have the ball and make the rhythm of the game.

They got their goal on twenty minutes. Klose got away without being picked up properly and headed his fourth in two games.

At half-time we decide to accentuate the positive. We haven't played well but we have restricted them. This bunch do not deserve the respect we are giving them. Let's forget about the white jerseys with black trim and how intimidating they look. Let's go a step faster, a yard quicker. Let's take them on. Let's throw the bodies up to help Robbie and Damien. Before we go back out, Mick tells me to be ready, he'll be throwing me in.

He takes his time. I watched their defenders in the pre-match warm-up and would love to get among them. You can usually tell when you look at a guy how you'll do against him. Sometimes you see a sweet ball player and you know that you'll outjump him all day long. Other days you see a guy who's not the quickest but who's brave and can read a situation. He'll hit you with everything he has every time. Today I see two nice ball players designed for an era other than the one I grew up in.

I grew up in the time of Briggs and Shotton. Back in the Arsenal days, we were playing Oxford one time and they had two centre-halves, Briggs and Shotton, who had a reputation like the Jesse James Gang. That was bad enough but for corners I was told to mark Billy Whitehurst who was madder and badder than Briggs and Shotton put together.

I remember picking him up for the first corner at the near post and he hisses at me, 'Whoever marks me at this corner is going to regret it; I'm going to smash them. If you want it to be you, then stay here.'

I'm the sort who's afraid to go into a dark room, so I catch David O'Leary's attention and I wander off as casually as I can. 'Dave, Dave,' I shout. 'You pick him up for this one.'

I played when Terry Hurlock ran the manor at Millwall. We played against them when I was at City and I remember Hurlock chasing Michael Hughes around the place while the game was going on. He was like a greyhound coursing a rabbit and while the chase was on they seemed to exist outside of the match altogether.

Finally, with little more than a quarter of an hour left, Mick calls me from the bench. I'm itching to be in this one. Robbie and Damien are beginning to play very well up front but we're not getting through to the territory just in front of their goal. Gary Kelly comes off and I'm on. It's a tactical switch. We're throwing the kitchen sink at them.

When I come on to the pitch I ask the lads at the back to look up and notice where I am. Special words for the full-backs – you can hit it early but look for me. I'm the tall, lanky one and it's supposed to come off my head and in behind the German lines. Simple. Look for me, I'll get my head to it and send it on.

Suddenly, we're getting some joy. The German centre-halves are barking at each other. A forward loves that sound. Oliver Kahn is roaring at them from the German goal. Kahn has been brilliant all day long. We're surprised to see him so excited.

They've given up on the idea of scoring another goal. They've hauled off the wretched Jancker, who has spent most of the afternoon whinging, and they've taken Klose off, too. They've added another midfielder and left the elderly Bierhoff up front alone.

I say to Robbie that maybe something is about to give here. I just have that sense. I almost play Robbie in, he spins his man but I've put it a yard ahead of him. The next one comes down a little behind me, I kill it and want to whip it but I slightly mishit it. If I'd put it in the other corner, it would have been better, much better. I don't know, though. Kahn seems so good, so on top of us.

Just at the start of the second half Kahn made a wonderful save from Damien and it looks as though that moment might define the whole game. Kahn is so confident and when he comes to make a smothering save he looks huge and aggressive. He makes the goal look like the one we use in five-a-side games. Damien's chance has been our best of the game. Even though we have them pinned back now, we're not cutting them open. Time is galloping past. You can feel the anxiety. The bench is screaming at us, the crowd are on edge. Tick tick tick . . .

We're into injury time. Please let something fall for us. Please. Steve Finnan, who has held his place at full-back, comes out with the ball. He's composed and cool, as he always is; he deals with everything as if he has ice in his veins. He sends a nice angled ball towards me. I've been through this with Robbie a thousand times on training grounds. He knows where I'm going to put it and he gets there on time. My part is done. It's all down to the kid now.

Robbie controls my headed pass exquisitely and the ball is his. From the side I can see Ramelow, the big German centre-half, coming in to kill him. Ramelow has this desperate look on his face. It would be better for him to take Robbie out than suffer the wrath of Kahn for not getting there. But Robbie is too quick and he sticks it past Kahn. The keeper gets some glove on it but the net bulges and the response in the ground is electric, deafening.

Robbie somersaults in celebration, as he usually does, and we pile on to him. Everyone is off the bench; above us there's a wild noise, an endless cheer. Ask me to pick and I'd say it's the best Irish World Cup moment ever – it's some kind of wonderful right there, a miracle in injury time in Ibaraki. We stay in a celebratory heap until Richard Dunne throws himself on us from about six feet away and we begin thinking of the little injuries we carry. What about my back? Better let me up . . .

Thankfully, the final whistle goes and we are off again. We run everywhere, darting off in different directions like twenty-two fire-works. For ten minutes almost, we carry on as if we have just won the World Cup.

This is the magic moment that every World Cup should have. Nothing I've experienced with Ireland before has been as intense as this. We've never scored a last-minute goal before to save ourselves. Typically this team has given them away. Robbie scoring, the final whistle, the noise in the stadium – it's the start of something. Damien Duff and Robbie Keane will be remembered for this game as clearly as Don Givens is remembered for the hat-trick against Russia nearly thirty years ago.

The interaction between ourselves and the crowd is a celebration in itself. To some extent or other, everybody has been through the Roy nightmare. Now it's truly over. There's no need for us to tell our weary selves that we should go and wave at the crowd from duty. We can't tear ourselves away from them.

Last February, Mick told me that he wanted me to be ready at the end of the season, that if I went to the World Cup it wouldn't be as a starter but he might just want me to come on and make one flick for Robbie. In the dressing room afterwards, that conver-sation floods back. Whatever mistakes Mick may have made along the way here, I hope I haven't been one of them.

Our attack on the racing world continued and for a while it looked as though Cois na Tine would earn us all a cushy retirement.

His third race was in Leopardstown, a listed race. He led, got passed half a furlong out and Christy Roche got him back up and just about threw him over the line. The commentator, Dessie Scahill, noted, 'Cois na Tine getting back up, as brave as a lion, nearly as brave as his owner.' I remembered the Oxford game and thought, with embarrassment, that the poor horse deserved better commendation than that.

We went to the Orchard Inn on the way back with Sam and his wife Helen and Christy Roche. Three wins out of three races. If only I'd thought of becoming a racing tycoon earlier in life.

His fourth race was a group three. By now we thought we were invincible. A guy called me and offered £150,000 for the horse. The condition was that he was not to be run at the weekend. I talked a good game. 'Well, it's either bought by then or we run it,' I said.

'OK,' he said. 'We'll get the money. And we'll have it tested by a vet tomorrow.'

Then I had a crisis of confidence. I have to discuss it with Gillian and Sam. I'm afraid to ring Jim Bolger. If a trainer has just done well for you, bailing out on him straightaway seems like bad manners.

We rang Christy Roche instead. Our share of £150,000 was more than we could have dreamed of at the time. We had a mortgage of about £100,000. I was earning £1,200 a week. The horse had cost ten grand and we were paying for half the training. The offer was too good to turn down but we were a little in love with the horse. We called Christy, hoping to be talked out of it.

'Don't sell him,' Christy said. 'I'll win on Sunday.' Right, Christy. We called the man and cancelled the deal.

The day before the race, Jim Bolger rings up and says he has a filly owned by Noel Keating, Ballyket Nancy, running in the race. He thinks this horse will win and he wants Christy to ride that. He says we're not to be disappointed, he's trying to get our horse a bit of black type, which means that if he finishes in the first three, it would add to his value. He says again not to be disappointed. We are devastated. Christy told us he was going to win. Now he's on a different horse.

I rang Christy. He said he was riding ours, he thought it was a better horse. I found out later that Jim and Christy had fallen out. In the end, Kevin Manning rode the filly for Jim Bolger.

Cois na Tine won the race and broke the track record. We were thrilled. Four wins out of four starts made him one of the top-rated two-year-olds in Ireland.

The man from the week before called again. He'd be able to get a bit more – £180,000. Cois na Tine had already won us £40,000 in prize money. Our eyes were bulging. We called Christy. The voice of caution came down the line again – 'No, wait. He's worth more.' The next bid was £200,000. 'No,' said Christy, 'wait.' Christy advised us to wait for one more bid and then put an end to it. The man offered £250,000. This time Christy said, 'Take the hand and all of him.' So we cashed in and I thought for a while I knew whatever there was to know about horses. Cois na Tine went off to the west coast of America.

The following year we were offered Cois na Tine's full sister, Eva Luna, for £50,000. We fancied ourselves this time, though, and turned it down. Eva Luna was far more successful than Cois na Tine and Jim reputedly sold a half share in her for £400,000 two months later. By then she was the top two-year-old in Europe and I was learning fast.

We bought another horse, Raghida, and we were off. We kept half the money from Cois na Tine to put back into horses. By the time I was injured for the second time, horse racing was all that I had to keep me occupied. We formed a syndicate, Sporting Quest, and at one stage bought eighteen yearlings. We named them all after Irish sporting heroes. There was Chunky O'Brien and another hurling related nag, The King of Cloyne (for Christy Ring, the hurler from Cloyne). The King of Cloyne was a success

– bought for £17,000, ran twice and sold for £120,000.

We had Hoppin Higgins. We bought her at Goffs where, a little while earlier, Alex Higgins had hopped around at the Irish Open with one foot in a cast. She cost £10,000 and we sold her for £120,000. We had the Chairman of the Boards (Eamon Coughlan), Melbourne 56 (Ronnie Delaney), Supersonic Sonia (Sonia O'Sullivan), Captain McBride (Willie-John, and just as slow), Heffo's Army (Kevin Heffernan), Clear Round Macken (Eddie Macken – the thing couldn't jump a twig), Christy Senior (we landed a fine gamble on that one) and the Clones Cyclone (Barry McGuigan).

I took a bad hit on one horse we had, The French Furze. He was running one day and I promised everyone in the syndicate that I'd get the money on for them in one lump sum so as to obtain the best price. Smart boy, I couldn't. The horse won. I'd got 5–2, a great price for a horse returned at 6–4. Unfortunately, I got only about 40 per cent on, but I decided I had to pay out everyone the full amount. What choice was there? It cost me £20,000. Generally, I'm not a big gambler and I'm a good loser but that choked me.

Running the syndicate was an exciting time with good horses always making up for the bad ones. Gillian and I were really doing it to see if it would be a viable option after football. We worked for nothing, swept along by the thrill of it. Now there are only five of us left in it and we pay somebody to look after it. The interest has waned somewhat but I still like studying the movers and the shakers. I like being around racing people, licking up the lessons from the care they put into their trade.

We have a horse at the moment called Halmahera. He's a seven-year-old I bought into and so far we've been a little unlucky with him. He's finished second in the Stewards' Cup at Goodwood three times. I've backed him a few times, which I shouldn't do. It has been getting to the stage where he owes me, big time. But luck always changes and just recently he obliged at Doncaster – and, yes, the money was down.

Racing is an enclosed world, like soccer. It has its own history, stories and inner universe, and its own archaic systems. There'll be one hundred million pounds bet on a Grand National and jockeys will get £40 after tax for riding in it. Bookies are protected at the expense of stable staff and the welfare of horses. I don't know how they live with that.

The syndication business is a huge plus for the sport. It means that people on ordinary incomes can be involved. It gets away from the idea that racing is a rich person's plaything.

In Irish racing, there has traditionally been a West British element who nauseate me. They have alienated people and prevented the man on the street from making it his sport. Lately, though, racing in Ireland is starting to become really enjoyable. It has come on leaps and bounds, and for that we can be particularly grateful to Jim Bolger. He took those people on, ultimately to his detriment. He should have trained for the Sheikhs, for Coolmore, for the best owners in America. His outspokenness and his willingness to stand up to the exclusionary element in racing has cost him. But finally he has won; he has beaten 'The Hats' and Irish racing now finds itself in the strongest position it has ever known. There is huge prize money, vastly improved facilities and thriving attendances, the envy of Europe. And yet, maybe some day, it might even boast men without hats.

With Cois na Tine's money we bought the house in Manchester. Ideally, we should have put it all into the mortgage but the horses have always been half an adventure and half an idea that might do us for the rest of our lives after football. I'm glad we went for it and now that the end of my career is within touching distance, I know that the future has horses in it.

There are good days with the punting, too. One bookmaker in Liverpool has been paying me in instalments although things aren't going so well with another bookies' in Dublin with whom I have an account. In a funny way, it's a pleasure doing business with both. You can't shed tears over money. Last September I had a once in a lifetime day. I'd backed Tipperary every two weeks on their run to the All Ireland in 2001. Come the day of the final, Peter Reid wouldn't let me go to Dublin. He knew what it meant and he knew the state I might come back in if Tipp won, so we went to an Irish club in Newcastle, fifty yards from St James' Park. The chat started, one word borrowed another and soon I was taking bets all over the place. When Gillian saw me leap nine feet in the air at the final whistle, I think she knew it wasn't just a love of Tipp and Nicky English that was getting me off the ground.

The horses will be a theme in my life for ever I think but when the football stops the betting stops. Good horses having bad days are among the easiest ways I know to get through a pension fund quickly.

While I was injured for the second time, we were on the verge of moving back to Ireland, to a house near Naas in County Kildare, with the intention of getting into breeding. We bought twelve mares. The most we paid for one was about £5,000. The bank in Ireland put me under unbelievable pressure to retire. They wanted the insurance company payout or the house paid off. Sunderland weren't in the Premiership and I was crocked. The bank saw me as just another washed-up old footballer.

In the end, we had to sell the house, and when I recovered, we sold eleven of the mares. The mare we kept was called Bereneice and we hung on to her because she was unraced and so was her mother. There wasn't a winner in sight on the pedigree. She is a lovely, sweet-tempered horse and she has been a star producer. Her first three foals have all won races. The prices go up and up. She's paying for a lot of the mistakes we've made.

At some stage, we hope to get involved in breeding at better levels. That's the future for Gillian and I. It could be some stage soon. Saudi Arabia, after all, could be my last match ever.

✳   ✳   ✳

At dinner, Mick is clapped into the room by his players. We have already been applauded by the hotel staff when we arrived back. It's a long, long night with no curfew. The FAI have kindly booked extra rooms for the players whose wives are here. Some of us exceed the sensible limit of six pints, and sing late into the night – players, fans, officials, some journalists. Damien Duff's little brother Jayo plays the guitar with Noel O'Reilly right through.

Gillian and I get to bed at 7.30 in the morning. There's a bus to Disneyland for family trips with the kids leaving at ten. We carry our sore heads down and Disney clears it all. It feels like a real holiday, a complete break from football.

It's late when we get back. There's a buffet set out for the technical staff and their families but we get into the dining room first and eat everything in sight. Eddie Corcoran has a seizure. He's livid. There's no humouring him out of it. He just storms out.

We go for the longest sleep and next day turn our faces towards the Saudi game. We need to win by at least two goals. We have never scored more than one goal in a World Cup finals match before.

CHAPTER SIXTEEN

ON THE EDGE OF SOMETHING

I'd sawn half-way through a plank. Now I can't see my mark. It's the fate of every carpenter to fade into his own woodwork.

PAUL MULDOON, 'THE WORKMAN'S CHORUS'

Yokohama, Japan's second city, seems to be a suburb of its first city. This afternoon we drove here from Chiba through Tokyo and we didn't pass an acre of countryside in between.

It's half-time in the Irish dressing room and we are a little bit overexcited. A few of us need to be shot with tranquiliser darts. We're playing in the stadium where the final will be held. It's big and sturdy rather than impressive. Before the game, we made jokes about leaving our gear in the lockers and collecting it when we come back for the final but those jokes seem to have been made a long time ago now.

We are playing a Saudi Arabian team who have played two games and lost them both, conceding nine goals in the process. They are missing their two best players today. We need to beat them by at least two goals. We have been 1–0 up since the seventh minute but have been playing like drowsy schoolboys since then.

What a goal it was to lull ourselves to sleep with, though. Stan takes down the ball in the centre circle and sweeps a beautiful left-footed pass forty yards to Gary Kelly in the right corner of the pitch. Gary hits it first time, a looping cross back into the path of Robbie Keane and the ball is in the net before those of us on the bench can get to our feet to see what Robbie will do with it. If we get through this, that goal will definitely make the TV teasers for our next match.

After the goal, we dozed off like men who'd had a good dinner. The Saudis are playing six across midfield, choking the life out of the game and we're letting them do it. Suddenly, Mick's face has clouded over and Shay Given is pulling off saves as if he's being paid for them by the half dozen. The Saudis are coming at us in furious waves. We've been snoozing and the half-time whistle wakes us with a start. We're all excited suddenly. Is that really the time? Only forty-five minutes left?

Everyone has an opinion. The dressing room is hectic. The thought of screwing up in this game . . . there will be murder . . . there will be bad blood . . . there will be resignations and there will be firings. This could be my last memory of playing international football, catching splinters while we go out to Saudi Arabia. Of course, there is also the huge storm still waiting to spill down on everyone over the Roy Keane affair. A whimpering exit like the one we are looking at today will bring that pot pouring on to our heads quicker than you can say the word 'hat'.

So we are all in the dressing room, shouting. Everyone needs settling. Mick has a plan and he seduces us with it. For the second half, Ian Harte is gone. Kevin Kilbane is pulled back to play at left full-back. Damien Duff goes home to the prairies of the left wing. I am to come in up front. Good plan, I think. No regrets, we all say. Another spin in an Irish jersey, I tell myself. No regrets at all.

I'm doing the job today that Frank Stapleton did when I was a kid. In that long spooled out thread of Irish forwards, my name is about to disappear as Robbie Keane takes his place in the line. I reckon Robbie is better and more confident than any of us. He's a product of the modern game. His goal in the first half tonight was his second of the tournament, so already he is Ireland's top scorer ever in a World Cup finals. It won't be long till he's Ireland's top scorer ever, full stop.

The wonder of it for me is that Robbie has to exist in a different world from the one I knew when I was getting my footballing education. I trained and then I dawdled, gambled, drank, idled, slept or ate. Robbie's life is different. He'd be tabloid fodder if he let himself be. Every move, every word is examined and analysed. So for a few years now, Robbie has let his agent, Tony Stephens, handle his affairs and speak for him in public while he figures out the lie of the land.

When I was older than Robbie is now, I ran away from football altogether, just scooted out to Heathrow on Christmas Eve and went home. Two days later, desperate to undo what I had done, I was back at Highbury, lying through my teeth to George Graham. I could never have handled Robbie's roller-coaster life.

When I started off, there was something romantic about being a footballer. Clubs were connected to communities and players weren't all that different from the people who paid to watch them. I'm ending my career at Sunderland where that bond still exists to an extent, where people expect the club to have the values that they have. That link is dying, though, and when we don't perform, the crowd can often turn on us quickly. It's not pleasant but what else can we expect? The gulf between what we earn and what the man in the street earns has never been greater, the difference between our lives and ordinary working lives has never been bigger, the esteem in which we are held has never been lower.

We moan about weekly wages that are higher than most people's annual pay, we behave badly in nightclubs and bars, we let people know that loyalty is for suckers. We don't stay and fight for our places any more; our agent engineers a move for us.

We have no need to apologise for getting a fair share of the football industry's profits. That share was denied to generations of footballers before us who built the game up, but we need to think about our place in the world and where the game is going. In that respect, my testimonial and the reaction to it shocked me. Then came Roy's departure and the billions of acres of newsprint that it generated. Mostly he was demonised. In some cases, he was canonised. Hardly ever did I see the Roy Keane that I know. We are all characters in a soap opera and it's taken for granted that nobody is up to any good.

I don't know how we fast-forwarded to this strange place. Not long after I became an Irish international, I played in Frank Stapleton's testimonial game and wondered if I'd ever achieve that landmark. When I did the football world was a different place. You needed fifty games back then to be awarded a testimonial and, in truth, players needed the money they got from those games. Careers were short and retirements were long. Great footballers went through their careers without financial advice and when they finished they went off to suffer bitter twilights, cursing the game that underpaid them and then forgot them.

I know plenty of guys whose personalities just shrank when football ended for them. They started to drink too much, started to mull over the past too much, stuck doggedly with the hairstyle that made them famous and clung to all the grievances they had stashed away from when they were busy playing.

People forget so quickly. One minute you feel you're indispensable, next minute nobody knows who you are. All that grumbling about your privacy? You've got a lifetime of it ahead now. Even the best names don't last long in the memory. A few years ago, Norman Whiteside came to see us at Sunderland. Norman is a podiatrist now and he was working on a project for the FA. I've known him for a long time and we arranged to meet for a drink in the afternoon. I decided to bring the young lads Kevin Kyle and Cliffie Byrne along so they could meet with one of the great names. We were sitting in The Shakespeare in Durham when Kevin asked Norman if he had ever played football himself. Steve Bould was with us and his jaw dropped. Norman handled it better than most former players would. He asked Kevin and Cliffie a trivia question.

'Who's the second youngest player ever to have appeared in the World Cup finals?'

The boys thought about it for a minute and then said incredulously, 'You?'

'Nah,' said Norman. 'It's some bloke called Pele. I was the youngest.' Two jaws dropped.

Since the time I've had kids, I've spent the years telling myself that football won't beat me up when I'm finished. I try to keep one step ahead of the resentment and the insecurity. I've made sure that I have another life waiting to happen the day this football thing ends. I'm in football for a short while yet, but when I go, I won't be sitting here grumbling about people and the way they do things in football. When I go, football is somebody else's business. I like to think that I'll walk away and get on with something else in my life, play a little junior hurling and ease back into the world. I've put a lot of time during the last few years towards easing the blow. I'll never be as young, as fit, as well known again. It's not as if you don't see it coming.

I was on my second or third cap at the time of Frank's testimonial and I said to myself that I'd make sure I was happy on the journey to fifty games, if I ever got there, and I'd give the money away. There was no great piety in it. Testimonials were plentiful, the economy was busted. Giving the money away wouldn't be a big deal. Not being sad and bitter would be the only way to stay sane.

Time passed quickly, of course. I won my fiftieth cap in Liechtenstein and was more worried about still having an international career than I was about a testimonial. Anyway, it became apparent that summer that fifty was no longer the magic number. You now needed seventy-five caps. There was talk of legal action but I hacked on. What the hell? I was enjoying myself.

With seventy-three caps, I needed the two games against Turkey in the play-offs for the European Championship. I was named in the team for the first game, which was to be played at home, but I had to get an injection in my back. When it didn't work, I had to tell Mick that I wasn't right. My head was half filled with regret. I knew if I just stepped on to the pitch for five minutes and then played the next game the following Wednesday, I had the testimonial.

But I decided not to play. They got a late penalty equaliser, which was enough to put them through after a scoreless draw in Bursa where I made my seventy-fourth appearance. We wouldn't be going to the European Championship.

Three days later an announcement came – no more testimonials for anyone. So I thought it was gone and it didn't bother me too much. Stan and Tony Cascarino, who were just ahead of me in the queue, had a letter from the FAI guaranteeing them a joint testimonial. Behind me were guys making good money in the modern game. It was not something I worried about. It passed. Stan and Cas had a good night. More caps came my way. All this was a bonus, added-on time in a career that I had thought was over.

One day Bob Murray, the chairman of Sunderland, invited about eight of us and our wives to the races at Thirsk. He was chatting to me and asked when was my testimonial. I explained the business with the FAI, how they seemed to be leading me on all the time and then saying no. I told him that it didn't upset me much. I'd been going to give the money away anyway. Bob Murray was interested and encouraged me to look into the process again. He has been a great supporter all the way through.

First I tried floating the whole thing past an FAI official. I can't name him although I'd like to. Mark Blackbourne, the Sunderland club secretary, and I walked in through the door of a hotel room in Dublin and the first thing that Mr FAI said to us was that when this meeting ended it would be as if it had never happened. I knew there was going to be a problem. Nobody says that at the start of a meeting they expect to go well.

Mark Blackbourne had advised me not to tell Mr FAI right off that I was giving all the money away. It was a sound tactic. We'd make as much ground as we could on the basis of a normal testimonial and then clinch it. So we said that Sunderland had given me a testimonial game. Would the Irish team be allowed to play? Mr FAI said no. In fact, he said NO!

He felt it would cause legal problems with other players wanting the Irish team to play at their testimonials, kids' birthday parties and so on. Mark Blackbourne said, 'Niall is thinking of giving the money away to kids' charities. If he did that, what would you feel?'

Mr FAI was clearly a man of exemplary compassion. He had to protect the Irish players from this. They were his players apparently. 'You can't have the Irish players,' said Mr FAI. 'It can't be the Irish team. You can't have the crest. It can't be called Ireland. We will give permission for Niall to speak to the other players about it. That's all.' As if his permission was needed.

'If it's nothing to do with you,' I said, 'I don't have to ask you.'

It was uncomfortable and quickly turning bitter. We withdrew before tempers got short. I shelved the idea. Nobody would go to a game versus Mick McCarthy's XI.

Some time later, there was a palace coup. FAI coups are like buses – wait a while and another one will come along. Mr FAI was among those who rode off into the sunset. Not long afterwards I was speaking to John Delaney who had another role in the new administration, just having a mundane chat with him about players' needs, and at the end of it I floated the testimonial idea past him. I told him the history of Mr FAI and me. John was interested. He said he'd look into it and go about things in a positive way. He was as

good as his word and two weeks later he came back to me. The
idea had been passed unanimously by the FAI Council. That was
just after Christmas, 2001.

So I had the OK, I knew it was going to happen, but I hadn't
thought much about it beyond that. It made sense to have the game
in Sunderland rather than at Lansdowne Road. Probably we'd get
a bigger crowd, and there would be no rent to pay to the rugby
people. I discussed it with the PR people at Sunderland and we
decided to announce it in March or April.

Best laid plans – one of the tabloids in Ireland did a big splash
soon afterwards. In a panic, we briefly denied everything. David
Walsh from the *Sunday Times* called and we played it down again.
We didn't have dates, we didn't want a very long run-in and, anyway,
Mickey Gray at Sunderland was due a testimonial first.

David came up to see me. He made the point that if the *Sunday
Times* broke the story and got behind it, it would make a huge difference. That was on a Thursday. David said a big piece would appear
in Sunday's paper.

I alerted the publicity people at Sunderland. We'd a big game
against Fulham on Saturday and at the press conference afterwards,
we told the local journalists about it so their noses wouldn't be put
out of joint when the story appeared the next day in the *Sunday
Times*. They looked baffled, made some notes and left.

The next day I turned straight to the *Sunday Times* sports pages.
As David had said, it was a big piece. Quite pleased, I closed the
paper and there was the story on the front page as well – the first
soccer story to appear on the front page of the paper that I can
remember in a long time without the word 'arrest' in it.

That is what has been so shocking about it – the fact that such
a fuss could be made, the thought that people expect so little of
us nowadays.

Television cameras followed me to Manchester that Sunday night.
We were going down to do a little training there and when we got

to the hotel, two different camera crews filmed me getting off the bus. There were aspects of the whole thing I was uncomfortable with. For the first time in their lives, Gillian and the kids got shoved to the fore. I whored myself a little. I allowed the shots of the family. Suddenly, they were projected out front. It was a risk and something I didn't like doing but we ran with the momentum.

The game needed promoting but doing it without looking pious or sanctimonious or judgemental about other players was tough. I kept reminding people of what football in general and Sunderland in particular had given me, this lease of life at the end of my career, earnings in the last three years easily eclipsing everything I earned in the previous sixteen. I have a great and happy life and I've been lucky. I sold a horse seven years ago for a quarter of a million pounds. I haven't even spent all my career at Sunderland. I've had signing-on fees and lucrative moves. I'd be a fraud to take the money.

Two communities made the night a success. Lots of people in Dublin, where half the money went, pulled their weight. There were so many aspects. I had to go back to the ground after training every day to help organise it. We made formal approaches to customs and excise to forgo the VAT. That was £175,000. Tax? Because I hadn't served ten years with the club, I was expected to pay 40 per cent, which amounted to £400,000. The tax bill was waived.

People bought non-attendance tickets, had collections, worked for free, just sent cheques. Nobody took money for the advice they gave. We got sponsors. We got bands offering to play. Barclaycard came in and put all their workers on two hours' extra shifts for free. The company that packaged and processed the tickets did it for free. Everything to do with the game was free. People gave the best of themselves.

The local Labour Club in Sedgefield rang me up. They'd had a do at the end of the season and come up with £2,700 on the night. Barclays Bank in the village matched it. Things like that happened. Dave O'Donoghue, an old friend from Manortown United, got something going where he works. They raffled flights to the World Cup and raised £6,000. A bookie gave me a £2,000 free bet. I had 7–2 on Ireland to get past the group stage. A letter came from an old lady enclosing £5 because she couldn't afford the £10 non-attendance ticket. Aer Lingus were brilliant. They put on a Jumbo at cost price. A girl I know who runs two hotels in Newcastle offered rooms at rock-bottom prices. We got 37,000 people on the night. Together with the donations and non-attendance tickets, that equalled a crowd of 60,000.

We had a police bill and the stewards had to be paid. That was it for the expenses column. I'll be writing thank-you letters for the rest of my life.

I know it was said in some parts of the game that I was spoiling it for other players who deserved testimonials, that I was grabbing publicity. I understand that attitude. The whole thing was a humbling experience.

I was offered awards, receptions and honours everywhere. I turned down the Freedom of the City of Sunderland and the club had to ask me to please take a Fellowship from the University of Sunderland in case bad feelings were caused in the city. There was no intention to offend anybody. I was just surprised and embarrassed by the whole thing. After the life I've had, people should have said that it was the least I could have done, the smallest bit put back. How could I be given the Freedom of Sunderland when there are nurses, doctors, social workers, orderlies, teachers, battalions of people out there who do real and meaningful jobs every day of their lives? How could I swan about in front of those people?

I feel embarrassed even talking about the testimonial now. Just as sometimes over the years I've felt embarrassed telling people what I do. It's like announcing that I'm cut off from the real world.

At the start of the publicity process, I found myself in the paediatrics ward in Sunderland's hospital having my photo taken. It felt cheesy and wrong. I knew I had to do it to sell tickets but I was conscious that it probably turned a few stomachs. There are lots of people inside and outside the game of football who go about that aspect of their lives quietly without telling anyone and without offering photo opportunities to the papers. But the nature of the event needed a face. I was uncomfortable but I couldn't find a way out.

In the end, the story wasn't me or football. It was people doing things for themselves, with football and me in between.

In Crumlin Children's Hospital in Dublin, Karina Butler is in charge of the infectious diseases ward. I'm in awe of her. She devotes her life to sick children, day in, day out. Nobody writes articles about what a good human being Karina is. She works more hours in a week than I do in a month.

I don't rack myself with guilt about it all but when I read in a paper that a player is going to walk out because he's getting £22,000 a week instead of the £23,000 he reckons he deserves, I wonder what people like Karina make of us all.

The money we are paid is silly, so silly it stuns me to think of it sometimes. At Sunderland, we get a £5,000 bonus for winning a Premiership match. For every place above the relegation zone that we finish, a huge amount of money goes into a players' kitty. For the two seasons we finished seventh, we divided up a million pounds between us each time. We have the best bonus system in the Premier League and yet the newspapers suggest that Sunderland are not seen as a 'big money' club.

I've been in and out of Crumlin Children's Hospital all my life in some capacity or other. I just never took the time to notice it. My best friend Dave Whelan married his childhood sweetheart, Brenda, who works there. She arranged my first tour with Karina. I was shown to a run down pre-fab that gets used as an office most of the time. They have to take the desks out for seven hours a week because they need the space for counselling the families of kids with infectious diseases. To counsel every family in Ireland who is in this position, they had seven hours a week in this little pre-fab.

On the way back, we came through the leukaemia ward and there were teddy bears touching the ceiling. It was a sad, touching place to be but it was well equipped. It took me a short while to understand the difference. Nobody gives to the kids with HIV.

Karina won me over. She wins lots of people over. We had a golf day at Druids Glen before the testimonial. All the celebrities and players came to the charity auction afterwards and Karina spoke first. She made just about everyone in that room cry within five minutes.

First thing we auctioned was a greyhound. We were hoping for 5,000 euros. The first bid was ten. In the end, Kevin Phillips got it for 13,000 euros and he doesn't know one end of a dog from another.

Football gets a bad rap, usually from me, but there are good guys out there. Robbie Keane took a collection in the Leeds dressing room, literally passing around a hat, for Gary Kelly's testimonial. It came back with £75,000 in it. Leeds were going through a bad time and there wasn't a whisper of that. Gary Kelly made the largest individual donation to my fund, even though he was running his own charity game at the time. For my event, several players from several clubs volunteered to help and donated vast amounts of money. I'll never ever forget.

In the end, all the fuss came down to a few cheques placed into envelopes and sent in the post with the hope that they'll make a difference. The publicity was over.

Someone once said to me that I had been handed a privileged life and abused it – it was true. I came to England at seventeen and was mollycoddled. I skipped the tough apprenticeship and just got myself a living playing football. I drank, I ran wild and when somebody brought me to another club I got given even more money. It's gone on for nineteen years, lucky breaks at just about every turn, more money for playing the same game.

ON THE EDGE OF SOMETHING

I have the best life, a beautiful wife and two beautiful kids, and enough fame and money to do me. So make the next article about Karina Butler or about the people in the paediatric ward in Sunderland or about John O'Shea's work with GOAL in Africa. They are the real heroes.

In Yokohama, we are awake again; up and about and busy. Damien Duff is turning the screw on the Saudis. We are pushing them back up the field, forcing them to defend. Our defence can hit balls earlier now that I am posted up front. We just have to wait for the break.

Finally, it comes. Kevin Kilbane is chopped down when he tries to overlap on the left. Stan posts a free kick across goal and Gary Breen, who has wandered upfield, darts out of nowhere and hits it with the outside of his right boot, sort of volleys it but spins it home at the same time. We're all a bit stunned. Centre-halves aren't supposed to do these things. Gary is a bit stunned himself I think. His celebration is just to raise his arm in the air as if he is calling for offside. It's 2–0 and we're cooking.

Word is that Germany are beating Cameroon. The cards are falling our way. We aren't nervous any more. The confidence is running through us and we can feel that we are the better team, that we have earned our place in the next round.

These are the best days, when you play and things fall right and you know that, as a team, all the things you have done on the training ground are paying dividends, and all the bonding and messing around together. We're working for each other, reading each other's games. We know where everyone will be on the pitch, and we know each other's capabilities.

We're safe now from the threat of disaster, beating a team who aren't as good as us. It's taken a long time for Irish football to have that sort of confidence. Traditionally, we've preferred to creep into games as the merry underdogs and take people by surprise with our passion and our endless running. We've seldom been comfortable playing against teams we are supposed to beat. In the past, on days like today, we've often depended on Roy Keane to drive us on. Playing without Roy, we've grown up a bit.

Three minutes from the end, we score again. Duffer gets the goal that his performance deserves. He cuts in from the left as usual and thumps it at their keeper who sort of flaps it over the line into the net – not the greatest looking goal Damien has scored, but he'll take it.

Damien's goal tops off his man of the match performance. Soon after that, the referee blows for the end of the game. We stay out waving to our fans for quite a while. For many of them, this is the end of the road; they've paid to come to the first-round matches and now they'll be going home. A different contingent will fly out for the second round.

For us, the journey continues. By tomorrow night we will be in Seoul, South Korea, waiting to see which opponents the second round will bring us. Another ending postponed.

CHAPTER SEVENTEEN

CLOSING TIME

I live the life I love. I love the life I live.
GEORGIE FAME

In Seoul, we train at a military base, a good bus journey from the hotel. To get there we travel through the opulent business district out to the fringes of this seemingly never-ending city. Scenes of incredible wealth are followed by a belt full of sour poverty with beggars and people living under bridges – we sit on the bus and watch it all go by.

The training ground is fine, but not great. It's not what we had in Japan but by now we are caught up in the World Cup. This is Seoul, a real living carnival.

In a million years I never thought I'd travel from Crumlin to here. Our hotel is a Westin, right in the centre of this sprawling city and beside a massive and chaotic traffic junction called the Kwanghwamun Intersection. When South Korea plays, the inter-section is closed to traffic. Almost a million people fill the space, and all the streets around, watching the games on big screens.

On the night we arrived, South Korea were playing Portugal. Stan and I left the hotel and wandered the fifty yards or so to the intersection. The sight was incredible – hundreds of thousands of people in red T-shirts, swaying and chanting. They policed themselves. They left pathways; they tidied up after themselves. They were in rapture. They got such joy out of a football match. I don't think Stan or I had ever seen anything like it.

There was passion and pride but no negative undercurrent. You never felt threatened. You never felt worried about what would happen if Portugal tore South Korea apart. There was a sense that football is a thing to be enjoyed and celebrated, that it is an innocent thing they could all share, only a game.

We are getting close to the Spain game. We have watched them in patches and begin to turn our minds to the problems they'll pose. The press are supposing that the Spanish centre-half partnership will be Hierro and Nadal, and we read that this would be a good thing because they are old. Well, I'm old and I remember Nadal. I played against him in 1989 and I sometimes wonder if half the aches and strains I have now introduced themselves to me that day. He went through me again and again as a short cut on the way to the ball. Half the time he battered me, the other half he just played as if I wasn't there. Anybody but Nadal, please.

We are getting bored. We've been away for quite a while, in each other's company for the longest time, and the meals are always the same. Some of us developed pasta madness the other night, broke out and got steaks. On the lam, we went to a karaoke bar, too. We took the chance to get the singing without the drunkenness. Gary Kelly sang a knock 'em dead version of 'Mustang Sally' in the style of Mickah Wallace from The Commitments. He almost knocked himself dead in the process, swinging the mike up in the required style and clunking himself in the forehead.

Today at training he was wearing a baseball cap all the time to hide it. Finally, Mick Byrne, alert as usual to all our ailments, spotted the cut. He nearly had a heart attack.

'How did you do that, Kells? Come here and let me see.'

Gary makes some excuse or other and Jason McAteer, who we've taken to calling Taggart because, like the Scottish detective, he's always first on the scene, innocently contradicts him. 'Nah, that's the cut from the karaoke bar last night.'

Diversions like that get us through the days. We watch videos, we walk, Duffer sleeps, some play cards, we give press conferences. It's like a distilled version of football life. We wait and wait for the next game to come.

This thing about being well known — I use it. I can knock up a place where I know I'll be recognised and they'll get out of bed to give me a late drink. I'll never sink to the do-you-know-who-I-am routine, though — too clever for that. I ring a car hire firm, say, and they'll answer, 'I'm sorry, sir, we have no cars available.'

'Oh dear,' I'll say. 'Nothing at all? You usually help me. The name is Quinn. Niall Quinn.'

'Hold on for a second. I'll check again.'

Also I get away with things. One time, I'm speeding towards Dublin airport, late for a flight back to training in England. I'm doing a hundred flat and the blue light starts swirling behind me. It's a policeman on a motor bike.

'I'm so sorry,' I say meekly. 'I know I was going fast but I have to make training at the club. I was afraid I'd miss the flight.' I can see he knows.

'Oh, Jesus!' he says. 'Niall! C'mon, follow me.' He gives me an escort to the airport.

I live in this bubble of privilege. I can go out on the beer all day so long as I turn up at a football pitch by 10.30 tomorrow morning. I can go to bed at 1.30 in the afternoon if I'm tired. I can even complain about it all and people will listen, a thirty-five-year-old man groaning about how badly his football game went. And I'm still getting paid for all this.

When Arsenal won the League all those years ago I was on £325 a week and after tax I had damn all. Now the game is paying out like a big fruit machine and I have both hands stretched out. So has everyone. We have fifteen- and sixteen-year-old kids with spotty faces coming to Sunderland, and this past while I've been trying to assess them.

'How long is he signed for?'

'Just two years. His agent won't let him sign for longer.'

How did this happen? Where have I been? Why didn't I notice?

And the kids are different – more cocky, less awed.

When I was a kid, if I had presents for my birthday and for Christmas, that was it for the year. Always they were sport oriented gifts. My own son is the son of a footballer but nobody gives him footballs. Life has changed. There are so many more distractions. You're welded to a Game Boy as soon as you have the use of your fingers, or you're a mind-slave to the PlayStation. Football is for somebody else. If you're going to do it, it's fun maybe, but you need an agent, an accountant, a lawyer and probably some PR people.

When I ask the young lads how it's going for them, they tell me things are so-so. The agent says he can get them first-team football. Really? Yeah, he can get them a pay rise and games in the First Division. The kid is eighteen going on nineteen and thinks that's what life is about – more money and worse football.

They are at Sunderland, the club of Len Shackleton, Charlie Hurley and Charlie Buchan, and it means nothing. Only suckers spend years fighting for their place in a team, working on skills day in and day out. It makes me feel old. Did I really spend a thousand afternoons kicking a ball against the gym wall at Highbury?

There's no adventure left. Kids don't come to football thinking they've had a close escape from the real world; they come with careers and money in mind. Perhaps it's not a bad thing but the

innocence has gone. A big part of football should be about innocence and escapism and daydreams.

Before Arsenal came knocking on my door, I could see the way
my life was going to go. I'd had a half-day off from school a while
previously to attend an interview for a job as a postman. This was
Dublin in the early eighties. Every job that became available had
thousands of kids scrapping over it. I had to take a public exam
to become a civil servant to be a junior postman. There must have
been 5,000 other kids taking advantage of the half-day away from
school. It was part of the routine of the times. Thousands and
thousands of kids doing exams to get into the bank or the civil
service. Fifty of us were picked for the junior postman jobs. I was
going to be a postman. I was thrilled. I had it all planned out. I
thought to myself that if I could persuade my parents to let me
leave school early and become a junior postman, I could do my
work in the mornings and earn enough money to keep myself while
playing football and hurling to a decent standard.

The profession I ended up in hadn't changed much from the
fifties when I joined it. I went to London wide-eyed and clueless
but determined to make the most of it. Looking back, that's what
I've done. I thought being a footballer would be a great life and I
made sure it was. A huge part of me still regrets the fact that I
never hurled for the Dublin senior team, and that I wasn't around
to be part of the 1984 Dublin Minor Football side, but those
postal rounds – I haven't missed them.

In truth, we played the football of cavemen a lot of the time.
We trained in a basic way and never looked after ourselves once we
got beyond the gate of the training ground. Those were the times,
though. Now we have so many tests and measures of fitness that I
often forget we are footballers. It's like training to be a Navy SEAL
or an astronaut.

Maybe it all started with Willie Young and the aerobics. Willie
Young was a legendary Arsenal defender in the seventies. He used

to make his own track through the cornfields at London Colney during pre-season. The lads would take off on a big loop and Willie would plough a path through the corn, just trampling and ripping it out of his path – straight through, he went, like a tractor.

He left Arsenal the summer I arrived but his legend lived on. The previous summer, the club had introduced aerobics into the training routine. One morning apparently, a girl instructor arrived at London Colney, stuck on a backing tape and started to teach the movements.

'No way,' says Willie.

'If you don't do it, Willie,' says manager Terry Neill, 'you're fined £20.'

'Fine.'

'Willie, if you don't do it, the fine is £50.'

'Bollocks. Never in a million years, Gaffer.'

'A hundred quid, Willie.'

'Suits me, pal. I'm never doin' that.'

'Two hundred quid, Willie.'

'Weh hey,' says Willie, bursting into a jig. 'I'm dancing. I'm doing it. Yippee!'

In a game in which almost everything hinges on getting the right break at the right time, I've been snowed under with blessings. Pat Rice came to Arsenal and saved my career. I was called back from a loan spell at Port Vale minutes before I left and made my debut that Saturday. Players got injured at just the right time for me to benefit. Every move I made between clubs worked out for me. I ran into managers all through my career who believed in me – Jack Charlton, Howard Kendall, Peter Reid, Mick McCarthy.

I've seen greater talents than mine go to waste or cut down. Paul Lake and David White, who were with me at Manchester City, were sublime footballers. The game was tough on them.

It was all on a plate for Paul. He should be coming into his prime now. His earnings would be huge; he'd be the key to England's

World Cup squad in Japan. He must find it hard even to watch. After years of injury struggles he quit and studied physiotherapy instead. I see him occasionally when he calls to Sunderland, selling physio equipment.

David White works with his father. They are scrap metal people in the north-west of England. Injury took the best time away from David, too.

When I say I've been lucky, I know what I'm talking about. Dave and Paul had more ability, dedication, desire and athleticism than I had. They got through the early rounds of the lottery, they were spotted, played well in trials, made the first team and still it was pulled away from them. I shouldn't have been on the same team as them, especially Paul, yet it happened for me and it never happened for them.

Often I think of Dave Rocastle and that first day at Arsenal when I left my duffel coat back at the ticket office. We weren't close but we were good friends. I remember one disastrous night out we had when Dave was seeing an Irish girl called Ruth. She had a friend, Esther, and Dave couldn't let it lie. He had to match me up with Esther. So we all went out one night in Lewisham and ended up at a dance club. I remember Dave moving about the dance floor with the same elegance he had on the football pitch and me trying to move about the dance floor with a little bit more elegance than I have on the pitch. They didn't know whether to laugh or cry. A couple of years ago, Brian Marwood, our old team-mate, rang me to say that Dave had died of non-Hodgkin's lymphona at the age of thirty-three.

The standard football words like 'gutted' or 'sick' don't describe that cold shudder of sorrow and regret. I was with Dave at Arsenal and again at Manchester City. How many times did we train together, travel together and laugh together? Yet I never kept in touch. Hearing that he was gone was a shock, a kick in the gut, and it left me feeling that the game was up, that all the time I assumed was left to me could never be taken for granted.

Apart from Dave Rocastle, I lost track of Tony Adams, Paul Merson and dozens of other people I worked and played with. If you were to ask me who my friends from football will be when I leave the game, the list would be short. Stan probably, although I dread meeting him on my own – it's a day or two lost because we never seem to go home – Kevin Kilbane and Kevin Phillips I hope, and Peter Reid.

If you had asked me the same question when I was leaving Manchester City, I'd have given you a long list of names, people I liked, people I thought would always be in my life. I can give you a long list of names of people I like now but I know that teams are an illusion. We're close when we play but whether you disappear for a while with an injury or for ever through retirement or transfer, your old team rolls on without you.

When I left Manchester City, a club I loved, the truth is that I stayed in touch with nobody. Footballers move on. We're more fickle than fans. We value our friends outside of football more. I'm in more regular contact with guys I've known all my life than I am with football friends.

When I look back over this stretch of nineteen seasons, I can't help but notice that a river of alcohol runs through it. Again, there have been victims. Many of the people who have passed through my life during this time have been alcoholics. I could have a separate index of the people mentioned in this book who have been wounded and tormented by drink.

I'm not one of them, touch wood. I'm conscious that I could be seen as a poster boy for alcohol but I've had nothing but good times over the years. It's never been a problem. I've swum in the river without getting wet – another piece of luck, I suppose.

I offer no excuses. I come from a different time perhaps, and from a family who drank. I grew up in a culture of drink in a country of drink and left as a kid to go into a business where everyone drank. Sport and drink were always mixed in my mind.

One of my favourite memories is of the time I played hurling against my father. It was a pub game between the Culchies and the Dubs, who drank in the Laurels Pub at home.

The first time I was ever drunk I was about sixteen years of age. Paddy Hughes from across the road and I got into some Poitín that Paddy's father had been given. As if we were the first to think of it, we replaced what we drank with water. Poitín can make you crazy and when we'd drunk enough of it, we decided we needed more drink. We went across to my house and up to my sister's room. Anne Marie, or Ambie as she was known, was the wild one in the family. At the time she was brewing her own beer.

We removed one large bottle and brought it downstairs where it exploded with disastrous consequences for the sitting room. Soon the authorities were on the scene in the shape of my parents and Paddy's parents. We pointed the finger at Ambie's bedroom. Another explosion came from there, cutting short the inquiry into the state of Paddy and myself. Ambie had made a mistake in the brewing. She'd put all the beer into screw cap bottles and the gases had reached a level where the pressure was just beginning to make the bottles explode.

My first night drunk was spent watching a delicate bottle disposal operation from my sister's room and it's been stories, songs and yarns ever since.

I have listened to Roy Keane preaching like a temperance minister against players drinking, and implying perhaps that he is the last true professional in football. I think he misses the point. Like any of us, his view will be coloured by what's best for him. He has had his problems with drink and it's brave of him to battle against that now. I know it's a tough, white-knuckle ride for him sometimes, and the discipline he brings to it is part of his make-up, part of what makes him what he is.

I have drunk throughout my career to escape football, to be free of the worry of whether or not I was good enough. I have done it because I could. Sometimes I've done too much of it, sometimes I've used drink in the wrong way, but I've got by and I still love a good pub, a place where people meet and talk. The world hasn't enough of those places.

I drink to keep myself sane in what is a narrow, shallow world. Very little in football is authentic. We live in a bubble. We stay in nice hotels and our bags magically get to our rooms without us carrying them there. Hands up how many Premiership foot-ballers travelled on public transport this year. How many of us have had to queue for anything? We've quarantined ourselves from the world.

The pub has been my escape. I can go to the Dun Cow in Sedgefield and talk about horses all night. I go to The Shakespeare in Durham and talk about the next golf trip. I go to The Phoenix in Seaham and chuckle at Newcastle United.

The Phoenix is a big Sunderland supporters' pub. When I'm in there, I get to know what people are feeling about the team. Mostly, I get belly laughs. On days when Sunderland aren't playing and Newcastle are on the telly, a big crowd will gather in The Phoenix in the hope of seeing Newcastle lose.

One evening when Newcastle were away to Norwich, things got a little low. Newcastle were winning 4–0 at half-time. Big Adie, the proprietor of The Phoenix, had an idea – he'd ring The Strawberry. Newcastle fans will know The Strawberry. It's right next door to St James' Park and when Newcastle play away, hundreds of fans gather there to watch the game on the telly.

At half-time, Big Adie puts in his call in the guise of an Australian technician for Sky.

'You getting our new crystal-enhanced big-match vision service?'
'Nooo.'

'Well, you'll have to adjust the dish a little. I can talk you through it.'

'Alreet, man. Mary, get ooot the ladders.'

288

Mary gets out the ladders, climbs up and begins taking roared instructions.

'Tell her to move it about thirty degrees. North-westerly direction.'

'Aye. Mary, move it thirty degrees north westerly. Ooh, it's gahn all fuzzy, man.'

'OK. Don't worry, turn it almost the other way around now.'

'OK. Aye, Mary. Turn it the other way round he says.' There are loud angry shouts in the background. 'The dish has stopped working altogether now.'

'Well, stick it up your arse, you black and white twats.'

And a great roar goes up in The Phoenix in Seaham, this little piece of the earth getting a rare one over on Newcastle.

I wouldn't ever lock myself away from all that. That contact, that mixing, is the only way I could survive in the game.

I'm not a midfielder like Roy. I don't put mile after mile on the clock. I work in a tight place. If I drink nothing for a year, it's not going to help me keep the centre-half's elbow out of my face on Saturday. It's not going to help me direct my headers or add finesse to my touch.

I have drink because that's the way I am. I can't take the responsibility for others and I can't preach to them about what they should do. I think professionalism is about getting yourself right for the game on Saturday.

Everybody finds their own level. Roy would be critical of what he'd see as my lack of passion for the game. I feel that way sometimes about other players. What would Roy have done had he seen two Sunderland imports chasing Gus Poyet down the tunnel looking to swap jerseys moments after we'd given away a goal which cost us a precious point at White Hart Lane? We had been attacking, trying to get the goal that would give us three potentially lifesaving points. We lost possession, they poured forward and Les Ferdinand scored the winner. I trooped off scarcely able to speak.

Supporters see it differently. They see the shell of the game.

There's guys in football who are here to collect wage cheques and the jerseys of famous players and they are feted. And there are guys giving sweat, blood, tears and more and they are in the stocks the whole time, being pilloried.

I look at a player like Kevin Kilbane. I know first hand how intensely he feels things, how he fights and dies for Sunderland football club and still people somehow pour scorn on him. I know it hurts. I was walking up the tunnel that day as Poyet's jersey was being tugged at. Kevin Kilbane was beside me. I don't know how he felt but the sight of the Poyet incident made me cringe. Still does.

Right now there's a lot being said about professionalism. Roy has a lot to say to us. Are we the most professional team at this World Cup? Probably not. Are we the most talented team at this World Cup? Definitely not. But we have gone further than Holland, Portugal, Cameroon, Argentina and holders France to name a few. We are through to the last sixteen in the world.

So how do you measure professionalism? By how much pasta you eat? Bleep tests? Abstinence? The ability to get on with it no matter what the circumstances? Walking out on your team before the biggest games of their lives?

We all get through things in our own way, get to the same point in our own style. The only difference between Roy Keane and the rest of us here is that Roy thinks there is a difference.

We made a million mistakes in the way we handled things. Should we have had a meeting in Saipan? Shouldn't I have interrupted Roy right at the start of his rant, just pulled him back from the edge? Should one of us have gone after him when he left the room? Should we have had a press conference that night? Should senior players have gone to that press conference or stayed away and tried to conciliate later? Should we have asked him to come back? Should we have watched a tape of his interview? I have asked myself a million questions, been through a million different scenarios and I wish Roy Keane had played with us through these last few games.

It's like the drink, though. We all take responsibility for ourselves. Roy left us, not the other way around, and he punished himself more than any of us by not coming back. For what it has done to him, I have him down as another victim of the game. He wouldn't see himself that way but when is the last time you saw the guy look happy?

We will go home soon. Without Roy there's not really a chance of us winning this thing. Before the new season starts, everyone who played in my testimonial will receive a letter from a child who benefited from the game – usually players give each other Rolex watches for such favours. I have the letters and Michael Kennedy has all the addresses. I'll address each letter to the player and his wife and I hope they'll both open the letter. Maybe one or two will stay in touch with the kids who have written to them. Some of the lads have already been asking for their letters.

At home, I have a letter in the kitchen from a little girl in India, thanking us for playing a game of football. Some of the proceeds are going to her village. Underneath her letter there is a note from the relief agency GOAL, just to say that by playing our little game of football we've rescued this girl from the life of prostitution that she has had since she was eight years of age. I can't think about that for a moment without welling up, without wanting to reach for my own eight-year-old, Aisling.

Let me tell you about my friend. I know he'll have watched these past three games. He's a young lad from Dublin. I can't tell you his name. That's part of the secret. He plays hurling, Gaelic football and soccer, all the things I played when I was his age. We've met a couple of times and he has written to me, thanking me for the game. He has a secret that he doesn't tell to just anyone. In fact, nobody knows except his parents, his doctor and me. His life is different from mine at that age in one big way. He comes to Crumlin once a month for injections because he's HIV positive. That's his secret and he frets that if any of his friends found out, they would never play with him again. He rings occasionally for a chat. He makes me laugh but he leaves me in tears.

We all know stories like that; we've all come across sorrow like that. I know that Roy has similar tales he could tell and, in his private way, puts things back. But what do most of us get out of doing that? We can't live these privileged existences and go around slaughtering each other across the tabloids. We can't scowl our way through the lives that we dreamed about having. When we do, it's a kick in the teeth for everyone who pays to see us, for every kid who collects the soccer cards like we did, who dreams the way we did.

Jack Doyle, my hero, happens to have come from Cork, like Roy does. I don't know if everyone who leaves that county gets supplied with his own personal demons but Jack rode to the top and down to the bottom not once but twice. He took an excess of everything – drink, sex and gambling – but the nature of his pride was such that he always turned to the world with a smile on his face.

When success came, my da would say to me, 'Don't do a Jack Doyle on it,' and it took me a long time to appreciate the tragedy behind the great romantic story that I loved. As I got older, what I took from the Jack Doyle yarns was not just the morality tale of a life gone wrong twice, but the quieter things such as the sense of dignity and elegance the man carried. He had his demons but he talked to them alone. He didn't rail at the world when he discovered it wasn't perfect. He made the most of it. He sang, he danced, he saw in many happy dawns. I've tried to do the same.

On Sunday night, this Irish team will drive the hour or so from Seoul to Suwon. We'll play Spain for all the chips on the table – winner goes through, loser goes home. We'll pitch our group of over-performing players against their superstars. We'll hurl ourselves at them and they'll try to parry us.

For us as a team, it will determine how we are remembered and judged. If we lose badly, we will be failures and there will be calls for Mick to go. If we win and march into a quarter-final in Gwangju next week, we will tip the country over into a delirium from which it might not recover.

All shades of things might occur between those two options. We might lose unluckily or heroically. Who knows? We'll represent the place we are from. The Spanish team will do the same for their country. Billions of people will watch. There's a wonderful excitement about it. There's nothing quite the same in the whole world of sport, nothing.

For me, it will be the last game, or the second last – in my dreams, maybe the third last. I can't dream beyond that. We wait and wait. The same things still stir my head in the mornings – the thought of Sunday night, the noise of our shouts as we leave the dressing room five minutes before kick-off, walking out past the blazers and walkie-talkies, the sound of our studs clacking as we start up the tunnel, the guy in front of me shaking the kinks out of his shoulders, the guy behind roaring, and we're walking quicker towards the floodlights, the immaculate green pitch and the lusting roar of the crowd. We'll get between those white lines and the world will be ours again.

When it's over, whenever it's over, I'll fly back to the real world.

I live in Sedgefield with Gillian, Aisling and Michael. I live with twelve horses, four cows, three ducks, five hens, a cockerel, two goats, three dogs and two cats. I don't have millions and I don't have many medals but I am happy. Soon, we will probably live in Ireland again, and we'll miss this place and this time.

Almost twenty years in the profession and I'm still as happy as when I started out. That's the secret – being happy. That's the dues we pay for the privilege of our work being a game, for the money we are paid, for the dreams we have realised, for being given the escape we always yearned for.

You only go around this world once and being a footballer is about as good as the trip gets. The least we can do is wear a smile and say thanks.

Thanks.

AFTER HOURS

You spend a good piece of your life gripping a baseball and in the end it turns out that it was the other way around all the time.

JIM BOUTON, *BALL FOUR*

September 2002. We played Manchester United on Saturday. It's never ordinary against them. Saturday was extraordinary. Lingering ghosts and unsettled accounts. The new season has exploded for us.

Ireland's World Cup finished ten weeks ago. Despite the promises, we players were treated to a débâcle of a reception in the Phoenix Park. To drown the embarrassment, we spent the night in Lillie's Bordello, the Dublin nightclub managed by Gillian's sister Val.

Gillian and I arrived home in Sedgefield the following evening. It was summer and the fields were green and busy with life. These were going to be our last weeks here. The phone was backed up with messages from Sunderland Football Club – I was to see Peter Reid at his home the next morning to speak about my future, and

I was warned not to speak to anyone from the press before then.

I assumed that the club were going to lowball me on my retirement plan. Gillian and I spent the night talking about the settlement we'd look for. My mind is made up; I'll be leaving football. The next day I drove the twenty minutes to Peter's house in Yarm, rehearsing my speech – thanks Peter, thanks for everything. Now let's talk softly about hard things. I want to walk away. What can I walk away with? Peter is a friend and as a friend I have a list of things I want to tell him about the miserable season just gone by.

When I get to Yarm, he lets me talk awhile. I speak about how we ended last season. The team was fractured and bitchy, the fans were on us, we played nervously and without unity. I tell him he needs to put the dressing room back together, the players need to discover again what Sunderland means, what the values and the essence of the club are. The team needs to be a Peter Reid team again.

'Yeah,' says Peter. 'I want you to help me fix it. I want you to become player-coach.'

I was surprised but I wasn't gracious. I interrogated Peter, looking for ulterior motives. Couldn't find any.

Player-coach? Me? Not what I expected.

Player-coach? Peter has put me on the back foot, thrown me.

I ask for time to speak to Gillian, and to Bobby Saxton, whose job I will effectively be taking.

I know I'll feel good about taking the job. I want to knock walls down for Peter Reid. He comes on strong about needing me, so I rearrange life overnight. It's a footballing life, though, made for rearranging.

I'm not sure I'll be content until I'm sure Bobby is happy. Bobby is an old-fashioned football man, my cup of tea in that respect – no heart monitors or kilojoules per megahertz – and he has been my friend for a long time. He has a pure football brain and was instrumental in the coaching that took us from the brink of the

Second Division to the Premier League. He filled our dressing room with spirit; we drew much of our morale from him. If we want to resurrect that spirit, I can't see how we can do it without Bobby. I call Bobby again. I'm not completely convinced but he tells me to take the job, removing the last barrier that's stopping me accepting. I throw away twelve days of summer holiday to make a start.

First day, I decide to get changed with the players and stay in the dressing room. I don't want to be the textbook guy. I don't want to hang out with the coaches. A few years ago, Paul Bracewell tried this job and after a little while he was bringing a briefcase in. I'll learn from the bitching that went on about that.

So I go into the players' dressing room as usual. Everybody's there except our five World Cup players who aren't back from holiday yet. Silence falls. They all shut up and continue changing in silence. Finally, I break.

'For fuck's sake, lads, speak to me.'

My early tasks are dealing with old friends. Tommy Butler. In July, Tommy's contract expired and he earned the right to go wherever he wanted. This wonderful midfielder whom we've practically hand-reared might go off to be appreciated elsewhere. So we needed a little movement on the club's side.

Thomas did well for us at the end of last season when nobody else was doing well and, looking at it with a cold eye, he should do well again. He might get more money elsewhere but he'll get foot-ball here. He can get his claws into a place and he can keep that place if he shows that he wants to play. Thomas stayed. He started the season in the team. A week or two later, he made his senior debut for Ireland.

And Cliffie Byrne is still with us. I can't believe the man he has become. If I were a manager I would build a team around him. He has those qualities, that ability to inspire and push and look after his own stuff into the bargain. People don't see it in him yet but I evangelise on his behalf, I go around converting people to Cliffie.

He's got a new contract. He'll be a hero for this club someday.

So that's my job – getting into people's heads. I have to remember the words and ways of all the people who helped me get this far and what they said. I have to borrow their words, recycle them.

Right now, I'm a bit like the student teacher coming in each day knowing that this class will make or break him. I watch while at the other end of the training ground Adrian Heath and Peter have the pre-season stopwatches out doing bleep tests. I can't be a hypocrite. I hate that stuff.

There's good news, like there should be before the start of every season. Young Sean Thornton, a new signing, has tied with Mickey Gray at the top of the bleep tests. Everyone is impressed. Phil Babb is here, three years older and wiser than the last time I played with him for Ireland. We've employed him to calm things at the back. Every day we are linked with some new player; every day we retreat and make our plans and talk football. Physically, my pre-season has been manageable. I'm surprised still to be here. We have our backs to the wall. We know that. *Butch Cassidy and the Sundance Kid*, final scene.

It's been hard to adjust. We played Blackburn on the first day of the season and I knew I'd be on the bench. My back was feeling good, though. Start of a new season and the usual basket of good intentions to carry around. Peter asked me if I could get to the ground before eight that morning to make sure the bus was stocked with everything we needed. He thinks sometimes I came up the River Wear in a bubble. I passed the message on to one of the kitmen, bought myself an extra hour of sleep.

We get by like that. Peter is the bookies' favourite to be the first Premiership manager sacked. We are widely tipped for relegation. Until transfer deadline day, the new strikers we wanted to sign wouldn't come here. Some people thought we had the mark of death.

We'll survive, though. We'll scrap. It was Manchester United on

Saturday and we pulled a point out of it. I couldn't help wondering again how it all got so serious so late in my career. And ghosts still linger of course.

A few weeks ago I saw Roy Keane in a magazine wearing United's new Nike kit. I thought back then that when the season started it would be business as usual for us all. I was wrong.

I spoke to Michael Kennedy last Friday. Michael talked to me about the sense of isolation Roy feels, about what he has been through, about the mix of anger and reflection he has inside him. It's been a rough three months for him. Michael reckoned that Roy was ready to build some bridges.

Much of the anger has been channelled into his autobiography. On Saturday before the game Jason McAteer brought the book into our dressing room. For Jason it is *The Satanic Verses*. At one stage he asked one of the young apprentices to go next door to the United dressing room and ask Roy if he wouldn't mind signing the book for Niall, Stan and Mick. The poor kid just got saved at the last minute.

On Saturday when I watched Roy Keane out on the field at the Stadium of Light, his afternoon suggested to me all that I envy in his life and also all that I could never handle. He was running the game with his usual throbbing fury, the best footballer on the field, but he was also having sticks poked at him from every side. The crowd were jeering. Jason was tweaking his tail. They were turning his troubles into a carnival freak show.

I was sent on as a sub towards the end of the game. Having spoken to Michael on Friday, it was in my mind to go to Roy afterwards and shake his hand and say to him that we've all lost out this summer, that enough is enough. For all the good times and for all the extraordinary games he has played, he deserves more than this undignified circus.

And then he got sent off. Jason had been winding him up for a long time and Roy cuffed him on the ear as he went past, a big brotherly sort of cuffing I thought. But the referee had no time to consider context or character or history. Red card.

As Roy was making his way off the field I realised there was going to be no opportunity to make contact. Roy would disappear into the United dressing room and tomorrow the headline writers would be back kicking him to death. So I ran to him and shook his hand and just said, 'It's been three months of shit, Roy. Enough is enough.'

And Roy shook my hand. It wasn't a 'peace in our time' moment, and many said it was opportunism on my part or the right gesture at the wrong time. Anyway, I immediately got the hairdryer treatment from Alex Ferguson who arrived on the scene hissing expletives, having completely misread the situation. He and I expressed our differing opinions a bit more forcibly in Peter Reid's office afterwards.

I'm glad it all happened, though. We've never been close, but Roy and I have been through a lot together. For the rest of our lives to be about blame and recrimination would make a mockery of the good days. I'm glad we shook hands in public, too. What was happening to Roy, what was happening between Roy and Jason, what is happening even now between Roy and Mick, none of it is good for Irish football.

A new season just blossoming. We're back at Whitburn and the wind is cutting through us, reminding everyone that we are headed for the long slog of winter. Four games down. Thirty-four to go. A drama in each one.

Roy is down but not out, facing suspensions from what I think is a vindictive FA. He'll be back and he'll be stronger. The terrible isolation of a great player is beginning to come to an end now, I hope. His genius deserves the dignity of respect. I'll say it once more: I hope someday soon to pay money to see Roy Keane play in an Irish jersey again. I don't know how that can happen, but it must.

At Whitburn the players are beginning to talk football instead of holidays, there's that little edge now. Train. Play. Train. There's that feeling in the stomach, what we can do, what we have to do.

I'm smiling. This fortunate football life rolls on for another while at least. I can't wait to see how it all turns out.

INDEX

Note: 'NQ' indicates Niall Quinn.

Adams, Tony   57, 111, 114, 118–21, 124, 196–7, 286
adidas   144
advertising   66, 204
Aer Lingus   274
agents   67–9, 130, 268, 282
Ahern, Bertie   24
Airport Hotel, Dublin   116, 186
Aldridge, John   66, 93, 138
All Ireland junior championships
        football   32
        hurling   37
Allen, Clive   34
amateur sport   37–8
Amblehurst Inn   155
Ard Ri ballroom   155
Arsenal   12–14, 39, 48–9, 52–6, 69–74, 78–80, 84, 91–2, 96, 105–6, 121–5, 136, 144, 148, 157, 178, 231, 282–5
Ascot   39
Aston Villa   210, 213
Australian football   42, 50–1
Austria   213–14, 217–19

Babb, Phil   65–6, 210, 298
Bailey, Gary   85
Bailey, Roy   145–6, 155, 194, 202
Ball, Alan   212–13, 219–20, 250
Ballinascorney   30
Ballyfermot   216
Ballygowan Water   192
Banks, Tony   188–9, 193, 195, 199, 202

Barclaycard   273
Barclays Bank   273
Barlow, Colin   222
Barry's Hotel   219
Beasant, Dave   148
Beckham, David   43, 89
Beefeater Bar   46–9, 51, 54, 57
Bell, Colin   147
Bennis, Richie   235
Bereneice   262
Bermuda   117–18
Best, George   234
Blackbourne, Mark   270–1
Blackburn Rovers   130, 239, 298
Bolger, Jim   235–7, 258–61
Bolger, Paddy   237–8
Mr Bollan   245–6
Bonner, Packie   37, 64, 104, 138, 160, 172–3
Book, Tony   144–7, 156–7, 202
Bould, Steve   119, 269
Bracewell, Paul   297
Bradley, Brendan   234
Brady, Liam   13, 25, 27, 129–31
Breen, Gary   5, 116, 186, 228, 242, 277
Briggs, Max   254–5
Brightwell, Ian   154
Brown, Michael   87
Browne, Max   187
Buchan, Charlie   282
Burridge, John   226
Burtenshaw, Steve   49–50, 53, 92, 131

Burton, Terry 55, 70
Butler, Karina 275–7
Butler, Tommy 11–12, 67–8, 70, 73–4, 297
Byrne, Cliffie 11–12, 73–4, 269, 297–8
Byrne, Mick 20, 65, 81, 99, 110, 139, 165, 215, 225–6, 281

Caesar, Gus 56, 69, 84, 124
Cahill, Dessie 218
Cameroon 110, 129, 228–30, 238–40
Campbell, Gary 56
Cantona, Eric 88
Captain McBride 260
Carnell, Nigel 244
Carruth, Michael 179–80
Carsley, Lee 134–5
Cascarino, Tony 122, 138, 270
Caton, Tommy 69
Caven, Alan 74
Celtic 37
Chairman of the Boards 260
Charlton, Bobby 234
Charlton, Jack 47, 65–6, 81, 92–8, 114–15, 122, 136, 138, 162, 202–3, 208–10, 213–19, 284
Charlton, John 214–15
Charlton Athletic 6, 148, 247–51
Cheltenham Gold Cup 123
Christy Senior 260
Clark, Lee 250
Clarke, Wayne 231
Clear Round Macken 260
Clemence, Ray 147
Clones Cyclone 260
Clough, Brian 82, 249
Coca-Cola 204, 218
Cois na Tine 236–7, 257–61
Coleman, Tommy 55, 69–71, 74
Connolly, Dave 5–6, 66, 129–32, 166, 243–4
Corcoran, Eddie 3, 65, 77, 167–8, 263
Cork, David 56
Coton, Tony 154, 212
Cottee, Tony 220

Coughlan, Eamon 30, 77, 260
Coventry City 233
Coyne, Tommy 202
Craddock, Jody 247, 249
Croke, Paddy 31–2
Croke Park 31
Crumlin 13–14, 92
Crumlin Children's Hospital 275–6
Cunningham, Kenny 6, 167, 240, 243
Curle, Keith 147–8, 212
Customs and Excise 273
Cyprus 26

Daish, Liam 208, 233–4
Dalglish, Kenny 79
Daly, Gerry 234
Daly, Jon 25–6
Dalymount Park 26–7, 192
Dandy, David 190, 193–4, 202, 233–4
Darby, Bill 48
Davis, Paul 80, 124
Davis, Steve 112–13
Delaney, John 271
Delaney, Ronnie 260
Delhi Times 128
Derby County 154–5
Dervan, Cathal 19–20
Deyna, Kaziu 146
Disneyland 262–3
Dixon, Lee 132
Doherty, Gary 25–6, 28
Donnelly, Tony 55, 86
Doyle, Jack 2–4, 7, 292
Doyle, Mick 36
Doyle, Mike 147
Drake, Ted 80
Drimnagh Castle school 30–1
Duff, Damien 3–4, 64, 66–7, 178, 185, 227, 254–7, 266, 277, 291
Duff, Jayo 262
Duffy (Arsenal player) 54–5
Dunne, Richard 227, 230, 257
Dunphy, Eamon 230
Dunwoody, Richard 123, 237

INDEX

Eddery, Pat   235
Egan, Gabriel   172
Egypt   137
Eircom   168
Ellis, Gordon   244
Ellis, Sam   180–1, 184–5, 236, 258
England national football team   26, 137
English, Nicky   218, 261–2
European Champions League   18
European Championships   26, 136,
    162, 209, 211, 213, 270
Eva Luna   259
Evans, Ian 'Taff'   63, 160, 166, 174, 228,
    239
Everton   187, 213, 231

FA Cup final   29–30
Fallon, Johnny   107
Fallon, Richard   230
fans   11, 290
Ferdinand, Les   289
Ferguson, Alex   82, 89, 102–3, 160, 300
Finnan, Steve   99, 229, 256
Fitzgerald, Walter   13–14
Fleming, Curtis   222
Flitcroft, Gary   199, 212
Football Association of Ireland (FAI)   10,
    24, 38, 45, 107, 110, 121–2, 161, 163,
    168, 186, 204, 215, 262, 270–1
Francis, Trevor   231
The French Furze   260
Frisk, Anders   5
Frontzeck, Michael   88
Fulham   33–6

Gaelic football   27, 31–2, 36–7, 42
Gallagher, Dermot   188
Garner, Tom   153
Garton, Billy   84–5
Gary (Manchester City supporter)   146–7
Gascoigne, Paul   189
Gaskin, Liam   160
Gateaux   204
Gavin, Robbie   76
Geraldine Cup   31

German, Paul   56
Germany   238–42, 254
Gidman, John   84
Giles, Johnny   25
Gillespie, Frank   81
Given, Shay   62, 139, 228–9, 266
Givens, Don   27–8, 257
Givens, John   168, 172
Glanville, Brian   80
GOAL (relief agency)   277, 291
Golden Boot award   252
Gorman, Tommie   160
Graham, George   94–5, 105–6, 117–18,
    124, 131–2, 136, 267
Gray, Mickey   250–2, 272, 298
Gresty Road   29
Grobbelaar, Bruce   80
Groves, Perry   113
Gullit, Ruud   50, 138

Halmahera   260
Hammond, Nicky   56
Harry Ramsden's   216
Harte, Ian   4, 49, 54, 229–30, 239, 266
Hartigan, Pat   234
Hawaii   41–3
Hayden, Paddy   14
Hayes, Martin   56, 124
head tennis   145–6
Healy, Colin   37, 65, 89, 203
Heath, Adrian   145, 195, 298
Heath, Jane   195
Heffernan, Kevin   260
Heffo's Army   260
Helen (Manchester City supporter)   147
Higgins, Alex   260
Hiroshima   129
Hoey, Kate   13
Holden, Rick   181–3
Holland   121, 136–9, 210, 217
Holland, Matt   6, 134–5, 227, 229, 242
Holloway, Darren   247, 250
Hoppin Higgins   260
horse racing   260–1
Horton, Brian   186–8, 190, 202, 210, 212

Houghton, Ray   93, 217
Howe, Don   69–70, 79, 84, 92
Hughes, Emlyn   123, 137, 139, 154
Hughes, Mark   232
Hughes, Michael   255
Hughes, Paddy   85, 92, 287
Hurley, Charlie   25, 252–3, 282
hurling   14–15, 31–2, 35–7, 218, 234, 269, 283
Hurlock, Terry   255

Ibaraki   242, 257
Iceland   26
Ilic, Sasa   6, 250
Inter Milan   239
Inverdale, John   182
Iran   26
Irish Independent   79, 99
Irish national football team   16, 62, 93, 122, 175
        for the World Cup   43–5, 64–7, 72–3, 103–4, 139, 257
The Irish Times   98–100
Irwin, Denis   37, 66, 214, 218–19
Isaacs, Tony   56
itineraries   10–11
Izumo   110, 127–8, 141, 149, 159, 161, 163, 170, 175, 185

Jancker, Carsten   242, 255–6
Jennings, Pat   37
Johnson, Joe   112
Johnston, Allan   247, 250
Jones, Vinnie   119–21
JVC   124

Kahn, Oliver   255–6
Kavanagh, Mick   86, 92
Keane, Mossie   76–7
Keane, Robbie   3–5, 46, 49, 51, 63, 66–7, 72–3, 77, 185, 227, 254–7, 266–7, 276
Keane, Roy   18–26, 38–9, 45–7, 51, 63–6, 73–90, 95, 98–110, 116–17, 121–2, 125, 128–31, 134–6, 140–1, 150–2, 160–77, 185–8, 203, 208, 226, 228,

266, 268, 278, 287–92, 299–300
Keating, Noel   258
Kelly, Alan   64, 89, 104, 106, 140–1, 167, 243
Kelly, Gary   49, 51, 65–6, 104, 166, 210, 216, 228–9, 255, 266, 276, 280–1
Kendall, Howard   132–3, 152, 154, 186–7, 284
Kennedy, Michael   19, 65–6, 89, 110, 121, 129–36, 148, 150, 154, 159–60, 169–74, 187, 204, 210–11, 221, 291, 299
Kennedy, Mick   94
Kennedy Smith, Jean   237
Keown, Martin   56, 94
Kernaghan, Alan   214, 218
Kiely, Dean   103, 226–7, 243
Kilbane, Kevin   4–6, 74, 229, 240, 266, 277, 286, 290
Kimmage, Paul   172
The King of Cloyne   259–60
Kinnear, Joe   203
Kinsella, Mark   6, 134–5
Kipling, Rudyard   7
Kirk, Albert   163
Kiwomya, Chris   220
Klose, Miroslav   238, 242, 254, 256
Kyle, Kevin   68, 269

Lake, Paul   189, 199, 231–2, 284–5
Lawrenson, Mark   79–80, 96
Lee, Francis   147, 187–8, 200, 202–3, 210–12
Leeds United   51, 276
Leicester City   35
Liechtenstein   213, 217, 269
Limerick   214, 217, 234–5
Lineker, Gary   138
Little, Brian   213
Liverpool   79, 105, 123–4, 136, 179, 219
Lodge, Steve   232
Logan, Adrian   163
Lomas, Steve   212, 220
Lombard, Carole   7
Lotto   144

INDEX

Lucozade   204
Lukic, John   231
Lynch, Jack   15

McAteer, Jason   65–6, 99, 121, 129, 149,
   210, 229, 239, 281, 299–300
McBride, Willie-John   260
McCarthy, Mick   4–6, 12, 25, 45, 58,
   62–5, 81–2, 98–107, 110, 115–17,
   121–2, 129, 131, 135–6, 141, 149–52,
   160–74, 186, 203, 207–9, 213, 219–20,
   228–9, 238–42, 254–7, 263, 266,
   270–1, 284, 293, 300
McCourt, Graham   237
Macdonald, Frank   28
Macdonald, Malcolm   33–5, 49
Macedonia   209
McGinley, Eddie   32
McGrath, Paul   85, 116
McGuigan, Barry   260
Macken, Eddie   260
McKenna, Brendan   163–4, 168
McKenna, Joe   235
McKenna, Tommy   155
McLoughlin, Alan   188
McMahon, Seanie   214
McMahon, Steve   178–85
McManus, J.P.   160
McQueen, Gordon   17
Maddocks, John   184
Mail on Sunday   141, 150
Manchester City   34, 87–8, 131–3, 143–8,
   152–8, 178–82, 186–8, 194–6, 202,
   204, 209–13, 219–22, 231–2, 245,
   285–6
Manchester United   18, 26, 30, 36, 47,
   65–6, 83–8, 102, 106, 130, 144, 186,
   188, 234, 295, 298
The Manhattan   191–2
Manning, Kevin   259
Marbella   117
Mariner, Paul   69–70, 78–9, 84, 94
Martin, Con   25
Marwood, Brian   285
Mboma, Patrick   229

Meara, Skinny   35
Medcalfe, Neil   245
Melbourne   56   260
Mendonca, Clive   249, 251
Menton, Brendan   168, 170, 173–4
Merson, Fred   111
Merson, Paul   39, 48, 71, 110–14,
   117–19, 124–5, 286
Mexico   208
Milford, Roger   106
Miller, Greg   50
Miller, Paul   85
Milligan, Mike   156
Millwall   255
Moran, Kevin   30, 37, 81, 84–5, 188,
   190, 218–19
Morrison, Clinton   3
Morrison, Van   178–9
Moss, David   202
Murphy, Molly   31
Murray, Bob   270
Murray, Ciaran   165

Neill, Terry   13, 50, 53, 69, 284
Neuville, Oliver   242
Newcastle United   288–9
News of the World   89–90
Nicholas, Charlie   49, 69, 79, 85, 123–4
Nicol, Steve   79
Nielsen, Kurt   85
Nigeria   24
Norwich City   245

O'Brien, Andy   240
O'Brien, Chunky   234, 259
O'Brien, Liam   94, 215
O'Brien, Vincent   235
O'Byrne, Benny   80
O'Connell, Mick   235
O'Connor, George   218
O'Connor, Turlough   234
O'Donoghue, Dave   273
O'Donovan, Tom   41, 44
O'Dwyer, Mick   235
O'Dwyer, Noel   35

O'Hehir, Michael   32
O'Leary, David   13, 84, 93, 129–32,
    137–9, 178, 192, 255
O'Leary, Seanie   36
Olsen, Jesper   84
Olympic Games   179–80
O'Muircheartaigh, Michael   32
O'Neill, Martin   37
Opel   192
Ord, Richard   252
O'Reilly, Noel   263
O'Shea, John   277
O'Sullivan, Sonia   260
Oxford United   245, 254

penalty kicks   5–6, 249–50
Perez, Lionel   249
Phelan, Terry   212
Phillips, Kevin   247–52 passim, 276, 286
The Phoenix, Seaham   288–9
Piggott, Lester   235
play-offs   248
Player of the Month award   27–8
Player of the Year award   154
players' pool   203–4
Port Vale   246, 284
Portugal   211, 217
Poyet, Gus   289–90
Prophet, Mike   155
Puma   144
Purdie, John   56
Push the Pennies Over   157

Queens Park Rangers   27, 85, 231, 246–7
A Question of Sport   157
Quinn, Aisling (daughter of NQ)   200, 203,
    205, 245, 248, 291, 293
Quinn, Anne Marie ('Ambie'; sister of NQ)
    287
Quinn, Billy (father of NQ)   2, 14–15, 32,
    35–6, 287, 292
Quinn, Gillian (née Roe; wife of NQ)   9,
    20, 157, 170, 181–4, 190–203 passim,
    211, 220–3, 236–8, 243, 258–62, 263,
    273, 276, 293, 295–6

Quinn, Mary (née Condon; mother of NQ)
    15, 36, 50, 243
Quinn, Michael (son of NQ)   200, 201,
    205, 220, 293
Quinn, Niall
    at Arsenal   50–6, 70–4, 78–80, 84,
        91–2, 96, 105–6, 111–14,
        123–5, 131–2, 136, 148, 178,
        231, 282–5
    charity game   16–19, 51, 124, 141,
        268–74
    children (Aisling and Michael)
        200–5, 245, 248, 273, 276, 291,
        293
    cruciate injuries and septicaemia
        189–90, 193–204, 220, 230–3,
        262
    disco pants   182
    drinking   118–20, 196–7, 214,
        286–9
    father (Billy)   2, 14–15, 32, 35–6,
        287, 292
    gambling   85–7, 92, 112, 114, 196,
        260–2
    houses and flats   75–6, 92, 157,
        200, 261–2
    hurling career   35–7, 283
    interest in horses   200, 234–8,
        257–9, 261
    international debut   93
    journalism   95, 245
    at Manchester City   131–3, 143–8,
        152–8, 178–82, 186–8, 194–6,
        202–4, 209–13, 219–22, 231–2,
        285–6
    mother (Mary)   15, 36, 50, 243
    schooling   29–33, 48, 50
    sister-in-law (Val)   295
    sisters   76, 116, 287
    at Sunderland   182, 212, 220, 224,
        229–33, 244–54, 262, 267–8,
        272, 275, 282, 290, 295–8
    television appearances   116, 157,
        182, 203
    trial with Arsenal   48–9

trial with Fulham 33–5
Uncle Mattie and Aunt Ailish 52, 76
Uncle Niall 151
Uncle Noel 75–6
wife (Gillian) 9, 20, 157, 170, 181–4, 190–203 *passim*, 211, 220–3, 236–8, 243, 258–62, 263, 273, 276, 293, 295–6
work as a coach 296–8
Quinn, Philip 99–100

Rae, Alex 201
Ramsey, Sir Alf 123
Rees, Tony 56
Reid, Peter 59–62, 67, 78, 154–7, 178–86, 231–2, 244–7, 251, 253, 262, 284, 286, 295–6, 298
Reid, Steven 63, 66, 238–9, 242–3
Reilly, Paddy 123
Rice, Pat 70–4, 78, 106, 284
Rix, Graham 69, 79, 85, 155–6
Roberts, Graham 85
Robinson, Michael 93–4
Rocastle, David 52–3, 56, 71, 124, 220, 285
Roche, Christy 237, 258–9
Roche, Paddy 234
Roe, Johnny 200
Roe, Mick 200
Romania 139
Rosler, Uwe 88
RTE Television 203
Rudge, John 78
Rufus, Richard 249
Rush, Ian 79
Russo, Donato 56–7
Ryan, Gerry 30, 234

Sadlier, Richard 25–6, 28
Saipan 10–12, 41, 43, 45, 60–3, 88, 95, 109–10, 129, 150, 290
Salmon, Eamon 194
Salt, Alan 195
Salt, Helen 195

Saudi Arabia 240, 262–6, 277
Saunders, Dean 154
Saxton, Bobby 246, 251, 296–7
Scahill, Dessie 258
Seddon, Dick 44, 50–1
Sedgefield Labour Club 273
Selangor 220–3
Seoul 279
Setters, Maurice 93, 96–7, 122, 138, 214
7 Up 66
Shackleton, Len 282
Sharpe, Lee 88
Shearer, Alan 190, 193
Sheedy, John 36
Sheffield United 247
Sheffield Wednesday 188
Sheron, Mike 247
Shotton, Malcolm 254–5
Sivebaek, Johnny 84
Sky News 185
Smith, Alan 106, 131, 136
Smith, Tommy 137
Smith Eccles, Steve 237
Smithy (apprentice at Sunderland) 59–60
Smurfit, Michael 237
snooker 56
Spain 1–5, 280, 292–3
Sporting Lisbon 211–13
Sporting Quest syndicate 259–60
Stadium of Light 16
Stapleton, Frank 13, 17, 27–8, 71, 84, 93, 266, 268–9
Staunton, Steve (Stan) 37, 47, 81, 104–8, 121, 135, 140–1, 159–63, 167, 211, 228, 230, 242–4, 266, 270, 277, 280, 286
Stephens, Tony 267
Stockport County 68, 74
Stynes, Jimmy 51
Summerbee, Mike 147
Summerbee, Nicky 247–50
Sunday Times 272
Sunderland 11–12, 59, 62, 67–8, 73, 212, 220, 224, 231–3, 244–54, 262, 270, 282, 290, 295–8

Sunderland, Freedom of the City of 274
Supersonic Sonia 260
Suwon I, 292
Swales, Peter 187

Talbot, Brian 72
Tango ball 79, 123
Taylor, Gordon 244
Texaco Award for soccer 235
Thatcher, Margaret 252
Thirlwell, Paul 88
Thomas, Micky 124
Mrs Thorburn 75
Thornton, Sean 298
Tipperary 14–16, 31, 35–8, 151, 234–5, 261
Toss the Feathers 156–7
Town and Country Club 123
Treacy, Sean 37–8
Turkey 209, 270

Van Aerle, Benny 138
Van Breukelen, Hans 138
Venables, Terry 234
Veysey, Kenny 56
Vickers, Steve 222

Walsh, David 272
Walsh, Martin 45, 100
Mr Weeber (surgeon) 244, 245
Whelan, Dave 30, 197, 275

Whelan, Liam 25
Whelan, Micky 123
Whelan, Ronnie 79
Whitburn training ground 62, 300–1
White, David 85, 148, 154, 284–5
White, John 63
Whitehurst, Billy 255
Whiteside, Norman 268–9
Whyte, Chris 79
Wilkins, Ray 130
Wilkinson, Paul 232
Williams, Steve 69
Wilmot, Rhys 56
Windsor 118–19, 123
Woodcock, Tony 69, 78, 84, 94
Woods, Jonathan 56
World Cup
    1990 competition 47, 131, 136, 139
    1994 competition 188–90, 202–3, 209–10
    2002 competition 1–6, 10–12, 16, 20, 24–8, 38, 95, 129, 149, 162, 185–6, 203, 205–9, 226, 242–3, 254, 265–7, 279
    see also Irish national football team for the World Cup
Wright, Ian 157

Yokohama 265, 277
Young, Willie 283–4